Taking Care of Asta

by Sue E. Costello

TAKING CARE OF ASTA

This is a work of non-fiction,
but names and places have been changed.

ISBN: 979-8-218-21544-6

Dedicated to Annie,
With Love.

TABLE OF CONTENTS

PART I

JANUARY 2018—DECEMBER 2020

CHAPTER 1
BACKGROUND

THE PROMISE

"Promise me you'll take care of Mama," my dad asked of me shortly before he died. Although I understood that "you" meant me specifically, I hesitated to take sole responsibility. After all, my sister Elsa, the oldest, had just moved into the house next door for the express purpose of taking care of the two of them in their old age. I was in the process of relocating to Southern California, and Chris, the middle sister, was getting ready to move out of state.

"I promise," I said. "We will take care of her," deliberately committing all three of us. Collectively, we would do whatever was necessary, of course, to take care of our mother.

After Daddy died, the true extent of Mom's dependence on him quickly became apparent. She didn't drive, was going blind, and living alone was more difficult for her than expected. It was no longer safe for her to use the stove, and the steps to the second floor were a constant source of worry.

Elsa took Ma to doctor appointments and occasional social outings, and ran interference when our mother had problems with her phone or cable TV, or needed help arranging and supervising workers for home repairs. Elsa agreed to perform a daily safety check and ensure our mother received a meal every day, our version of Meals on Wheels. Elsa didn't want Mom to know she was being paid for her services. She also didn't want the payment to come out of Mommy's money. We argued over who should foot the bill: Mommy, or Chris and me—Suey. This became the case of Who was Paying Whom out of Whose Resources, and Who Knew About it. It wasn't pretty.

Socially isolated, my mother sat and watched out the window, waiting for her daily visit from Elsa, watching as Elsa's married-to-someone-else boyfriend came and went. I called Mom daily to provide some telephone companionship. She was very critical of my sister's boyfriend, and was having difficulty managing her household, even with Elsa next door.

Elsa called periodically begging, demanding that I take Mommy to California. "You've got to take her off my hands for a week, a month, forever. I can't take this," she said. "She's impossible to deal with. She's nuts!" Chris and I had reasons to be concerned about our mother's safety under Elsa's supervision, but more on that later. The short list of daily tasks proved too much for Elsa, and we needed to make different arrangements.

My husband, Tony, and I had discussed having Mom live with us. We had in fact chosen a house with three bedrooms with her in mind when we moved. "Come live with us, Mommy," I'd say when she complained about Elsa or the boyfriend. But Mommy didn't want to leave her house. She didn't want to leave her cat. She didn't want to bring her cat. She didn't want to leave Daddy's ashes behind. She didn't want to leave the familiar for the unknown. Perfectly understandable.

And then we suggested converting one of our garages into a 'tiny home' for her. Granted, it wouldn't have a bathroom or a kitchen, but she would live with us, have a space of her own, access to 'her own' bathroom, and would never again have to worry about cooking, cleaning or home maintenance. Chris, who managed Mommy's money, said Mommy could pay for the conversion. My mother agreed.

It made sense. After all, I had spent a recent dozen years working as an adult home/assisted living administrator and had a few more years in elder care services under my belt. I understood what her needs would be, and I knew how to navigate the system. She'd been a very good mother to me. I could do this. I wanted to do this.

And so this saga begins.

Out of respect for my mother, and out of consideration for my sisters, whose privacy I respect as much as I do my own, I have changed all our names and locations.

January, 2018—Apr, 2018: "MAPARTMENT"

In January, we hired a contractor to build walls, replace a window and door, install a closet and ceiling fan, connect the fire alarm to our system, put in flooring, put up wainscoting and paint the apartment. We extended our heating and cooling systems into her room and remodeled 'her' bathroom for safety, replacing the tub with a shower and adding senior-friendly fixtures and hand rails. We upgraded the garden on her side of the house where the lemon and tangelo trees grow, leveled the bricks in her alley, and installed a hand rail into the pool. We split the costs as best we could according to what was strictly for her benefit, and what would benefit our house.

Chris and her husband came out in March to visit, inspect and evaluate. Together, we arranged U-Haul containers, bought airline tickets and planned this itinerary: On May 19th, Mother's Day weekend, I'd fly to Woodstock for a graveside ceremony that I would arrange for the burial of Daddy's ashes. A day or two later, Ma and I, and my former brother-in-law, Marty, would escort Asta to California.

Marty agreed to accompany us because my mother was planning to bring her cat, Heidi. I would need help moving my mother, her cat, and luggage all at the same time. Marty will also be able to help with last-minute handyman projects that might be needed upon her arrival. Tony and I are both very grateful to have Marty's help for the literal and figurative take-off and landing. He will be a huge help for the initial transition.

Fortunately, the plans to bring Heidi changed. Tony recommended the cat stay in Woodstock with Elsa since we have coyotes in the area. If Heidi were to get out—and Heidi is accustomed to being outdoors—and got lost or eaten by a coyote, Mommy would be devastated and quick to blame. A move to California would not be good for the cat, and would just be a stressor for Asta.

Chris broke the news to our mother, and to our relief, she agreed. In fact, she said, she had been thinking for a couple of months about leaving Heidi behind in Elsa's care, but Elsa had been encouraging her to bring the cat with her to California. You see, Elsa was already taking care of several cats. Some lived in her house, some feral cats living in her garage, and she took care of several other cats that stayed or frequented the porch outside her office. She wasn't eager to take on another cat. She thought bringing Heidi along would be good for our mother.

You can see that we're already on a collision course before we get out the gate.

Chris and I finally got Elsa to assure our mother that she would take care of Heidi. Ma is relieved to be travelling unencumbered by her cat, I will have Marty's assistance at the airport and for the trip, and Tony will have Marty's assistance and company for the first few days following Mommy's arrival. And Heidi will be safer and happier in familiar surroundings. It will be hard for Asta to part with her beloved Heidi, but she is looking forward, she says, to helping out with our little dog, Dawson, by letting him out to pee now and then.

May, 2018: PREPARATION

Ma is excited about making the big move out to California, and I'm feeling pretty happy about it, too. Her U-boxes arrived on Monday and Tony and I unloaded their contents into her 'Mapartment' and into an area we've set aside in our garage for her use.

We bought her (she paid) a lovely white-cushioned day bed, and I made it up with sheets over a mattress cover in case she has a bloody nose—which she's told me about—or has an accident of another sort, which could easily happen. We arranged her furniture so that she could move right in, and later rearrange to suit her tastes.

Construction to 'her' bathroom was completed on Tuesday, and we set up a little 'kitchen' area in the corner of the garage just outside her door. It has a mini-fridge, a Keurig coffee maker, and three cupboards that she can use for storage. She will be arriving to a beautifully appointed room in our lovely neighborhood setting, and we have plans:

- Tony will put fresh water in her Keurig daily and make sure her fridge is stocked with beverages or her favorite things.
- He will make her breakfast of soft boiled eggs and toast, put out a little smorgasbord in the afternoon, and have cocktail hour at 4 p.m. until I get home from work at 5:15, at which time we'll make dinner.
- Tony will encourage her to exercise with him in the pool. He'll take her on outings to landmarks when she's up for it, and try to encourage her to get into the routine of a nap in the afternoon so he can have his man-time.
- In the evenings, she'll keep me company while I (or we) make dinner, and then she and I will do something in the evening—maybe soak our feet or do nail care in front of the TV, or just watch TV and talk.
- On my days off from work, which are Mondays and Tuesdays, Tony will orchestrate some special outing or other for the three of us—a trip to the hot springs, or a bus tour, for example.
- We will throw a party at our house for her 90th birthday. Elsa and Chris will fly in from the East Coast, and most

of the grandchildren and their partners will attend. We'll invite friends and neighbors to help her integrate. She will love being the center of attention.

In spite of having Chronic Lymphocytic Leukemia (CLL), Ma is in pretty good health. I'm hoping for some quality time before she becomes ill or too frail. We want to make the best of what time she has left, and hope she will enjoy what we have to offer. I've given my mother this speech a few times leading up to her move:

"We all have to be prepared for disagreements and be willing to make some compromises. We'll get into routines that ensure everyone gets their own space. No matter what, we'll work it out."

With family at the top of our priority list, Tony and I are committed to taking care of her to the best of our ability. She will join our household naturally and seamlessly, and will be able to enjoy comfort and security in our care.

"I don't ever want you to go to a nursing home, but there are times when it can't be avoided—like for a short period after an injury or illness." I'm being honest with her. Our plan is to have her live here with us to the end. She plans to reserve the money from the sale of her house to pay for private nursing care at home should the time ever come that she needs it. That's a good thing to save it for.

The other night, Ma and I talked on the phone for over an hour, the way we used to do when I was young.

"I've been calling Chris my 'mentor' since Daddy died," she said, "but now that I'm moving, I told Chris, 'You're fired'." Just like on 'The Apprentice'. When she's happy, she's funny. I want her to be happy.

CHARACTERS

My story centers around five main characters. I'll introduce them here in the order of importance.

Asta: My mother. Born and raised in the Swedish countryside. Moved to America with her husband and three month old baby at age 25. With a few exceptions, for the sake of readability, her accent will be reflected only as 'yust' in place of 'just'. In case you're interested—and my mother was very interesting to listen to—her true accent sounded more like this:

"I'm tinking about trowing anudder birtday party for myself dis Yuly and want to know how you feel about eet."

Elsa: Queen of the Universe. Enough said.

Chris: Middle Everything. Multi-talented. Cringes at loud noises.

Tony: My Italian-American husband. Goes by Mr. Moderation, King of Hyperbola, and sometimes Master of Self-Restraint. In this story, he goes by Scape Goat.

Suey: Yours truly, Sue Ellen. The Doormat.

CHAPTER 2
NEW HOME, NEW LIFE

June 26, 2018: HONEYMOON'S OVER

As was the plan, I flew into Woodstock on Thursday, May 10th. We buried Daddy's ashes on Saturday, and on Sunday—Mother's Day—flew to Palm Springs. Marty was a big help and a super-supportive travelling companion. The trip was uneventful, and Asta was grateful to be pushed around the airport in a wheelchair. We got the job done and made it to our home, her new home, safely.

So far, she has been relatively easy to please. She has a good appetite and hasn't been complaining about our food. She usually keeps me company while I cook, then she and I watch TV together or go out to the pool for a dip, or I help her with her shower (set it up, get the water temperature just right), her feet, or with whatever she needs or wants done.

Shortly after she arrived, I noticed some redness on her legs. I took her to Urgent Care, where she was diagnosed with cellulitis. Tony was going to make sure she got her medicine on schedule while I was at work, but Asta protested.

"I don't want side effects, and I don't want Tony involved. I only want you to help me. No one else." To make sure I knew she meant it, she put on her 'ugly face,' the one where her upper lip is raised in the center while the corners go downward in disgust. It's a family-tradition kind of face.

Yesterday, Tony drove us first to her medical appointment and then on her errands. I appreciate his help and good attitude. As was her routine with Elsa in Woodstock, Asta often offers to take us out to eat as a way of thanking us after a day of driving her around. Sometimes we accept her offers, but just as often, we don't. We pay. I didn't expect it to become an issue.

And then I got an email from Chris asking that I call her 'when I was alone.' She wanted to discuss the dinners for which Mommy had paid. Were we taking advantage of our mother's generosity by letting her take us out for dinner?

She also wanted to talk about Ma's report that Tony has been touching her things in the garage or outside her door along the 'strip'—the brick path that leads from her door to the back yard—her 'garden'. Tony will be the first to describe himself as 'OCD,' but he genuinely thinks he's being helpful. My sisters feel compelled to intervene by 'addressing the issue' (they mean Tony) with me.

Other fears my mother has been sharing are her suspicions that (a) the pair of intercom phones I had installed (one in her room, and one in mine) were put there so we could eavesdrop on her, and (b) the smoke alarm in her ceiling was actually a camera that Tony was using to watch or spy on her.

I removed the phone from my room and showed her where in garage cupboards it would be stored, but of course I left the smoke alarm intact. Adjusting is difficult at any age. Trusting can be difficult, too.

My mother has never been shy when it comes to voicing her opinions, and sometimes she reveals a sharp tongue. After breakfast this morning, she described how I talk to people—including the dog—"in a business-like manner. Not sweet and friendly, but 'like a head nurse.'" We all know how she distrusts and dislikes head nurses from her days as a young LPN in Sweden.

"Yes, well, I've always been on the serious side," I admitted, taking her comments in stride.

"Yes," she agreed. "Elsa is more playful, fun-loving."

Or the other day, when I took her to the bank to get her new Health Care Proxy form notarized. A male couple sat opposite us in the lobby. My mother started talking. By the look on her face, I could see that she was getting ready to comment about the couple.

"Prata Svenska" (speak Swedish), I said. That's the strategy we've used all our lives when we spoke about others in public. She started to, but after two or three words slipped back into English. Again, she looked poised to say something rude or embarrassing—her filters for being socially appropriate aren't what they used to be—and I wanted to avoid it. I reminded her. "Prata Svenska."

Determined to say what she was thinking, she put her hand to her mouth to whisper. I motioned for her to put it down, so as not to attract attention.

"Shut Up," she snapped at me, loudly. In my family of origin, telling someone to 'shut up' is a cardinal sin, and it pissed me off. I shut my mouth.

She was gearing up for a fight in public and decided to throw a low blow. "How are you with Ronnie?" she said. "Are you compatible?"

Veronica (Ronnie) is my only child, and I worship her. We moved to California to be near her. I was not going to respond to such a comment. I turned the other cheek, another strategy my mother taught me growing up.

When we finally had our turn with the banker, he was unable to notarize the document because I only had a picture of my mother's driver's license on my phone. He needed to see the original.

"It's your fault. We left the house in too much of a hurry," my mother said.

"I take responsibility for not thinking ahead about that," I said.

We had several stops planned for that outing. Next, we drove to the craft store, where we were going to have one of her pictures framed. Being new to the area myself, I followed Siri's directions to a framing shop that turned out to be inside a mall. My mother would not have been able to manage the walking. Driving away, she berated me further for not knowing or anticipating this. Again, I apologized for not realizing the shop's address was inside of a mall.

We had planned on visiting the library to borrow some tapes so that she could learn Spanish, but by now our outing was ruined and she just wanted to go home.

"When I said the wrong things in public with Elsa," she said, "Elsa would yust laugh about it." Uh-huh.

"I understand that sometimes you won't like me, Mommy, and that's okay," I said.

On our way home from the mall, I noticed a frame shop in our neighborhood. We went in to place her order. She gushed to the salesperson at the counter at length about being Swedish and about his well-behaved golden retriever. He nodded politely until she was ready to take her cane and move on. As soon as we got out the door, she gave me a speech about how helpful a good relationship with the salesperson is when doing business, how he'll give her a better price because he liked her. She wanted me to know that it would behoove me to be more like her in that regard. Mm-hm.

Tonight I'm making crockpot corned beef and cabbage because she's been craving that.

"You're not cooking it right," she informed me.

"I'm following the slow cooker instructions on the package," I said.

"I think you should cook it on the stovetop or in the oven instead," she said. But I'm not going to turn on the gas stove and have it cooking for five hours when it's 100 degrees outside. The slow cooker will do the job just fine.

July, 2018: FRIENDS AND COMPANIONSHIP

My mother has accompanied us to a few Buddhist meetings and is getting to know and like some of the members in our group. She sees a few potential friendships for herself among them—the member who is 101 years old, the one who praised Mommy for her beauty, another who just returned from a vacation in Sweden, and my friend, Eddie, who enjoys listening to and talking with her.

We've taken her out for dinner on several occasions, including to our favorite Mexican restaurant, a fancy diner, a popular tourist spot, an Asian restaurant in downtown Palm Springs, a local burger joint, and a chain Italian restaurant.

We've gone swimming together in the evening after work on several occasions, and also once after dark. We've taken her to three doctor appointments, and taken her shopping. I've helped her unpack, hang pictures, move furniture, and buy things for her room online. I've been teaching (and re-teaching) her how to operate her Keurig coffeemaker and her phone. And we've made other modifications such as outlining the path from her door through the garage into the house with bright yellow duct tape on the floor. It's hard to believe she's only been here a month.

Today, while she napped, Tony and I swam together, enjoying some rare private time, talking in the pool and playing pool games. We talked about her health and our goals for her quality of life. We are on the same page. She has some sores in her mouth about which she didn't tell her doctor yesterday. I am concerned about infections, and falls are always a big risk. She's been aware of a narrowed carotid artery—the one in the side of the neck that feeds the brain—for years, but continues to refuse all treatment options. She has a new diagnosis of aortic artery stenosis. We can't predict her life expectancy, but I hope she will be able to enjoy living with us for at least two years. Mommy has said she would like to live to 100, or at least 95, provided her quality of life is as good as it is right now. We're happy to hear that because it tells us she's happy to be here.

Meanwhile, Tony and I would like to spend a day at the ocean. Although she nibbles from her dorm-sized refrigerator in the garage, if we want her to have a meal, it's pretty clear that someone will have to be here to prepare it and serve it to her. We think we've come up with a way to provide safety checks and meals while allowing her to feel independent. We'll hire our friend Eddie to 'walk the dog', and 'since he's here anyway,' have him prepare dinner that the two of them can eat together. She enjoys his company. Win-win.

July 10, 2018: THE SPLINTER INCIDENT

Recently, Mommy got a splinter in the heel of her foot. She woke me at 11 PM to take a look at it, but wouldn't allow me to touch it. She had a podiatry intake appointment coming up that she had asked me to schedule to have her toenails trimmed. She would ask the podiatrist then to remove it.

In the doctor's office, the podiatrist made it clear that he had no intention of trimming her toenails. (He was above that.) And he didn't want to talk about her 'neuropasy,' she calls it. Instead, he offered a neurologist referral.

"He'll test you for neuropathy," he said. "The test is long and uncomfortable. Could even be painful."

"What about the splinter in her heel?" I asked.

"You'll need a separate appointment for that, if it doesn't work itself out on its own."

We will not be going back to that office.

Once we returned home, with a pin and a pair of tweezers in hand, I sat her down to remove the splinter myself. She kept jerking her foot back, screaming and moaning, carrying on as if I were amputating her foot without anesthetic. Tony stood nearby for support.

"Almost done, just a little more," I tried to reassure her.

"I'm moving back to New York!" she hollered, putting on quite a performance until I got it out. I'd like to think she learned that she can trust that I'll take care of her in spite of her capacity for high drama.

July 15, 2018: PUSH-PULL

Mommy is getting more comfortable here and recently took the liberty of rearranging all the 'prydnader' (Swedish for knick-knacks) on my dining room shelves while Tony and I were out on a date. She did an amazing job and it was a lovely surprise. I sent pictures to Chris and Elsa of her primping proudly in front of her achievement.

We've been swimming in the pool together almost every day. She feels more secure in the child-sized inner tube Tony bought her and has dared to venture away from the steps to kick her feet a little. She's no longer saying—while paddling in the pool—that she feels just as trapped inside by the summer heat as she was trapped inside by the winter cold in Woodstock.

Asta is getting along beautifully with Tony, and sits with me every evening for a couple of hours in front of the TV. She has both of us at her beck and call for anything she might want or need, and we are able to deliver pretty quickly. She's a part of the family and household.

Despite my encouragement, however, she is unwilling to open the kitchen refrigerator, as if that would be crossing some boundary. She's reluctant to shower and hates that she needs my help getting it started. She insists on showering with her underwear on, which is ridiculous in my opinion, but Asta can be very stubborn.

Today, she and I took a celebrity bus tour to learn about the famous people who once lived or currently live around Palm Springs. In the evening, Tony invited me out to dinner.

"Maybe Ma should come along," I said, hesitating.

"I was hoping for some time just for us," he said.

So I informed my mother that he and I were going out for dinner and I'd make her dinner either before we left or when we got home, her choice. She gave me the evil eye. Tony then invited her to join us, but she refused, and it got awkward.

Ultimately, Tony and I went without her, managed to enjoy our dinner out and brought a take-out meal home for her. She sulked and refused to eat, while lecturing me to ensure I'd feel guilty, which I did, both on her account and on Tony's. I'm only one person, being pulled in two directions, or three, if you consider that I might prefer going out for dinner without having to cook anyway.

When I later did gongyo (evening prayers), I prayed for peace and calm, for family unity and happiness, and for all of us to be pointed in the same direction. She can choose to sulk, and I can choose to feel guilty, but it doesn't accomplish anything. I put my feelings aside and invited her to join me in front of the television, which she did for a few minutes before giving me an angry stare and leaving to go to her room. I chose not to get sucked in. I'm tired and am going to bed with my husband, a good man who deserves for our life to go on as a couple in spite of having his mother-in-law move in as a dependent.

Aug 6, 2018: CHINA CUPBOARD

Mommy and I reorganized my china cabinet as an activity for her entertainment. Here are some of its contents:

- My mother's family's plate of lacquered World War II rationing coupons;
- My father's grandfather's yellow jug in which he carried tea or coffee to work in the mines, and which might still have his DNA on it; the jugs my grandmothers used to preserve their pickles and herring;
- Two ceramic dogs my great-grandmother received as a wedding gift.
- The binoculars that belonged to Daddy's great-great-grandfather Anderson, a watchman on the platform in the sea between Sweden and Denmark whose job it was to signal—with red or green lanterns—safe passage to the boats.

- The silver alarm clock my mother's parents bought as new-lyweds. Its job was to wake them at 4 a.m. so they could go milk the cows; the silver candleholders my grandmother purchased from a catalogue for Asta when Asta was little.
- The blue ceramic 'lerjuk' whistle. The housemother required Asta and her fellow nursing students to go up to the mountain at 4 a.m. to hear the lerjuk bird sing. Asta placed colored toothpicks in it like tail feathers.
- The porcupine bank was a gift Asta received on her 18th birthday from friends at the hospital in Styrse, Sweden, where she worked.

I'm treasuring my forbears' memories by taking care of the objects that held some meaning in their lives.

Aug 27, 2018: RESENTMENTS BREW

In her daily phones with Asta, Elsa lays on thick how much she misses having Mommy next door. The whole town misses Mommy. Heidi sits on what was used to be Mommy's porch. Elsa suggests an ocean beach-house vacation (Asta's treat). Everyone would come to see Asta. They discuss my marriage. Elsa confides to Asta how she never liked Tony and feels Tony doesn't like her. Elsa feels I owe her an apology for not allowing her boyfriend to speak at our dad's funeral three years ago (I had reasons). Asta feels sorry for her and campaigns on Elsa's behalf. The stage is set.

Last night over dinner at a restaurant, Ma criticized Tony as if she'd been planning it, waiting to seize an opportunity to cut him down a size or two. I give him credit for how he parried with an apology for whatever it was she took offense to. At home in the driveway, Ma apologized to Tony for lashing out at him, and he again to her, and the three of us took an amicable dip in the pool together.

This morning, when I brought her morning cup of coffee in to her, she was seated at her desk, eyes red, sniffling. She quickly covered the writing she was working on in front of her.

"Have you been crying?"

"No," she denied. But I know my mother. She'd been brooding about her exchange over dinner with Tony. I'm not going to add fuel to that fire.

"How long have you been up?"

"All night," she said, "I couldn't sleep."

I observed that her ankles were a little bit swollen. "Let me help you into bed. Lay down and raise your feet, rest your eyes."

"I think I'll sleep all day, since we don't have anything special to do today. Don't wake me up for breakfast."

"Have you eaten tonight?" In truth, I knew by the crumbs on the floor by her bed that she wouldn't starve for not eating breakfast.

"No, not really."

"I'm going shopping today, maybe for clothes. Would you like to come along?" I asked.

"No," she said. I let her sleep.

I'm going for a walk and hope to enjoy the day more or less independently of Mommy this morning. I'll try to spend some of the day with Tony, who deserves better than her blame and resentments.

Sept 3, 2018: THAT WAS EASY

Tony has a 'That Was Easy' button that sits on our kitchen counter. We cracked up when Asta pushed it away and quipped, "That wasn't so easy."

Tonight's menu:

- Grapes as appetizers
- Grilled sausages, skin-on mashed potatoes

- A side of fresh sliced mozzarella cheese
- Strawberries in cream for dessert

Over dinner, Mommy shared some insights she's had about me since moving in. "Your wardrobe is more relaxed than it used to be" (when I was an executive). And "I'm surprised to see you wearing my slinky hand-me-down red pajamas." My mother and I are about the same size and I've worn her hand-me-downs for years.

We talked about why things are difficult between Tony and I and Elsa, whether or not she'd like a family-reunion-type vacation, if she would like to go walking in the neighborhood for exercise, the book she's writing, and the meal. Tony has a gift for engaging her in conversation, raising topics she might be interested in, and asking questions that get her started telling stories. After dinner, he played a Diana Krall video on TV to see if she'd be interested in joining us to go see Diana Krall in concert. She wasn't.

For my part, I'm looking forward to our friends and neighbors getting to know her better. I'm proud of how witty she is and how much fun she can be to spend time with. Last night we typed the last installment to her story, 'Do Not Cry for Me, Tina'. She creates, and I do the typing. Next, we'll work together on the story's timeline— who got married to whom, who was born when, to whom, etc. And then tomorrow, we're going shopping for a book to help her learn Spanish. My mother is determined to be able to communicate with our gardeners. She's a gracious and social woman and I've always been proud of her.

Sept 14, 2018: ATTACHMENT

Two days ago I was laid off from my job. Mommy is downright gleeful. Looking for cues from me as to how she should think and feel, first she reacted with anger, then sadness, then pity, trying feelings on like outfits. Which was the right one to wear?

"Everything's okay," I assured her. "We're okay, there's nothing to worry about." Today when I brought in her morning cup of coffee, as is our routine, here was our conversation:

"How do you feel about being home with all this time on your hands?" she asked.

"Good," I answered.

"Why?" she asked.

"Because I get to spend more time with you!" I said, and I meant it.

"Good answer," she said, grinning. Just a few hours later, things turned in a different direction.

Since Mommy can't walk (much), she often asks for assistance in getting this or that. I genuinely don't mind, and she seems grateful. She asked for a piece of yarn, which I delivered with, "At your service". We grinned, and I went back to my own business in my office. Five minutes later she came storming into my office wearing a broad, fake smile.

"If you think I'm asking too much of you, then I'm in the wrong place," construing ill-meaning where there was none. We got through it without an argument, but it is evidence of how fragile her good attitude is, how hasty her judgments are.

It's only day two of unemployment. At various times throughout the day, I invite her to keep me company, yet still try to preserve some time to myself for paperwork, errands and such.

She's in relatively good health, but needs meals, help with showers, entertainment, and supervision. Earlier today, I heard a big crash in the garage and ran to the rescue. She had moved three large storage bins to access the contents of her big yellow trunk. From it, she had withdrawn and dropped a ceramic ghost. Relieved that she hadn't fallen, I cleaned up the shards so she wouldn't cut her feet.

She needs an arm to hang onto because she's too proud to use her walker. I did manage to persuade her to use her seated walker last week when we went shopping for clothes, and she discovered how convenient it was to sit while she shopped. But when we went to the HOA meeting, she insisted on taking the cane in one hand

and holding onto my arm with the other. The walker would've given her more freedom and independence, but the issue is vanity, pride.

She doesn't want to hang onto Tony's arm. Only mine. Doesn't want to swim with Tony unless I'm also in the pool. The word is 'possessive.' I wish she would be willing to distribute the weight of her needs a little more between the two of us. That said, having her here has been going fairly smoothly. So far.

Sept 19, 2018: TLC

On Saturday, Mommy had an upset stomach, refused to eat, and had to be coaxed to drink a sip of water or tea. She hung her head over the wastebasket and tried to throw up into it. Didn't want to go to Urgent Care. I took her temperature, no fever.

"I think I'm constipated," she said. Maybe she just needed fluids.

I catered to her all day and then at bedtime gave her a foot massage. "We're doing reflexology. I feel a knot where the colon spot might be," I told her like a bedtime story. And then she slept. On Sunday I was supposed to accompany Tony, Ronnie, Angi and Angi's cousin to the LA Rams game, but stayed home to keep an eye on her. I wasn't going to leave her alone when she wasn't feeling well.

By morning she was much better, saying the foot massage did it. In the afternoon, I made 'garbage soup' (family recipe of cabbage soup with vegetables and skin-on chicken), her favorite, and she ate two big bowls of it.

The next day, I took her for an appointment with her new eye doctor. That she was blind in one eye and going blind in the other was no surprise, but the cause of her blindness was upsetting: poor blood flow to the eyes, possibly due to her carotid artery blockage (she calls it her 'corroded' artery). For the next couple of hours we talked about life and death, philosophy, religion and living, and then after dinner, sat at my computer and put the finishing touches on her book. Working together on a project or shopping on the computer always makes her happy.

I spend quite a bit of time with her, more on some days than others, but often four or more hours a day. She's glad I'm unemployed. Unlike in Woodstock, she doesn't have to watch for me out the window, wondering when I'll drop in. I help her shower and wash her hair, check on her and make sure she has what she needs at bedtime, put a clean cup and fresh water in her Keurig machine, and a cold bottle of water at bedside. I take out her trash, do her laundry and fetch whatever she asks for or needs. Beyond that, she's content to rest in her room reading or writing, or when we're not home, in the living room with Dawson watching the news on TV.

Tony is refereeing tonight so Ma and I are on our own. We'll be going to a Buddhist meeting where I hope to recruit someone to check on her, for pay, when Tony and I go out of town. Mommy is agreeable to having someone assist in this way, provided she knows and feels comfortable with them. But first, liverwurst sandwiches.

Oct 18, 2018: POLKA DOTTED PANTS

When it came to doing laundry, my mother had made it an art form. Her whites were white, colors bright, and her towels and sheets were soft and inhale-worthy. It was one of the things I looked forward to when visiting her home. She was glad to relinquish the chore when she moved here, but is particular about how it gets done.

Initially, we combining her laundry with ours.

"I don't want my clothes to end up in your closet," she objected. So we began washing her laundry separately. "I want my clothes washed in Woolite, not your brand of laundry detergent." Again, we complied. But there've been other laundry issues as well.

- When she couldn't find her favorite black polka-dotted pants, she blamed Tony, who does the bulk of our laundry.

"Maybe they're still at the dry cleaners," she said—not believing it, but trying to give him the benefit of the doubt. She refused to allow me to check her closet or drawers. "I know what I have and where I put it."

- She found a black beaded top hanging in her closet with a matching skirt, but was convinced that the top she brought from New York had a different style of shoulder straps.

Mommy is offended when I suggest that maybe, just maybe, she might have misplaced it. She refuses my invitation to inspect my closet for her clothing. When she later finds an item, she suspects that Tony or I put it back when she wasn't looking. Since she doesn't want to blame me, she blames Tony. Like today:

"I think he's taking my things to make me think I'm going crazy," she said. Nothing I say changes her thinking. "Of course you would defend Tony."

There's no point arguing with her, so I tried a different approach.

"Well, I hope that someday you'll come to trust him, because we need him, and he's doing everything he can to make you as comfortable as possible, as am I," I said.

She continued to struggle with missing the pants, and later, appealed to Tony: "I modeled those pants for you before the Willie Nelson show. Remember?" she asked. He wasn't so sure.

A few days later, Chris found Ma's black polka dotted pants in a box labeled 'winter clothes' that Ma had asked her to forward when winter approached. When I showed her the picture of the pants in Chris's text, Ma got hand-wringingly upset.

"It's not possible that those are my pants," she said. She's afraid to admit that she made a mistake for fear it would signal dementia. "Chris must have bought a replacement pair and put them among my things. Why would she do that?"

"Because she loves you and would do anything to make you happy," Tony said.

"You understand, Tony," she said. He does.

Oct 19, 2018: FALL RISK

In their daily phone calls, between Mommy's kibitzing with Elsa about things she can't find and their gossiping about Tony and me, Elsa lays her affection on thick. She is Mommy's best friend and confidante, and is trying to persuade Ma to return to New York "for a visit. But you'll have to be nice to Tom" (her boyfriend). Note the condition.

The topic of my mother's travelling to New York comes up often. I've made it clear that I'm opposed to her making such a trip because:

- A flight could bring on another case of cellulitis, like she had after traveling here, and a visit would mean she'd have to fly twice—there and back.
- New environments are often responsible for falls in the elderly, and falls can cause broken bones.
- Ma has trouble with steps and would be stuck in Elsa's house. Here we have no steps at all, and Ma has her own private entrance/exit and garden that she can independently access.

But Elsa sees it as a competition, I think, one she intends to win. I'm very frustrated with her.

Oct 20, 2018: THINGS WE LEARN FROM OUR MOTHERS

"I don't need to be entertained," my mother boasted to Chris, who was visiting for a long weekend. "Some nights I watch the shadows on the ceiling of my room and sees the shapes they take."

"When I close my eyes I see white lines cross my field of vision," Chris added.

"When my eyes are closed, I see worms and parasites," I said. "I guess we learned that from you, Ma. All we need to entertain ourselves is a dark room."

Entertaining yourself is a skill.

Nov 11, 2018: ELSA'S F-U VISIT

Prior to coming out for her visit, Elsa encouraged Tony and I to go away for the weekend and asked to borrow one of our cars while we were gone. We considered taking advantage of her offer until I learned she was planning on having a dinner party while we were gone. I didn't feel comfortable having her play hostess to my neighbors, in my house, in my absence. When she arrived and I informed her that we had decided to stay home, she made a sour face and complained to Asta about it. It wasn't a good beginning.

Tony, meanwhile, is still hurt by Elsa's past interference in our marriage. It is true that she encouraged me to divorce him, even sent me several unsolicited divorce self-help books. He knows she's gossiping about us with my mother. He's aware how Elsa is complicating Asta's adjustment and tarnishing her interactions with us.

So when he saw me and Elsa talking out by the pool, he suspected her of criticizing how we take care of Asta. He came outside, chest forward.

"I don't want you talking shit behind our back," he said. "Stop interfering." There, he'd said it: what he's been wanting to say to her for years. Elsa gave me her "See what I mean?" look. The three of us went to our own corners inside.

Privately, I explained to Tony his mistake, that she had not been criticizing us or him. "And anyway, no lecture anybody could give would cause Elsa to change anything. We just have to get through the visit." He promised to be polite, if superficial, for the duration of the visit.

I went and talked to Elsa.

"Mommy feels like a prisoner in a gilded cage," Elsa said, using a phrase Mommy has also been using lately. "It's too hot to leave your door open, and the air conditioning is on," she said. That's right, Captain Obvious. "She needs friends other than you," Elsa said, presenting herself as if for service.

"If it had been so great in Woodstock, Elsa," I said, "Mommy wouldn't have moved here."

Elsa brought out the guns and aimed at my marriage. "I feel sorry for you, Suey," she said.

"Fuck you, Elsa," I said.

"Fuck you, too," she said.

"Don't sabotage what we are doing here for Mommy, and don't turn her against Tony. She's living in his house, for Christ's sake, and he helps take care of her. You're only confusing her."

"Don't tell me what to say. I can say anything I want to her," she said.

"Yes, you can. But keep in mind that Tony and I are here for her sake. You want to help? Stop talking shit about us, and stop enticing her back to New York. Let's play nice for her benefit."

The next few days were strained but tolerable. Tony and I went on bike rides and to the movies, allowing Elsa alone-time with Mommy. We drove them where and when they wanted to go, and treated them to a show (which they loved) at the McCallum Theater, where Tony and I volunteer as ushers. Elsa must have told me ten times how much and how deeply she misses Mommy. I nodded, "I'm sure you do."

Her visit finally ended.

"Elsa said her visit was painful," my mother said. "You owe her an apology. She's pressuring me to go stay with her in New York."

I didn't remind my mother how, when she lived next door to Elsa, Chris and I were concerned for her safety. I didn't bring up how, after Ma had fallen and broken three ribs, Elsa had delayed taking her to the doctor for days. She didn't think anything was wrong, or maybe it wasn't convenient.

Mommy is safe here and we're taking good care of her. I wish Elsa would just stop.

Nov 18, 2018: INTERCEPTED LETTER

"You might want to intercept a letter I sent because I don't want Tony to see it," Elsa texted. "On the other hand, if he sees it, I'm okay with that too."

The letter came. In it, after griping over how we hadn't gone away as we had said we might, didn't lend her a car and how she'd felt unwelcome, she went on to describe Tony with seven angry, hate-filled adjectives. I didn't have the stomach to write them down. I got rid of her letter.

Mommy summoned me to her room. Elsa had sent her a copy of the letter and my mother was upset.

"I yust want everybody to be happy and love each other," she said, "and *forgive* each other. Because we are blood, we are family."

"I forgive Elsa," I told her, "but I don't owe her an apology, and I'm not asking for one from her. Tony doesn't owe her anything either. They don't have to like each other. Elsa can come and visit, but in her letter she made it clear that she would make other arrangements. Her choice."

It was inappropriate of Elsa, on so many levels, to send our mother a copy of her vicious letter. But I will not respond to her letter. I will not join the stage for her performance.

Dec 1, 2018: HOSPITAL STAY

On Tuesday, after a breakfast of French bread with butter and jam with Mommy, Tony and I ushered at the McCallum. When we came home around 1 PM, Ma was in bed. She had vomited. I offered to take her to urgent care.

"No way," she said. "I haven't pooped and I feel bloated and nauseous." I took her temperature. It was normal. We agreed to wait and see. In the evening, she had some chicken soup and kept it down. I gave her tea that's supposed to help her poop and took her temperature again. Again within normal limits. I set my alarm and checked on her twice during the night. At 5 AM she pooped and said she felt better. Crisis averted, we thought.

In the morning, she had a light breakfast and was cheerful, so I confirmed my plans to meet Ronnie for some outlet shopping. When I went to say goodbye, my mother was throwing up again. Still no fever, and again she refused to go to the doctor. Tony would be home so she'd have supervision, so I left according to plan. But by the time I reached the Interstate, I had called Ronnie and cancelled. I turned around and drove back home.

I went into Mommy's room. "I'm taking you to urgent care," I said. "It's not okay for you to lay here in pain, suffering, and not knowing what's going on or what can be done about it. Let me help you get up and get dressed. We'll head over there now." Reluctantly, she cooperated.

At urgent care, they took a urine sample, found blood in her urine but no infection. They referred us to the ER. We drove to the hospital, waited an hour in registration, and an hour more after her blood was drawn. She was her charming self with staff, even witty at times, as she likes to be with medical personnel. When one medical assistant in the ER asked, "What brings you here today?" she answered, "Well, to see you of course!"

I kept my sisters informed as things developed. Elsa sent all-too-frequent syrup-y sweet texts, which I found ingratiating and annoying. Chris called me to talk.

"I'll be on a plane tomorrow, if you need me," Chris said.

"I know, but that isn't necessary at this point," I replied.

Over the next several hours there were more tests and exams. Ultimately she was admitted for observation and given a room. I followed her to her room and waited until she saw a doctor and got the diagnosis: kidney stones. They gave her pain medicine and hydration. I went home for the night at 10 p.m.

In the morning, I returned at 8 a.m. More tests, more exams. We waited all day expecting to be discharged. I helped her take a shower, helped her go to the bathroom, kept her company, asked and answered questions of staff with her permission and on her behalf. I repeated or restated to her what people said, and explained it again after they left. We looked things up on the internet (via my phone) and wrote down additional questions.

At 8 p.m. it was determined she would not be discharged after all. She would have another test or procedure in the morning. I went home and slept well, woke up in the middle of the night as usual, and wrote down some middle-of-the-night notes.

By morning, her IV had been removed and we were told she would be discharged. We captured a sizable kidney stone in the urine filter and celebrated, reporting to staff. They gave us a container in which to keep it as a souvenir but with instructions to give it to her urologist next week. I helped her out of the hospital gown and into her clothes.

The doctors, nurses, housekeepers and dining staff had all treated her with dignity and provided quality care. She especially enjoyed the volunteer's escort through the lobby and was impressed by the magnificent chandeliers hanging there. She discovered a whole new attitude towards hospitals and medicine. No more fear and suspicion.

"I'm willing to take the medication they ordered and go to their follow up appointments," she announced.

I'll take some credit for the positive outcomes, for how I kept her company, explained things, kept everything objective and in perspective. Once again, my mother wanted to talk about life and death.

"Everyone dies," she said, pragmatically. "There's no avoiding it. It's yust my turn. Well, not yet, but it's inevitable."

I agreed, and said, paraphrasing Nichiren Daishonin's words in his Letter from Sado: "Even horses and cattle cling to life, why not humans?" We talked about death as the shedding of a body, about hospitals, nursing homes and hospice facilities.

"I'd like to spend my last days in the same hospice that Daddy was in," she said.

"If you get to the point where you need hospice care, Mommy," I said, "you won't be able to travel 3,000 miles. We'll get you whatever care you need here." She could have hospice care here at home with visiting nurses.

On the way home from the hospital, we stopped for a brunch of lingonberry pancakes at Elmer's, then picked up her new medication. At home while she rested, I organized her paperwork, made phone calls and scheduled her follow-up appointments. Tony picked up Chinese food and the three of us sat down for dinner. Ma put her story-telling strengths on full display.

She told about the whispering man who, wearing lots of bracelets and necklaces, came into her room at 5 a.m. and took more blood. He was friendly, but she was frightened. The moment he left, she pushed the call bell for someone to come so she could ask "Who was he?" With her expressive face, voice and gestures, and added details, her telling of the story was captivating.

But the whole hospital experience had been overwhelming, she said, and now she was 'crashing'. "But I'm grateful and have a whole new outlook about hospitals." I'm so incredibly proud of her.

Before bed, she came out calling my name.

"I yust didn't want to go to bed without thanking you for all you did for me the last few days. You were wonderful," she said. Clearly, we have a two-way fan club going on here.

I'm still not working, so I can attend to Ma's needs without too much stress. Tony is supportive. Ma wrote a thank you note that I will deliver with a can of Pepparkakkor (Swedish ginger cookies) to the hospital staff later today.

My niece, Lisa, called and said she and her partner were on their way to Palm Springs 'for an event' and would be arriving within the hour. I'd wager she is coming as Elsa's delegate or proxy. I love

Lisa, and she is welcome. But nobody asked me, and Ma would have preferred a few days before having to receive visitors. At any rate, she's putting on her game face and preparing to entertain. Tony went out to buy heavy cream for me to whip up and serve with the lemon cake Elsa sent to Mommy through the mail last week.

Dec 25, 2018: HOLIDAYS

Ronnie and Angi arrived for their holiday visit. They and I spent the afternoon shopping at the outlet malls, and after dinner Tony took the five of us out to see the new Mary Poppins movie. Asta slept through most of it.

On Christmas Eve morning I delivered, as Ma requested, her silver tray breakfast carrying a bowl of cereal, a small pitcher of milk to pour on top, a cup of coffee, a glass of orange juice, her pills in one dessert dish and some apple sauce in another. She took her time getting dressed and joined the party when she was ready. Ronnie, Angi and their dog entertained us all throughout the day with their company and conversation.

Our Christmas Eve menu included:

- Three varieties of fancy cheese with crackers for the appetizer
- 'Lazy Man's Lobster,' a Costello tradition, made with lobster tails, scallops, extra-large shrimp and pieces of skin-on salmon, Ritz crackers and lots of butter
- Mashed potatoes
- Snow peas
- Tangerine cake (made of fresh tangerines from our tree) for dessert

After dinner and a light clean-up, the five of us moved into the dining room and distributed gifts in front of the fireplace, sounding the requisite ooh's and aah's and snapping thank-you photos to send to the givers. Sated, we went to bed around 9 or 10 p.m.

Around 3:30 a.m., Tony woke up with an upset stomach. Probably too much butter and cheese. At 4:30 a.m., I drove the girls to the airport for the continuation of their journey, came home and climbed back in bed.

Then came a phone call from Mommy. I ran to her room and found her on the floor on her knees.

"I got up to go to the bathroom, got dizzy and fell back onto the bed," she said. "I had to crawl to the telephone to call you." I helped her up and to the bathroom, then back to her room, and cleaned up the pee on the floor. Back to bed. Just as I was falling asleep, Ma called again on the phone.

"I'm afraid," she said when I arrived in her room. "I thought I was having a stroke. Maybe it's a side effect from the heart medicine they put me on. Those doctors make you sick so they can make money."

"It may be a side effect," I admitted, "but I'm sure the doctors are trying to help."

"In case I die before I can tell you again," she began, "here's how I want you to distribute my stuff…" I listened while she talked at some length about her knickknacks, artwork and clothing. "Would you sleep in my room?"

"Okay," I said, wanting to allay her fear, and tried to get comfortable on her too-short red velvet loveseat. "We'll call the doctor in the morning, tell him your symptoms and ask if you should continue with that heart medicine."

"Don't call the doctor," she said.

"We'll look the medicine up online in the morning," I countered.

But my mother wanted information now. I retrieved the pharmacy's Rx information sheet from my office and read it to her. Yes, dizziness was a side effect, we confirmed.

"Tony isn't feeling well either," I told her. "He's having trouble with his stomach." Telling her this was a mistake, because now she would compete with him. Which of them would be sicker, which would need me more, who would I make my priority? My mother doesn't want to share my attention. She wants it all for herself.

Neither of us was getting any sleep, and she wasn't having a stroke, so I excused myself and went back to my own room to doze.

In the morning, sulking and critical, she exaggerated, "No wonder he doesn't feel well. He did 15 loads of Ronnie's laundry this weekend."

I extracted myself and returned a few minutes later. "What would you like for breakfast?" I asked, and "Would you like it in her room or will you come out and join us in the kitchen?" I always try to give her choices. She wanted bacon and eggs and would join us in the kitchen, it being Christmas, after all. I had to return twice and send Tony in once to remind her it was time to come over.

Meanwhile, Tony and I cancelled our plans to have Eddie over for dinner. Tony wasn't in the mood to entertain with his upset stomach, and I didn't want to have to be chauffer, cook, and conversationalist all at once. Too much effort and pressure. We broke the news to her over breakfast.

"It's my fault," Tony offered, so she wouldn't blame me, "for our change in plans today."

Surprised by his equanimity, she laughed. "Tony, I can't help but like you. Even when I don't want to."

"Good attitude!" he answered. "And anyway, you're stuck with me."

After breakfast, we re-read the medication information sheet, discussed her options and best course of action, and she decided to continue taking the medication for now. She'll ask her blood doctor's advice when she sees him on Friday.

Asta returned to her room to rest, and Tony laid down in ours. I took my first walk in two weeks and was able to relax for a bit before beginning to cook our Christmas dinner of turkey legs and roasted vegetables.

When I went in to check on her, she was sitting on the edge of her bed tapping her heels against the floor as she often does.

"Cramps," she complained, looking miserable.

Jan 6, 2019: MEMOIR CONTEST

Recently, Asta submitted an entry to the Rancho Mirage Library Writers' Guild Memoir contest. We had spent many hours together in front of my computer trimming her memoir to bring it to within the word-limit guidelines.

Tony, especially, talked up her entry to friends and family. Several of our friends and neighbors are also writers, so they have something in common. In any event, entering the Rancho Mirage Library Memoir contest is a pretty big deal around here.

So all of us—Asta, Tony, Ronnie, Angi, two neighbors and I—attended the awards presentation fully expecting her to win. She neither won nor placed, but it was an exciting night out and we enjoyed celebrating her efforts. I'm encouraging her to start a new project—maybe a children's book about Lollipop, my coworker's dog who had a very traumatic Christmas. We could work on it together.

Jan 7, 2019: NUISANCE COMMUNICATION

Sometimes I get a text from Elsa while I'm at work. "Ma isn't answering her phone," they typically say. "Tell Tony to check her phone."

I ignore such requests. Sure, I'd worry too if I were far away. When she was living next door to Elsa, I worried that Ma had fallen and wasn't able to reach a phone. I worried that her phone was broken because she lived alone. But here, when I'm at work, Tony is in the house and checks on her often. Elsa's 'emergency' is not my emergency, and I'm not going to make it one.

While I'm at work, Elsa and my mother are on the phone airing their grievances about me and/or Tony, cooking up trouble in their cauldron.

Today, for example, when I came home from work my mother said, "Elsa told me you owe her an apology, because she didn't feel welcome here during her last visit." They talk about this a lot.

"I don't owe Elsa an apology," I said. "Maybe Elsa owes me one. In any event, telling someone to 'say you're sorry' is childish." As is pouting for the apology that isn't coming.

Jan 20, 2019: SANDWICHED

Tony got upset when Ma and I teased him about turning lights off behind us.

"There's nothing wrong with turning off lights when there's no one in the room," he said. He's right, of course, but we've been teasing him over it for weeks and he's fed up with it. "What is this, two against one?"

I've got him on one side, fussing—OCD-like—over the lights (the cost of electricity, the waste) and Asta on the other, saying it makes her feel like she's in the way.

She doesn't like how he's expressing his frustration. The target on his back is getting bigger. I try to explain that he's just letting off a little steam.

"Don't worry. He likes you. He'll get over it," I tell her. "And it's not about the lights. It's about feeling ganged up on and teased by us."

Tony's never liked being teased. I'm not giving him as much time or attention as I used to. He's having to get used to that. I tell him all the time how much I appreciate his help.

And I feel like I'm in the middle, mothering both sides, trying to un-ruffle feathers, trying always to make everything okay for everyone. It's tiring.

Feb 14, 2019: SUSPICION AND GUILT

Ma is unhappy that Tony and I have been busy. She doesn't like that Tony is her 'caretaker' while I'm at work, or that some nights we have pizza for dinner. She doesn't like that I'm not always around.

"He says things to people in the neighborhood that make me look bad," she accuses, on absolutely no evidence. On the contrary, when he's saying anything at all about her, it's about how cool she is, how she's a writer and how she's from Sweden. How much more cool can you get than that?

She interprets his invitation that she 'watch TV and keep Dawson company while we're ushering at the McCallum' as a command. She conjures a suspicious motive behind his efforts to make conversation. Why would he take an interest in reading her Woodstock Sentinel (the newspaper Elsa is having delivered to our house), for example? Dare I defend him in any way makes her angry with me. Every day is a delicate dance.

"Of course you defend him," she says with contempt, then follows it quickly with an odd 'poor me, I'll be a good little girl' performance. "I have no voice here," she continues. My mother is oblivious to the fact that her needs and opinions are front and center in all our decisions.

Tony, unaware of all the mean, fearful, critical, miserable things she said about him to me last night, gave her a Valentine's Day rose and box of candy today. Which made her feel guilty. To balance the scales, she gave him the bottle of wine she'd been saving in her closet for a special occasion, so long as I promised to get her a replacement bottle for some future occasion. Of course I will. I'm on it.

When we came home from ushering, Tony demonstrated for her the Celtic dance moves he saw performed on the stage. How could she not love this guy?

Feb 16, 2019: A CONCESSION

We're planning my mother's 91's birthday party. "Elsa told me she needs you to invite her here in order for her to feel welcome," my mother said.

Elsa has become high maintenance. Not what I need in my life right now. But I'll reach across the aisle. I sent both her and Chris a formal invitation to the party by text, for the weekend of my mother's birthday. We would reserve the neighborhood clubhouse.

"Could we make it the weekend before?" Elsa wrote back.

"Because?" I wrote back. I didn't want to change the date, but added, "Anything's possible, but I'd prefer the weekend of the 26th."

"That weekend is just before my arts festival and it would be hard for me," she wrote.

I waited a few minutes to answer, thinking people who are invited to something should work with the invitation given, not try to make it revolve around themselves. Once the steam had cleared from my ears, I answered, "Nothing's easy :(Lemme think on it." Ugh. Another battle.

She blinked first. "Fuck the job, I'll make it work," she wrote.

Feb 23, 2019: HANDS-ON CARE, HANDS ON DECK

I had to be in Pasadena for three days of training for work this week. At the same time, our great-nephew, Russell, came visiting. Tony both entertained Russell and took care of Asta while I was gone. When I called Ma on a break to say hi, she informed me she had a loose front tooth. I scheduled a dentist appointment.

Once I returned home, Tony and Russell left to spend a couple of days in LA, have fun with family and live like tourists.

So it was just Asta and me at home and we decided on a little pampering. I fixed her an Epsom salt bath in the master bathroom. She wanted me to keep her company while she sat in the tub in her underwear. Getting in and out of the tub was hard for her, even with help, but it warmed her up and was worth the effort.

It had been a long day. I went to bed exhausted.

At midnight, Ma came into the hall calling my name. She was having a bloody nose and was worried. I had her sit down on my great-uncle Andy's green couch (a family heirloom) and made us both a cup of chamomile tea with honey. Her bloody nose stopped. We tried to search the internet for 'when does a bloody nose become an emergency?' but the internet was down on all devices. We agreed to ask her blood doctor the next time she goes to see him.

Before going to work in the morning, I took Ma for a CT scan that had been ordered to see if she had any latent kidney stones. Tony came home early from LA to help out, and drove her home from the appointment so I could go directly to work. I was busy that day at work but managed to get away and meet my mother and Tony at the dentist's office at 11:30 a.m. There we learned there is decay around the screw that is holding the loose tooth in place. The dentist could would try to repair it, but she might need a permanent bridge. Once again, Tony took her home and I returned to the office. I worked late to make up my missed hours.

To my surprise, my employer gave me a bonus that week that apparently I had earned. To celebrate, I took Tony and Ma to the Red Lobster for dinner. I loved watching Tony and Asta interact:

- How he reached over and took a piece of steak from her plate for the doggie bag, thinking she had finished when she hadn't, and how they dealt with that awkward moment,
- How she held onto his arm as he escorted her to the car, the two of them laughing,
- How they bantered with each other; how he inspires her sense of humor.
- How the two of them can talk about difficult issues, like cancer, and life and death. She likes the way he thinks, she says; likes him in spite of herself.

Over dinner Tony told her, "Suey gave me a sticker for keeping up with the laundry. Maybe someday, Asta, you'll give me a sticker too."

"When the time is right—if it ever is," she laughed, meaning, 'don't get your hopes up.' She's not about to give him any credit.

Today she informed me there is something wrong with her eyes. We made an eye doctor appointment. Tony will help with transportation and conversation.

Feb 24, 2019: TOXIC

Mommy came to our side of the house because she was bored and feeling lonely. I welcomed her, gave her dessert and a cup of coffee, and opened up a new package of 'skorpor' (Stella Doro sponge cookies).

Cue the Meddling Music. This is what she told me over coffee:

"Elsa sent me the book 'Narcissist,'" she said, explaining "because she knows I'm interested in psychiatry and because it will help me interact with people."

"What people?" I asked, knowing full well that Elsa means Tony. She has come up with a theory or diagnosis and is spreading it like peanut butter. I read the definition of 'narcissist' to Mommy. "Maybe it's about her," I suggested.

"Yeah," she said, "maybe it is." But my mother will dutifully read the book so she and Elsa can further tar and feather my husband. Elsa should be ashamed of herself.

Mar 2, 2019: COMPANY

Tony's sister, Enie, arrived for a few days' visit. One night, I took Enie and Mommy to Drag Karaoke. We sat at the table closest to the stage so Ma could see. Unfortunately, The MC (in drag) seemed to feel we had come to gawk. It was a boring show, but Mommy didn't want to leave. For her, it was a night out. For me, it was a work night and I was exhausted.

The next evening, Tony and I were ushering for the show 'Stomp,' so we bought two tickets and brought Asta and Enie along.

Enie is a natural caregiver, and Asta enjoyed telling her stories about herself … and me.

Yesterday, the four of us drove up to Joshua Tree with Ma and I in the back seat. She voiced one displeasure after another, with a smile, as if that would make her bad attitude go unnoticed:

- "California's not what I expected."
- "It's prettier in the high desert than in the valley where we live."
- "Wasn't today's drive as far as driving from Elsa's house in Woodstock to Chris's house in York?"
- "If I didn't have a loose tooth and numb feet I'd love to live alone."

Not getting a reaction out of me, she tried a direct attack.

"You are so stubborn," she said. "Where could you possibly have gotten that from? From whose side of the family?"

"I was born this way, Mommy. It's my karma," I said, accepting full responsibility for my nature. Her digs kept coming. Finally, I asked her in Swedish, "Are you mad at me? Have I done something wrong?"

"No, no, not you", she said.

"Are you mad at Tony? What has he done to make you mad?"

"Nothing, nothing. Forget it. Whatever."

I mean, it was ridiculous, having to parry one lunge after another. It must makes her feel powerful. This morning I asked Tony, "Is it me? Am I doing something that would bring this out in her?"

"No, I've noticed it too," he said. "Your mother has gotten more negative lately." He can avoid her, but I can't.

Mar 16, 2019: ZOO

Today, the three of us went to the Living Desert Zoo and Botanical Gardens. It's comfortable this time of year: not too hot.

Asta kept insisting this outing was on her. I stopped protesting and let her think she was paying, but Tony and I took care of it. We rode the tram around the zoo maybe three or four times, got off here and there to browse. Mommy wanted to see the reptiles, Tony wanted to see the Rams. We brought her seated walker and she enjoyed having us push her around in it, as if it were a wheelchair. We had lunch at an outdoor restaurant/grill inside the zoo, and to top off the day, she bought herself a souvenir at the gift shop on our way out—a wide-brimmed white hat with a leopard-print ribbon around it. It looks great on her.

Apr 8, 2019: COMPLAINTS

Elsa was here for a long weekend. On the evening after her departure, Ma pointed to an unopened box in the garage—the commode I'd purchased with her consent after her recent hospitalization.

"I don't want to be a patient here," she spat. "I want to go back to New York to live with Elsa."

I had been storing the box inconspicuously in plain sight and was surprised, first, that she noticed it at all with her eyesight, and second, how it angered her relative to the timing of Elsa's visit. I transferred it into Ronnie's room and stored it under my sewing desk. And then I called Elsa.

"Have you and Ma been talking about her moving back east?" I asked.

"We talk about it all the time. I want her to know she has an option."

"Mommy is too frail for a trip across country. Please stop encouraging that line of thinking. It confuses her and is not helpful. She's fine here, safe, and being well taken care of."

"Yes," Elsa agreed, "but she needs to vent."

"Maybe redirecting would be more helpful," I said. "For the most part, she complains just to have something to talk about when you call."

"It's my role to listen," Elsa said.

"I understand," I said, "but think about the fact that Ma is living here with us, and we have to clean up your mess."

The two of them talked on the phone that evening. At 1 a.m., Mommy called me on the phone. I went to her room and found her crying.

"What's the matter?" I asked, looking for signs of injury or illness.

"Nothing."

"Why are you crying?" (No response.) "Did you call me?"

"Yes."

"What's wrong?"

"Nothing. I yust wanted you to know I'm upset." And then she appealed dramatically, tearfully, arms outstretched, palms up, to Daddy in Heaven, "Is dis what you wanted for me?"

My mother was feeling sorry for herself, torn over where she should live. She had to take it out on somebody. That somebody would have to be me or Tony, of course, who are here, not 3,000 miles away in Paradise. We can't compete with Paradise.

Not one inclined to throw or attend pity parties, I said, "Try to get some sleep. You'll be seeing the dentist tomorrow and I need to go to work."

Having failed to snag me with sympathy, she aimed her guilt gun and shot. "Don't you think you could tell your boss that you have to take time off from work for this emergency?"

I didn't fall for that either. "This is not an emergency," I answered. "A dentist appointment is not an emergency. I will take time off for an emergency."

Apr 19, 2019: JOB LOSS AND RAINBOWS

Earlier this week I got in trouble at work for trying to leave to meet my mother at a doctor's appointment. Luckily, Tony was able and happy to take her without me. He has repeatedly urged me to do whatever my bosses asked, at whatever the time of day, but I've made it clear to all of them—my employer, my mother and my spouse—that:

- I would attend all my mother's informational medical appointments,
- I cannot be expected, on short notice, to cover shifts at work when people call in, and
- I will provide for my mother, and require for myself, a stable and predictable daily routine.

After my subsequent refusal to abandon my mother to cover a call-in, I got let-go, fired. This benefits Asta, of course. I'll be able to ferry her to Spanish lessons at the senior center where we're hoping she'll make some friends. But she needs to get used to the idea of having Tony take her, because I want to and will return to work.

For now, with extra time off, we can turn our attention towards getting her hearing aids cleaned and starting those Spanish lessons.

CHAPTER 3
SETTLED IN

May 25, 2019: ANNIVERSARY

This week we celebrated Asta's one year anniversary with us by taking her to a fine restaurant in Rancho Mirage. For another outing, we took her to the Palm Springs Art Museum. There, she sat in her wheeled walker and enjoyed being pushing around. Tony wasn't used to maneuvering the seat with her in it and bumped its wheel against the elevator doorway, which made her mad.

"I don't want him driving it. I want you to drive it," she said, speaking to me. "After all," she justified, "you're my daughter." It doesn't matter to her that he's stronger, or that it might help me out for him to be doing the pushing.

At the museum, all she wanted to look at was anything that might be Swedish. She's obsessed with all things Swedish. Nothing rises to her standards unless it's bona fide Swedish. When the docent came by to explain the big collage at which we were gazing, Asta asked. "Is there anything in there (the collage) by a Swedish artist?" It took an enormous effort for me not to roll my eyes.

Standard family stuff.

June 4, 2019: TRUTH AND PRETENSES

Early this morning, my mother came looking for me. I had not yet gotten out of bed.

"I'm dying to see people," she said.

"I'm glad you came to get me," I said. "What's going on?"

"I've been sitting outside in my yard with a cup of coffee since 6 a.m. Where are all the people walking their dogs?" she asked, giving me a big, fake smile. Sarcastic Asta. But it's true, that was an expectation I created while persuading her to move out here where the dog walkers are our neighborhood social group.

I answered her literally. "Oh, they usually walk their dogs between 7 and 9 a.m.," and then reading her like a book, asked "Are you feeling like I brought you here under false pretenses because I said you'd see people walking their dogs?"

She spun around and stormed off, calling out, "Tony, what's wrong with Suey?"

I had blown her fake smile cover. But she is 90 years old and my mother, so five minutes later, I went over and talked with her.

"I understand that you're bored and lonely, and I'm sorry about that," I said. Of course she's bored and lonely. Unable to walk, nearly blind, hard of hearing and dependent does not a picnic make. "Come on over for breakfast. I'm going to be starting it soon," I said.

She did. In the afternoon we spent some time in the pool together, and Tony brought home an Alfred Hitchcock movie that the three of us watched together after dinner.

June 5, 2019: TUG OF WAR

Asta overheard Tony and I arguing about dental clinics, and was eager to divulge her interpretation to my sisters. I tried to get ahead of it by calling Chris. She and Elsa had already heard.

"Everything is fine," I assured her. "Every couple argues. It's okay that Mommy gossips—she just needs something to say." Our call didn't last long. I could sense there was something else that Chris might not be saying. In the morning, I called her again.

"Elsa and I are in a dilemma because Ma is so unhappy," she said. "We're discussing moving her back to New York."

"I think she should stay here," I said, "but if she convinces the two of you that she wants to go back to New York, I won't stand in her way."

"Look at it this way," she said. "If she were in New York, it would only take me about seven hours to drive there." Chris thinks she's selling me on the idea of moving Asta to Woodstock.

We didn't discuss whether or not, or how often, Chris would drive seven hours through rain and/or snow, or how soon Elsa would demand that *we* (Chris or I) *do* something *now* because she (Elsa) can't handle it any more or needs a *break*. Speaking from experience, some things don't need to be said.

"It would take you only seven hours to fly here too, so that argument doesn't hold water," I replied.

"For now, we're holding to course," Chris said. In other words, I may have won the battle, but the war isn't over.

Asta and I are on our way out to her Spanish lesson in a few minutes, and will go shopping at Revivals after that. Tomorrow, a couple of our friends are coming over with their dog for a visit. We'll all enjoy their company.

June 13, 2019: MENTAL GYMNASTICS

Over breakfast, Asta was telling me about the Kennedy family. She'd been listening to a book about them on her Kindle. Ethyl had 11 kids, John F Kennedy was her first son, and Ethyl was pregnant when John F Kennedy died.

"It's not possible for her to be pregnant more than 40 years after her first son was born," I said, confused.

"Why don't you believe me?" she asked. "I'm telling you what the book said."

"Well, who was Rose?" I asked.

"That was the matriarch," she said.

I looked up Ethyl Kennedy on my phone. "She was married to Robert Kennedy, the brother of John F."

"That's what I said," she said.

"Oh, I misunderstood," I said, happy to let her off the hook.

"That's what's wrong with people today," she bemoaned. "Dey always have to sheck der computers. Dey don't believe when someone tells dem de trut." Clearly, I was the 'people' she was referring to today.

"Well, I have a lot more wrong with me than that," I mused, like handing her the shovel with which to bury me. I wasn't expecting her to swing it at me.

"What's wrong with you that you have so little confidence in yourself?" she demanded. "Doesn't anyone compliment you?"

"Like who?" I asked, because Tony compliments me all the time and she knows it. Maybe I should have handed her a mirror and seen what she'd do with that. Again, I yielded. "Well, I did check my phone. I misunderstood what you were saying."

On another matter, I would not yield. Tony will be taking her to a doctor's appointment this afternoon because I'll be at a job interview.

"Well, you tell Tony not to talk to people," she said.

"You can tell him yourself," I said. "Tell Tony you'll speak for yourself in the doctor's office. He will be there as your ears, not your voice. Hey, how about if you put in your hearing aids today? I'll help you change the batteries this morning."

She didn't want that. She'd rather hold someone else responsible.

June 24, 2019: REASSURANCE

It was time for Asta to come over for dinner. I went in to let her know. She was weepy and sulking. I must not have paid her enough attention this afternoon when we were out lounging by the pool.

She assembled her face for the dinner table. After dinner, I persuaded her to watch TV with me, but after a short while she withdrew to her room. I checked on her three times. Her light was off and she appeared to be sleeping. I checked on her one last time before going to bed at 10 p.m. This time, she was awake and asked me to sit down.

"Do you and Tony *really* want me here?" she asked.

"Mommy, you've asked me that very question at least 30 times," I said, "and the answer is always the same. Yes, we want you here."

"But you and Tony can't live the same way you used to live: going here, going there. Why do you want me here?"

"It's true that we don't live quite the same as we did before you came, but Tony and I agree that it makes us feel good that we can help you this way." The words Tony and I use between us is that we are 'creating good karma.'

"But do you really *want* me here?"

"The answer is yes, and it's not going to change. You can stop asking." I want her to feel safe and secure.

July 10, 2019: BOUNDARIES

When Ma and I came home from a four-hour outing, she found her ceiling fan had been turned off.

"He should stay out of my room," she complained. "He needs to respect my privacy," and blah, blah, blah, blah. We've had this discussion many times.

"He's not coming in here to snoop, Mommy," I said. "He's just opening the door and flipping the switch. That's it." But Asta was determined to be angry. I texted Elsa and Chris to alert them, and asked for their cooperation so as not to make Tony a scapegoat.

"I'm sorry, Suey," Elsa texted back, "but he should not go in her room. It's not about the fan or turning off her lights all they time. It's about her privacy."

"I disagree. He's not snooping in her room. Just flipping the switch inside the door."

"He needs to leave it alone," she wrote.

"No, he doesn't," I wrote back. Now I was mad. I asked Chris for help. Chris called me back to warn me.

"Elsa is planning a confrontation with Tony," she said

"If she does that, I'll never speak to her again. Elsa has no right telling Tony or me what he/we should or shouldn't do in our house, even when it comes to Mommy. She had her chance to take care of Mommy and couldn't handle it. We'll take it from here." I made myself clear.

"I'll deliver your message," she said.

July 13, 2019: SATURATION POINT

Asta told me that Marty had called her to thank her for the magazines (that I'd shopped for, selected and purchased) we sent him for his birthday. She said they talked about "Everything, including Tony." Especially Tony.

I didn't want to hear the details. I shouldn't have to listen ad nauseam to her finding-fault about Tony, and I told her as much. To her mind, my unwillingness to listen to her air her grievances about Tony shows my 'bad attitude.'

"I have to talk to *somebody*," she reasoned.

"Call Elsa. She loves talking bad about Tony," I said, "but I don't want to hear it."

July 19, 2019: SNEERS, FEARS and FRUSTRATION

Asta's sneers are maddening. She wears them all the time, including when:

- Tony is refereeing volleyball. She thinks he's lying and going somewhere else.
- Tony isn't feeling well. She doesn't believe when he has diverticulitis or its symptoms.
- Tony and I are going somewhere, like the hardware store, together. "Tony should go on his own," she insists.
- I tell her I'm running errands. She thinks I'm working at a secret job or doing something to help Tony, who surely should be helping himself.

"Tony and I are thinking of going to the ocean on Sunday," I mentioned.

"You're trying to cram it all in," she complained. What she means is, she doesn't want a 'caretaker' to come over. Nor does she want to be home alone. She wants me to stay home with her.

Lately, she's been making vomiting sounds when I suggest she have an egg with her breakfast, or eat a mid-morning snack, or try rice with her dinner instead of potatoes. I don't understand the theatrics.

The other day, she wanted to rearrange her furniture so we spent two hours at it. I explained how certain arrangements might not work because of her lamp, phone or coffeepot, but we put things where she wanted them. By morning, she wanted to put it all back.

"No problem," I said. "We'll do it this afternoon." But by the afternoon, she had moved all the furniture herself. She was proud of herself, but angry that she didn't have help.

Focusing on the positive, "Good for you!" I praised.

I avoid sharing my frustrations with Tony because it would only upset him. I wouldn't dare confide in Elsa. She'd use it to orchestrate a coup. Chris is loaded with solutions: "tell her this," "suggest that," "distract her with cards, games or outings," "cook her this," or "buy her that." If only it were that simple.

It's a lonely enterprise, taking care of Asta.

July 22, 2019: NONSENSE

Asta refused a dip in the pool, refused my invitation to watch TV with me, and went directly to bed after dinner. I checked on her three times and all her lights were off. Knowing she'd wake up in the night, I left some snacks on her desk, and at 10 p.m. I went to bed. Soon after, she slammed the door coming in for the bathroom, and slammed it again going back. I went in to see her.

"Go back to your husband," she spat. "He's your priority".

"Okay, I'll see you in the morning." I wasn't going to engage. I knew what was behind her tantrum. She had mentioned it during dinner. I texted Chris.

"FYI," I wrote, "Elsa is still trying to persuade Mommy to become a snowbird. During dinner she asked Tony directly if he wouldn't be happier if she weren't here. He assured her that she is no trouble at all and we are happy to have her here."

"It's just talk at this point," Chris wrote back. "Just talk."

"Just curious," I answered. "Does 'just talk' include remodeling Elsa's bathroom, building a ramp to her front door and buying a new low bed?"

"Yes," she said. 'Just talk' has gone pretty far.

"Ma is confused," I explained. "She's torn between making Elsa happy vs. ensuring her own safety and security." Elsa is fanning the flames, making the fire roar, coaxing Asta with lipstick and syrup right into the fire.

"It's Ma's decision," Chris claimed.

"I don't believe she can make an objective decision. Maybe we should have her tested and see how she scores on a mini-mental.

Asta's relying on the three of us to make the decision for her. And since Elsa and I are on opposite sides, it'll be up to you, Chris." As power of attorney, it's ultimately Chris's call. "But safety trumps resident rights, and I don't trust that Elsa can take proper care of Ma, and I don't think it's safe for Ma to travel 3,000 miles at 91 years of age."

"I understand and you're probably right" she wrote, and "... I understand how you feel."

"I feel like I'm fighting an uphill battle," I wrote.

"You don't need to beat me over the head here..." she answered. "I get it."

Apparently, she didn't, because later that day she sent an email to Elsa and me announcing she'd had an epiphany and come up with the perfect birthday gift for Ma: round trip air tickets to Woodstock. "No need for Elsa to make any major adjustments to accommodate Ma for that short amount of time," she wrote. "I want it to be a surprise." As if a 3,000 mile trip for a frail 91 year old made any sense whatsoever. Chris was giving me the finger and putting Mommy's health and safety at risk.

New environment, frail, can't see. Absurd. Ma wouldn't be able to get in the shower for the duration of her visit, or climb safely in and out of bed independently (the bed in Elsa's guest room is quite high), or walk out of the house without help because of the steps. She wouldn't be able to get up during the night and make coffee and have a pastry, as is her routine here. But they're baiting her with Heidi the Cat, and promises of fun, fun, fun.

Deliberately, I spoiled the surprise for Asta. "Chris is buying you airplane tickets so you can go visit Elsa."

"I'll call Chris right now and put a stop to it," she said. "I'm probably responsible for their good-intentioned plotting, but I don't want to go now. I may want to go later, but I want to be involved in the decision. If I do decide to go, it'll be because I don't want to deal with the hot summer. I want to have a say in the timing."

"That's a good idea. Postpone it until maybe next summer. But please don't expect me to escort you there because I don't think you should go. And keep in mind that once you're there, something could happen and you might not be medically able to come back, like if you fell and broke your hip, or had a stroke while you were there. If you'd had kidney stones in Woodstock, Elsa would have given you herbal tea and you probably would have died at home."

"Ya, that's probably what would've happened," she agreed.

I'm fed up with this 'snowbird' nonsense and all the baloney that goes with it.

July 28, 2019: BIRTHDAY VISIT

We celebrated my mother's birthday with a party at our HOA Clubhouse. It had been months in the planning. Asta paid for most of it, but Tony and I covered the cost of renting the Clubhouse and of course provided the labor. Everything was 'Swedish.' The paper plates and napkins were blue and yellow, the tables were draped in plastic Swedish flags. The toothpicks for the meatballs had little Swedish flags on them. The very expensive birthday cake had blue and yellow icing flowers on it. The spread was fabulous, with meatballs, shrimp, caviar and herring, bruncål (which we usually only make for Thanksgiving and Christmas), cucumbers in sugared vinegar, knäkkebröd and butter. We included chicken wings (too 'American', Asta protested), hired a Scandinavian accordion player (she was delighted about that) and offered akvavit, which made me incredibly nervous, as people would be driving home.

It was a family reunion. Elsa and Chris came from the East Coast, Ronnie and Angi came in from LA, and Lisa and Jane came from Orange County. Everyone who could make it was here, and everyone helped. Elsa and Chris did a lot of the kitchen work while I did the running around, which made sense.

Asta looked smashing and glamorous in her white polyester bell bottom pants and matching top with bell bottom sleeves. We had about 30 guests, including friends from our neighborhood and Buddhist circles, and a few close acquaintances.

Elsa, having appointed herself Emcee, thanked everyone for coming and made all the announcements: "Now we're going to sing this, now we're going to do that, now we're going to have cake," that kind of thing. Chris played backup, engaged guests in conversation, and helped me keep an eye on the tables. Tony kept everything tidy. Ronnie and Angi ran errands, retrieved items from the house, served food on trays, and did whatever was asked of them. Ronnie urged me to sing my harmony with my sisters as expected. Dutifully (if reluctantly), I sang along.

The party was over and clean-up was done. Elsa walked beside me heading back to our house. Wasting no time to pursue her agenda, she said, "Keep an open mind about Mommy going back east for a vacation at my house.

"I get that you want her to come to your house for a visit," I said, "and understand that you could probably overcome some of the obstacles for while she was there—like equipment to help her get in and out of the tub, a lower bed to sleep in, and more—but the flight itself is dangerous for her. You can keep saying the grass is blue, but that's not how it looks like to me."

"I think it would be in your best interest to have a break," Elsa said.

"My best interests aren't the priority here. Mommy's best interests are. She's not a piece of luggage to be shipped around at her peril, and Tony and I don't need a break," I said. "I'm not getting on the grass-is-blue train." Why rush Asta to death's door?

Tony and I had a private talk with Chris. "Suey is providing impeccable care to your mother and you should kiss the ground that she walks on. She's that good," he said. "Your job is to protect your mother—and us—from Elsa's disruptive influence."

"If Mommy needs a vacation," I added, "Elsa can take her to Lisa's for a week, or rent a beach house in San Diego, or take her out on a boat and throw her father's accordion into the sea. Whatever. But please don't put her on a plane."

Aug 1, 2019: SWEET MEMORIES

Asta asked me to give her the Swedish flags that were used for the party. She didn't want the medium-sized flag that I had contributed, nor the flag toothpicks or tablecloth we'd ordered from Amazon. She wanted the flags Elsa brought. She suspected me of withholding them from her for some reason.

She was also irate that she couldn't find the CDs of Swedish music. "The CDs were wrapped in a rubber band," she said.

I recalled putting some CDs in the basket of stuff that Lisa had given her, but Asta insisted that she had organized the basket contents herself and the items she's looking for were not there. When I offered to help her look again, she became indignant.

"I know exactly where everything was. Look there," she pointed angrily towards her collection of CDs on the other side of the room, on my right. I reached out and touched a set of CDs that were rubber-banded together. She lurched with her cane across the room and launched into a lecture about what she put where, how it was organized, and how it wasn't here and wasn't there. I listened patiently for five (felt like 25) minutes.

"Okay, what can I touch?" I asked, truly just wanting to help.

"How dare you talk to your mother like that!" she exploded. I shrugged my shoulders, trying to understand her reaction and the question. Where was it even coming from? Maybe just the Land of Frustration.

"I'm going for my morning walk," I said, retreating. "I'll make breakfast in 45 minutes." She needed a cooling-off period and I could use the break.

Over breakfast, she picked up her thread and berated me for being impatient. "I'll try to be more patient," I said, conceding.

After breakfast, we spent a half hour examining her old tape/ CD player, trying to make it work. We inserted fresh batteries, tried different tapes, pushed all the buttons and combinations of buttons but couldn't get the tape player to work.

"Good news, though. The CD component works," I said, turning it on and off.

"I couldn't figure out how to turn down the volume, so I unplugged it and plugged it back in again, several times. It doesn't work. See?" she said, demonstrating, making me nervous with her fingers so near to the electrical outlet.

It was barely lunchtime and had already been a long day of accusations, protestations, hostilities and challenges. I crawled inside a protective bubble, inhaled sweet memory gas, and remembered the mother I love, still sitting in front of me.

Before leaving for work, I brought her a plate of cheese and crackers, reminded her she had food in her fridge, and encouraged her to eat. When I returned at 7 p.m., I saw that she hadn't touched the cheese & crackers, and looked like she hadn't gotten up all day.

"I'm not hungry. I'll eat on my own," she said.

"Mommy, come in and have dinner with us, please."

She did, and over dinner revealed that she had called Elsa and learned that Elsa had taken home the flags and CDs. "But I still have my brain," she said, pointing proudly to her temple. Tony and I nodded, obediently.

Aug 4, 2019: WEDDING BELL BLUES

Today is my parents' wedding anniversary. I invited Asta to accompany us to a Buddhist meeting. She'd be able to see people who had attended her party. "It's too early and I haven't washed my hair," she said, declining.

Back home after the meeting, I invited her to join me for a dip in the pool and offered, "Would you like me to help you with those thank you cards you've been talking about?"

"Don't rush me," she said, and remained in her bed.

"That's fine. Come out when you're ready," I said. I busied myself with other things. An hour or so later, she came out and commanded:

"I want to talk. Don't interrupt me." She gave a speech about how miserable she is, how she feels like a prisoner in her room, and how she's so incredibly lonely. She didn't want to be reminded that Rosalva was here visiting with her for two hours just last night, or that Eddie calls her on the phone. She didn't want me to talk at all, so I let her talk and cry... "I'm not trying to blame you," she said. "I know you're doing everything you can." Once it was out of her system, she went and got the thank you cards and we spent the next two hours at the kitchen table writing her notes to all who had come to her party.

When Tony got home, we persuaded her to put on her bathing suit so we could all take a dip together. Inner tube safely in place, she lowered herself into the water.

"So much effort to get into the damn pool," she groused.

"Mommy, are you serious?" I teased. Here we are, stepping into a luxuriously warm pool in our scenic back yard. I shook my head in amazement. She has round-the-clock supervision and support, companionship daily, gets all her needs—and then some—met. Can't change the weather, but that's what the pool is for.

We floated around for about 45 minutes to an hour, chit chatting (thanks to Tony) about Sweden and her early years in America. Since today is her wedding anniversary, I'm making kielbasa fried in butter and skin-on mashed potatoes. After dinner, I'll help her with a shower and wash her hair.

Aug 7, 2019: SABOTAGE

"I really don't like California. I want you to be open-minded about me going east," Asta said, parroting Elsa.

"You're going to make your own decision," I said, "but I won't endorse your getting on a plane. I believe it would be dangerous for you. So no, I won't be open minded about that."

"There are other ways," she said.

"Of travelling back to Woodstock? Taking a train? Driving in a car?" I asked.

"Well, no..." she said.

"I don't think it's safe for you to fly. That's one of my biggest objections."

"If I could walk, I would be happier here," she said.

"You wouldn't be able to walk any better in Woodstock," I said.

"Well, I'm not going anywhere unless you kick me out."

"I'll never kick you out. Never... Not even if you're mean to me."

"Or you to me," she said, "Because it's natural in a family. We get over it."

A package arrived in the mail to Asta from Elsa filled with thank you cards, stamps, and a letter in giant-sized font which began:

"I was so happy to see you enjoying yourself. It pains me so much to see you so unhappy, when you have options, where you have friends."

I'd call that sabotage. Wouldn't you?

Over dinner, Mommy commented, "How nice Eddie has it at his apartment, with neighbors right across the hall. He can yust knock..."

"Yes, it's very nice," I agreed. Eddie is younger than me, and independent.

"I guess that wouldn't work for me," Asta reasoned, "because I can't walk and can't shop, can't cook and can't see..."

"Let's take a dip in the pool," I said, bringing her back to the here and the now, and reality.

"I have to admit it feels good," she said.

Aug 9, 2019: TOOLS AND TEMPERS

"How about if we go to the Rancho Mirage Braille Institute today and see what tools they have that could help you with reading or writing? Rosalva suggested it after seeing how you use your magnifying glass," I said.

"This is why I left Woodstock," she blasted, "People talk about me behind my back. You're making me sick by treating me like I'm sick. If this is how it's going to be here, I might as well go back to Woodstock. Don't say a word. Don't talk to me, I don't want to hear it!"

"Okay, then you won't hear my explanation. I'm sorry for upsetting you," I offered, then added "but don't you think you're over-reacting somewhat?" I mean, we're talking about tools that could help improve her quality of life. And yes, I was calling her out for the drama. Nobody calls out Asta.

"Oh, shut up!" she yelled, refused breakfast and went back to her room. I delivered her breakfast on a tray. After breakfast, I offered to help her finish the cards she had started. We spent an hour just matching eight photos to her cards and envelopes. It was an exercise in patience.

Later in the pool, we talked about tomorrow's plans: Tony and I are driving to the ocean and Rosalva will come over from 3 p.m. to 5 p.m. to walk the dog, serve her dinner, and keep her company for a while.

Aug 24, 2019: REFRIGERATOR INCIDENT

Asta has been reporting to my sisters that my not putting deli meats in her little refrigerator is why she has lost some weight. Chris called and talked to me about installing a larger refrigerator in the garage and filling it with foods she can snack on. I explained to Chris that most of what I put in that's perishable spoils and has to be thrown out.

"Okay," I conceded, "I'll look around for a fridge. But first I'd like to monitor what goes in and out of her fridge for two weeks." Do a little reality check, gather some data.

"A couple of weeks is too long. Fill up the mini-fridge with new fresh deli fixings and give it a week, okay?" she said.

"I have to admit I'm bristling at being told what to do," I said.

"I'm asking, not telling. I think it should happen sooner, that's all," she said. It sounded like telling to me.

I informed my mother that my sisters want us to get her a bigger fridge.

"I heard from Elsa that there was talk about getting me a new refrigerator," Asta said. "I don't *want* a new refrigerator. I wish they would yust ask me."

And then over breakfast Asta said, "I'll only have one piece of toast for breakfast because I'm afraid I might have to go to the bathroom while we're out."

"That's why you're skinny. You don't eat," I said. "Tell that to Elsa and Chris. They're blaming me. They think it's my fault that you're not eating.

Meanwhile, I got an email from Elsa telling me how happy it made her that Mommy sounded happy the last few times they spoke. I don't need Elsa telling me when Mommy is happy or why, or how happy she is when Mommy is happy. I know when Mommy is having a good day/good week/good month. I just want my sisters to take Asta's reports with a grain of salt and stop campaigning to move her back east. I don't want them to tell me what to do, as if they could do it better. Elsa has already tried and failed, and Chris doesn't want the job.

Aug 25, 2019: FUNDAMENTAL DARKNESS

Asta was ready to leave for the Buddhist meeting an hour early and was annoyed that she had to wait. When it was time to get in the car she felt rushed. Apparently, I'd talked too fast.

"How long will the meeting last?" she asked.

"Maybe an hour and a half."

"That long?" she groused.

"Is that too long?" I asked. And here I got a little ornery: "Is there someplace else you have to be?"

She took this as her opening to blame Tony for my poor communication skills, hitting two birds with one stone.

We drove silently to the meeting. Today's topic: our fundamental darkness. Someone gave a presentation and members were asked to relate their personal experiences. The group leader asked me directly. Reluctantly, I complied. I described how practicing Buddhism helps me tackle my lack of self-confidence.

"I was completely humiliated," Asta told me in the car on the way home. "People will blame me for your lack of confidence, because I brought you up."

"It was not about you, Mommy," I said. "Not everything is about you. I've been on my own for over 40 years. If I lack self-confidence, it's my issue, not yours." But she was offended and wasn't giving an inch.

It had been an emotional morning. I waived the white flag of surrender. "I'm human," I said. "Just cut me some slack, could you please?" She couldn't. "I'll probably hear from my sisters. They'll have all the answers and will talk about moving you again."

"I won't say anything," she said. "I wouldn't dare."

"Well, I don't believe that for a minute."

We got home and she went to her room. I went to the supermarket for ingredients for tonight's dinner, came home, and started making lasagna. Her friend, Cary, dropped in to visit her. I went to get her.

"I can't see him," she cried.

"What should I tell him?" I asked.

"Tell him I'm crying."

"Are you sure that's what you want me to tell him?" The mother I knew would never let anyone outside the family see her in tears.

"Ja."

I told Cary she wasn't feeling well. He and I chatted for a bit, and just as he was about to leave, she came over, still crying, and invited him to visit her in her room. He followed her and stayed for 20 minutes. The two of them traded books they each had written.

Asta spent the afternoon lying in a fetal position on her bed, making sure I could hear, each time I checked on her, that she was still crying, sniffling.

We all have fundamental darkness.

Sept 5, 2019: HUSBANDS

Eddie told us he was going to take a bus here to visit Ma. Asta waited all day. When it was clear he wasn't coming, she blamed Tony.

"It's Tony's responsibility to take care of Eddie," she said.

"Eddie's an adult. He can take care of himself," I said.

"Ja, well, I guess it's yust all women's mission to take care of their stupid husbands."

"Was yours stupid?" I asked.

"No, of course not," she said.

"Well, neither is mine."

"Can't he go places with someone else? Can't he do things himself? Can't he ever give you a break? You need to relax, do things you enjoy," she said. Asta wants me all to herself.

"I enjoy going places and spending time with him," I said.

"Is he really at volleyball? Or is he out with friends?" she asked.

"What is it you suspect? That he might be having an affair? That he's not where he says he is? He's a volleyball referee and earns a little money doing it. I understand that you may not understand how refereeing works, but he drives to matches, referees for however long it takes—an hour, maybe two, could be three. Sometimes it's farther away, and sometimes the games are cancelled. I love you, but that you keep asking me these types of questions about my husband is just bullshit. Really."

"Ja, well, it's none of my business," she said.

"It's okay, Mommy. He is where he says he is, and he's never given me a reason to doubt him."

Sept 12, 2019: RESISTANCE

Saturday:

- "I have a sore in my nose. My nose is tender," she said.
- "Let's go to Urgent Care tomorrow and have them take a look."
- "We'll see," she said.

Sunday:

- "Let's talk about your nose. It would be easier if you'd let me take you today because (a) we'd get it looked at sooner, and (b) on Monday I have to go to work."
- "Not today," she said, and slept all day. I took her temperature. No fever, so I didn't worry too much.

Monday:

In the morning, she ate a full breakfast so I went to work as per normal. When I got home from work at 2:30 p.m., however, she had a temperature of 101 degrees.

"Mommy, I'm taking you to Urgent Care. Go ahead and comb your hair and we'll head over there now."

She was diagnosed with cellulitis of the nose, given a shot of antibiotics, two antibiotic prescriptions, and instructions to return the next day for another shot. She weighed 106 pounds, down 14 pounds since she arrived.

Tuesday:

I brought in her medicine, which she's supposed to take an hour before meals, at 9:45 a.m.

- "Here is your pill. Please take it now and then we'll have breakfast in an hour," I said.
- "Put it there, I'll take it later," she resisted.
- "Mommy, I need you to take it now so we can have breakfast in an hour. It's already 9:45 a.m."

Angrily, she sat up, took her pill with a mere sip of water, hating me for urging her to drink more and spat, "What kind of camp am I in here!?" I gave her time to get herself up, and returned an hour later.

- "Time to come over for breakfast."
- "Can't I have it in here?" she whined. A hassle for me, but I didn't want to argue.
- "Okay, I'll bring it in."

Just as I finished putting together her breakfast tray—an egg, some bacon, a piece of toast, coffee, juice, and her potassium pill with applesauce—she came to the kitchen.

"I thought you wanted breakfast in bed?" I said. She denied it. Whatever. She ate breakfast and went back to her room.

Two hours later, before leaving for my afternoon shift, I brought her back to the kitchen for lunch. She ate well and laughed about her 'camp' joke. I was glad she was feeling better. But by the time I got home and went in with her medicine, she was as grumpy as ever.

"Are you mad at me? Have I done something wrong?" I asked.

"I called Eddie and *he already knew* I've been ill," she said, assuming Tony had been talking behind her back.

"Yes, well, he texted me last night and said he would be calling you to schedule a visit," I said, taking responsibility. "I let him know that you were on antibiotics but would love to hear from him."

How could she be angry about that? I do everything I can to support her independence and privacy, offer her choices at every opportunity, include her in our daily activities, facilitate her development of friendships, and make sure that her needs are met. She does everything she can to blame Tony for anything and everything.

She took the pill in protest, turned off her light, and laid down with her back to me. I will have to go in and get her again when it's time for dinner.

Sept 20, 2019: GOOD SOUPS

Asta has been sleeping a lot lately, and talking a lot about dying, so we were both pleasantly surprised to learn from her oncologist today that her blood work shows no change since she moved in with us. Instantly, she cheered up and bragged to the doctor how active and independent she is, how she's taking Spanish lessons and writing books. Delightful to see and hear.

"Can I get on a plane for a five or six hour flight?" she asked the doctor. She knows I'm against it because of her leukemia and overall frailty. Elsa, like an evil monster lurking in the closet, has been coaxing her, confusing her, singing the "Hot Summer Where You Are" song. Chris, evidently, has also been encouraging Mommy to make the trip. That they are actually advocating for her to go and think she should take the risk is beyond comprehension to me. Just going to a doctor's appointment is a big deal and tires her out.

"I don't recommend it," her doctor answered, "because of all the germs in airplanes. And with leukemia, that could be very dangerous for you."

"Now I can tell Elsa," she said on the way home. "The doctor told me I shouldn't go." And since she was going to live, she would focus on food.

"You're a good cook, but you don't cook what I'm used to," she said. "If I were at Chris's, I'd be complaining about all the vegetables. At Elsa's, well, I'd be fatter. Elsa cooks what I'm *used to*." Elsa is a wonderful cook, but eats a lot of fast foods, fried foods, pizza, Kentucky Fried Chicken, donuts and soup. "Elsa makes the best soups," she said.

"Yes," I agreed. "Elsa makes good soups." I picked up four pricey yogurt cups to celebrate her happy news with a special treat. We each had one after dinner and put the other two in her fridge for later.

Sept 28, 2019: LIVER AND GRAVY

Tony and I recently switched to turkey bacon, which is lower in fat and price. Asta voiced her objections to Elsa and Chris, and soon she received a package from Burger Smokehouse containing four pounds of pork jowl and six packets of gravy mix. I understand that they want me to fatten her up and their intentions are probably good, but my sisters know I don't like to make gravy, and I don't appreciate being pressured into it.

Further, Elsa emailed an article to Chris and me claiming that chicken liver is good for neuropathy. Chris quickly responded by sending her famous chicken liver recipe. They've given me the tools; now it's my job to cure our mother with chicken liver, gravy and bacon. I replied back as follows:

"Hi Goils, the chicken liver recipe looks yummy. I may try it one of these days. Her bacon did arrive, by the way. Best bacon in the world. Will put the gravy packets aside for when you guys are here."

Of course I want Mommy to be fat and happy, but I don't run a restaurant, I can't make her eat, and I'm not going to make stupid gravy.

Elsa's quack cures give Mommy hope that this or that consumable will cure her ailments. On the positive side, they may encourage to eat, but making chicken liver out to be a miracle cure for anything is just plain dumb, and conscripts me into the position of Cook on the ship *Charade*.

We discussed the medical merits of chicken livers that evening over our chicken liver dinner. Tony playfully suggested, "Why don't you eat it every night for five days in a row?" He is the King of Hyperbola, after all.

"No," she answered, "I yust wanted to try it once." Asta the Pendulum, swings.

We put the leftovers in her refrigerator for her to snack on later that night, or to nibble on during the day.

Sept 29, 2019: COMPANIONSHIP

On Wednesday, I took Mommy to the Senior Center for her weekly Spanish lesson with Rosalva. On Thursday, a friend from our Buddhist group came to visit her and stayed a few hours. Eddie is coming over on Tuesday.

My mother understands that I hire companions when Tony and I go out of town, but doesn't know we also hire them for social visits. My mother benefits from the companionship. They call her directly to work out the dates and times. She doesn't need to know they are paid.

Yesterday, she expected a visit from Rosalva and was disappointed when Rosalva didn't show up. I had Ma keep me company while I cut fabric for some projects I'm working on. She talked endlessly about the formative years of her life and about the book she is currently writing.

Oct 5, 2019: CHF and CLOWNS

"Look at my ankle. It's swollen," Asta said.

"How do you feel?" I asked.

"Not good," she admitted. It looked uncomfortable and felt warm to the touch, but wasn't red. I took her temperature, no fever. No pain, no shortness of breath. She didn't want to go to the doctor.

"Lay down and elevate your foot above your heart and let's see if that helps," I said. It did.

I notified my sisters. No fall, no injury, no twist or sprain. I'm no doctor, but it looked like CHF to me. I texted Chris and Elsa.

"I'll take her to the doctor to be evaluated, but it doesn't seem like an emergency," I said. "It might be okay to wait a day or so." Chris agreed.

"She should put ice on it," Elsa wrote. "I say do nothing, since Ma wouldn't accept any treatment anyway."

After talking with Elsa, Ma asked for ice, which I provided. The next day, her foot swelled up again so she laid in bed most of the day. She still didn't want to go to the doctor, and I still didn't feel we had an emergency on our hands. The next afternoon, however, I took her to urgent care to have her ankle looked at.

"I have no intention of taking any more pills," she repeated over and over in the car and while we sat in the urgent care waiting room.

"I think I might be dying. I yust hope it's quick." I took out a pen and notebook and started writing her questions down.

"This is to make sure we get answers to all of your questions," I said, giving her power and control.

She was seen by a nurse practitioner who avoided the words 'heart failure' but described CHF and diagnosed pedal edema. No, ice packs would not help. No, Vick's Vaporub would not help. Yes, she could take Tylenol. No, there are no foods she should seek out or avoid, but she should reduce her salt intake and wear compression stockings.

We went to Panera for lunch, then drove to a pharmacy for the stockings. Since the pharmacy was next door to a Revivals, we went shopping and she bought several new tops and another pair of white pants. On the way home, I was warmed when she spoke favorably for a change of Tony—how pleasant he is, how nice and thick his hair is, how understanding he is, how he pleases her with his thoughtfulness... and then surprised me with, "Are you sure he's not gay?" she asked, sounding exactly like Elsa.

This is how they entertain each other on the phone: in whispers and giggles, conspiratorially. That's Elsa in a nutshell: sweet and loving to your face, gushing in adoration, boasting about compassion, then laughing behind your back and spreading rumors. She likes to charm people into telling her their secrets, then divulges them for a laugh, or in purchase of someone else's affection. And yet she can't comprehend why I don't trust her.

"Yes, I'm sure," I answered, keeping it simple. I'm not going to entertain that clown. I just want to take care of our mother.

Oct 14, 2019: POTATOES

"I got a call today from an old boyfriend of mine," Elsa texted. "I could tell he was trying hard to sound like he had teeth! Anyway… I told him about Mommy's leukemia and he said she should eat potatoes every day. Baked potatoes, mashed potatoes, potato soup, potato pancakes.… any kind of potatoes! He also suggested clear broth… 2 cups a day. It was fun to talk with him…. Gotta run."

I waited for the steam to clear out of my ears before I put my foot down.

"Please resist the temptation to provide dietary cures and advice. We have modified our diet significantly since Ma moved here, out of respect for her preferences and in response to well-intentioned sisterly advice. However, I do not run a restaurant. I will continue to provide a well-balanced and varied diet, one that includes potatoes." And then I shared the back and forth texts with my mother, since she'll be hearing about them soon anyway.

"Well, I can eat pasta," she shrugged, with obvious disdain.

Sometimes we have pasta, sometimes rice, and sometimes we have potatoes. But potatoes are no cure for leukemia. Two weeks ago it was liver and gravy. Another quack cure. Clever interference in my kitchen. A bowel movement on my living room floor. More nonsense I have to negotiate. More pressure I would rather do without.

Oct 20, 2019: WHO'S COMING TO DINNER

Chris and Ma have been discussing Chris' upcoming visit. We purchased tickets for a show but Ma is complaining it will take too much time away from spending it just with Chris. She'd rather spend their time finishing Ma's book and going over her bank account.

Chris said she wanted to take us out for dinner as a gesture of thanks for taking care of Mommy. That morphed into the two of them talking about inviting friends. The dinner would become a performance.

"When Chris tells you the plan, yust say 'yes'," Asta instructed.

"Even if I have a different opinion?" I asked. "And anyway, what about your concerns about having to share what little time you will have with Chris? Earlier you said you didn't want the stress of having to get dolled up for the theater. Now you want to invite friends to join us out for dinner? I'm confused."

"Yes," she said. "You should go along with whatever I and Chris agree to." She talked at length about how important 'communication' is in the decision-making process, but there's really no room for an opinion that's different from hers.

"I would prefer it to go differently," I said, "but okay, I'll cooperate."

Later, Chris emailed me what a 'hoot' it would be to bring the two guests along, selling the change in plan. "Let's talk about it later by phone," I answered. I needed some time to process the contradictions in their messaging and to spit out the sour grapes.

Oct 21, 2019: PARTY INVITATION

Our neighbor is throwing a Halloween costume party on Thursday at 5 p.m. and Ma, Tony and I have been invited. Ma had Elsa send Asta's old gypsy costume. Elsa enclosed two jars of homemade potato soup in the package, driving up the cost of postage to $60. Absurd.

"I have to work until 6 p.m. so I'll meet you and Tony there," I told her.

"I'll wait until you can go with me. I don't want Tony to be my 'caretaker,'" Asta protested.

"You can wait for me if it means that much to you. Tony will also wait. We'll all go together."

"Why should he always want to go with you?" she huffed.

"Sounds like you're wanting to go with me too," I replied.

"Can't you switch with a co-worker?" she asked.

"Not for a Halloween party," I answered.

"You switched before," she griped.

"For a doctor's appointment, yes, but I won't ask to switch for the sake of a party. I can meet you and Tony there, or we can all go together when I get home. It doesn't matter to me. It's up to you guys."

She decided to allow Tony to take her at 5 p.m. rather than miss half of the party, and now she's happily planning and talking about the party non-stop.

"I can't find my red top," she said the next day. "Do not try to help by looking in my closet. I've already searched it completely and it isn't there. Tony must have taken it out of my laundry basket for some reason. Or maybe it ended up in your closet."

"It's not in my closet," I answered, "and no, he wouldn't have removed it from your hamper."

"Well, it's strange. It's the *only* top I want to wear with my gypsy outfit. I *need* that top," she said. We were treading on thin ice. I had to be careful not to suggest that she overlooked it or made a mistake.

I turned to her open closet and lifted a small pile to reveal a neatly folded red top sitting there.

"Could this be it?" I asked.

"Ja, that looks like it! How did that get there?"

Vindicated, I shrugged. Her gypsy costume was salvaged and that was all that mattered.

Oct 29, 2019: PITY

"Listen to these voicemail messages from Elsa," my mother said, "and leave them on there."

- "In honor of Daddy's birthday, I planted flowers at his grave… I'm feeling blue," Elsa said on the verge of tears. "I'll call back later."

- "I've just meditated and now I feel much better," she said in a message a few minutes later, cheerfully this time, adding some benign detail of daily life.

My mother is susceptible to Elsa's sympathy-seeking. Me, not so much.

I invited Mommy to join me a while to watch TV, catch up on the news and watch an episode of 'Botched'. Soon she was talking and talking about Sweden, Sweden, Sweden, and people and events of her teen years. At 8 p.m. (exhausted), we agreed to get ready for bed. But first, she wanted to slay me:

"*We* owe Elsa an apology," she said, glaring at me, accusing. "You don't call her. The two of you don't talk."

I don't owe Elsa anything. Is it my job to take care of Elsa? If she were grieving our relationship, she could put in some effort herself, instead of kvetching to Ma, making it my fault and my responsibility to fix. I can't offer her what she wants or thinks she needs from me. And I don't feel guilty about it.

"Let me help you with your Kindle before bed," I answered, ignoring the hook, line and sinker.

Nov 1, 2019: HALLOWEEN BASH

Chris was here for the weekend and helped us assemble our costumes for the party. For Tony, lederhosen, hat, suspenders and a beer stein; for me, a painted-up artist's smock on which Ma signed her trademark WWII Swedish '91 Karlsson cartoon drawing, a knitted beret, a painter's palette, and a couple of brushes. Asta will wear her gypsy costume and one of the wigs Elsa sent her. But she was anxious because she couldn't put the wig on independently. I would be at work when she was getting ready for the party, so this was a big problem. I tried to coach her, but after numerous attempts, she still wasn't satisfied. She went to bed angry with me for not taking time off work to help her get ready for the party.

Then, in the morning before I headed off to work: "I can't find my red scarf," Asta said. "Maybe Tony or you took it or moved it?" I helped her locate it in the bag with the wig. "I can't find the necklace I was planning to wear." I had no idea where she might have put that. "I don't think I'll be able to go because I'm too tired from staying up late last night struggling with the wig."

"Why don't you go wigless as Macy, or wait until I get home at 6:30 p.m.?" I suggested. "Remember, it's only a Halloween party. Would you rather wear my costume instead?"

Asta was miserable with stress. I alerted Chris. Chris called Elsa, Elsa called Ma, and soon Ma came out practically singing. "It takes Elsa to come up a good idea: Use a different sash over the wig," she said.

"Great!" I said. "Looks good!"

There were no emergencies during the day, and no alerts or notifications from Tony. Our friend Cary—who used to work in the wig business with the likes of Elizabeth Taylor—arrived just as Ma and Tony arrived and helped her adjust her wig before ringing the bell. Tony helped her find a comfortable place to sit, made sure she had food, and kept her company until other people joined her. I arrived as soon as possible after I got off work.

It was a lovely evening with neighbors and friends. When we returned home at 8 p.m., Tony helped her into the house while I took the dog for a walk.

At 6 a.m., I was awoken by a text from Elsa.

"How was the party? I can't wait to hear."

I put off answering until I got up, and then reported the bare minimum. "Lots of fun! Interesting people and costumes. We all had a good time, and Ma looked great!" Ma can tell her the rest on their phone call later today.

Nov 9, 2019: ER VISIT

Tony and I got up early for our annual neighborhood garage sale. We hadn't been gone for more than fifteen minutes before I got a phone call from Asta.

"I don't want to scare you, but there's something wrong with my heart. It feels like it's pounding out of my chest. I don't feel right."

"I'm on my way," I said, and we rushed home.

She was a little shaky, and frightened. She wanted me to check her out.

"Ma, I'm not a doctor. I can't tell you what's going on. We'll have to have you looked at by a doctor." I cancelled my plans to meet Ronnie and Angi for some outlet mall shopping, helped Asta get up and get dressed, and drove her to Urgent Care. Walking in, I said, "Well, you must not be too bad, because you're walking in on your own two feet."

She was seen fairly quickly and given some tests, including an EKG and a blood draw. Ultimately, the NP told me to take her to the ER for cardiac care.

On the way, Ma revealed me she'd had four cups of coffee overnight.

We arrived to the ER around 9:30 a.m. More blood was drawn and another EKG performed. In the waiting area, we amused ourselves by finding the Swedish sailor song on YouTube about a bee landing on his true love's chest. She sang along quietly, nodding, with her beautiful voice, remembering every word of every verse.

We discussed how lucky it was that she had taken a shower and washed her hair the day before, as this trip to the doctor was unplanned. I try to get her to shower twice a week, but asserting her independence and insisting she's clean, she resists. There in the ER, she admitted I had a point. "I think I could start taking showers on Thursdays and Sundays."

"That'll work. We can do that." I said.

Meanwhile, Tony delivered sandwiches to us in the ER. At 4:30 p.m. she was discharged with instructions: "Eliminate caffeine and follow up with your primary care MD in a couple of days." Nothing to worry about.

"It looks like I'll make it home in time to usher at the McCallum tonight," I said.

"You're only going because Tony wants you to go with him. Don't you think you should stay home in case I need you?" she asked.

"You're probably just going to go to sleep, and I'd just be knitting in front of the idiot box."

I brought her a cup of hot tea with honey and fixed her a sandwich to cat whenever she wanted. Tony and I left, did our ushering, went out for a drink and a snack, and were home by 10 p.m. She was still sleeping and had not eaten. I covered her up with her blanket, turned on the nightlight, and went to bed myself.

In the morning, I replaced all her Keurig coffee pods with decaffeinated coffee, reinstalled the second telephone in her room to give her better access in case she wanted to call me, and moved our Himalayan salt lamp into her room as a soft nightlight.

Nov 11, 2019: BUG SPRAY, SHOWERS, OPINIONS and COMPLAINTS

"In case you notice the smell in the garage," I explained. "I sprayed bug killer along the edges."

"Ja, and I thought I would gash," ('gag'). Asta suspected the spray was our way of telling her she smelled, was offended by it, and decided she didn't want to shower twice-a-week after all. "I was up all night thinking about how *I'll* be the one to decide when I have or don't have a shower," she said.

"Okay, Ma. Obviously I can't drag you into the shower," I said, "and I can't force you to wash your hair. It'll be up to you whether and when you take a shower and how often you wash your hair."

"I'm going to start keeping a diary," she announced. She would write down her thoughts and opinions about everything and everyone around her, draw conclusions, and inventory her opinions about Tony's and my marriage and family. She'd complain of boredom and loneliness, and how she doesn't want to be forced into a shower.

"Great!" I exclaimed, thinking it might make for some interesting reading someday. I offered some story-starters, things on which she lectured me last night: "You could write about all kinds of things, like marriage, family, regrets, alternatives, finances, or Trump."

"I expected to see more people here in Californian," she said, "have friends knocking on my door, but everyting is too private, everywhere is gates. Maybe I've been so down because of the thing with my heart. It makes me realize that I could go quickly."

"Yeah, well, that's understandable," I said. "And we're pretty quiet around here." I understand she's lonely.

"And maybe you want to get rid of me," she probed.

"No, Mommy, it's a privilege to have you here," I answered, and meant it.

She grinned, "Good answer."

Nov 18, 2019: FICTION

Asta is writing a novelette about a woman named Norma who lives with her daughter, Kaisa, and Kaisa's husband, Nick. Asta was having trouble keeping the pages and her changes organized and readable. I offered to type it but she refused, shielding the pages to prevent me from looking over her shoulder. "Chris will type it for me," she asserted.

Later, having made manual revisions to the typed manuscript Chris sent, Ma asked me to re-type it from scratch.

"I'll ask Chris to send me the electronic document. It'll be easier that way," I said.

"No, you have to re-type it from this," she insisted. Maybe she didn't understand how easy it is to share and edit files.

I texted Chris and asked her to send me the draft to spare me from having to retype the whole thing from scratch. I waited for her response.

Asta, meanwhile, became irritated with me for delaying the project and stayed in her room all day to prove it, then picked at her dinner to demonstrate her displeasure. Finally, I got a call from Chris.

"Ma wrote some things in the draft that she doesn't want you to see," Chris explained, "and if I sent you the file, you'd see them, so I'm not going to send it to you."

The characters in Asta's story are loosely based on me (Kaisa), an irritable woman who is controlled by her manipulative husband, Tony (Nick, whose name used to be Dick, until Chris persuaded her to change it). And then there's her best friend Val (Elsa), the person she has fun with and with whom she does witchy things, like cast spells on people.

I am well aware that Asta weaves her thoughts and opinions about all of us into her stories. I'm disappointed that Chris has so little faith in me that she would withhold the file and cause me to have to retype 38 pages because of a few paragraphs that would've come as no surprise, and about which I would not have made an issue with Ma or anyone else. I pocketed the insult.

Pivoting, Chris asked, "Do you suppose Ma's focus on 'abuse' comes from her experiences as a child?" Asta had never claimed being subjected to childhood abuse.

"No," I said "I think it's just a reflection of her lack of life-experience, and it's the only thing she can think of to make her stories 'spenande'" (Swedish word for 'exciting'). "She's dreaming up baloney and making a sandwich with it."

Chris had made up her mind and wouldn't budge. She refused to send me the file. "Okay," I said, annoyed. "I'll type the whole thing over."

A few hours later, I brought the new draft in to Ma. Eyes narrowed, she asked my opinion.

"Not bad. It'll need some grammatical corrections," I said, fully neutral and supportive. "For example, you start the book with, 'Norma find herself' when it should be 'Norma finds herself'. I could help you fix things like that, if you'd like. And it might be a good idea to break the book into chapters. It's up to you."

"Ja," she said, "I've been thinking about those things. The ending is good, though." Asta said, still gauging my reaction.

"Yes," I agreed. "The ending is the best part of the book."

I wasn't offended by her fictionalization of us. Writing keeps her busy. Having a creative outlet/project is good mental exercise, gives her something to talk about with everyone, and enhances her self-esteem.

Nov 24, 2019: TIS THE SEASON

The Lutheran Church in Palm Desert will be hosting a Swedish celebration/gathering for Santa Lucia day, and I asked Asta if she would like to attend.

"What will I wear that's blue & yellow?" she wondered.

"How about the new blue jacket with yellow piping?" I asked. "The one we bought last week at Revivals. It fits you beautifully."

"Perfect," she said. "Maybe you have a pair of pants I can wear?"

"I do. And if they're too long, we'll have them hemmed."

It's lovely to see her so animated, so convinced how it's going to be, what food they will serve. After all, *every* Swede knows *exactly* what to do to throw a *perfect* party, and surely, the *rules* are the same today as they were 50-60 years ago.

"I'll treat you and Tony for the dinner portion," she offered. "It will be educational for him." I emailed the RSVP and her check and put it on our family calendar.

We won't have many more opportunities to celebrate Santa Lucia day—the most Swedish of all holidays—together. As children, we participated in the Santa Lucia ceremonies at the Swedish Lutheran Church in Philadelphia. As young women, we dressed up and sang Santa Lucia and other Swedish Christmas carols at Daddy's company events. At least once, we really did deliver, singing, breakfast in bed to our parents on Santa Lucia day.

While Ma and I sat outside in her alley talking about the event, glass of wine in hand, Elsa called. Ma told her excitedly about it and Elsa said she was jealous. Elsa asked Ma to put me on the phone. Elsa wanted to talk about Thanksgiving.

"I heard you're freaking out about the Thanksgiving dinner you'll be hosting this week," Elsa said. This must be their latest gossip fodder. They want me to be stressed, but I'm not.

Coolly, I answered, "No, I'm not freaking out at all. It'll only be seven of us: me, Tony, Mommy, Ronnie, Angi, Angi's mom Brenda, and Eddie." At no time have I experienced any stress or anxiety in connection to Thanksgiving dinner. Yes, it involves extra planning and preparation, but it's a joyful event.

We chatted briefly, awkwardly, about her Thanksgiving travel plans, until Asta started wiggling her fingers for the phone. In Anderson-speak, we call it 'röan-dennan.' Translated, that's 'give me the red one,' or equally accurate, 'gimme'.

Nov 30, 2019: THANKSGIVING EXCITEMENT

Thanksgiving is over. Dinner was a success. Ronnie and Angi were here and gave Asta ample attention, as did Angi's of-Scandinavian-heritage mother, Brenda. Ma gifted to Brenda one of her heirloom needlepoint wall hangings. Floyd and Louise also dropped by for a visit. Because Asta doesn't wear her hearing aids, conversations sometimes go sideways. Somebody mentioned they were thinking about taking courses and Asta exclaimed, "Oh, you have horses?"

On Friday, after everyone had gone, I left Ma sitting on the couch watching Fox TV while I went to the library to stock up on second-hand books. She was still there when I returned home. Pooped from a chaotic weekend, I laid down on the couch, put my head in her lap and exhaled a heavy sigh.

"I'm going to miss all the commotion of having company," she said.

"Yup. Now we go back to our boring lives," I deadpanned. Because that was kind of her point.

The beauty of company is the excitement, and the benefit of their leaving is the peace and calm, made sweeter by the anticipation of the next explosion of activity. When there's something to look forward to, periods of boredom can be enjoyable. They allow Asta to catch up on her sleep, listen to audio books in her Kindle, or practice her Spanish.

One of the things I admire about my mother is that she doesn't want to miss out on anything. She enjoys spending time with company, as long as her room—her sanctuary—is easily within reach. She basks in the energy of company, and when it's not her responsibility to entertain, she can relax and enjoy herself. It's hard for her to go out, but she loves it when the party comes to her. She does complain, however, of the pressure of having to get dressed; having to think, plan her outfit, and put on her eyebrows.

"I understand that sometimes thinking can be stressful, but I'm sorry, Mommy, with all due respect," I said, "I'm not going to accept your calling 'getting dressed' stressful."

Our next big project is Christmas. I will provide her with wrapping paper to wrap up whatever treasures she is giving away. She will help plan Christmas dinner, help me make the brunkål (her legendary Swedish fried cabbage dish) and her traditional Swedish rice pudding.

Asta's Rice Pudding

Ingredients:

- Long grain rice, one pound (River Rice brand)
- Gallon whole milk
- Sugar (to taste)
- Cinnamon
- Half and half

Place rice in an iron pot. Add just enough water to cover it. Bring to a boil.

Reduce heat and cook until water is absorbed. Stir continuously.

Add milk, a little at a time to keep it smooth. Continue stirring for 45-60 minutes until rice grains are soft and texture is porridge-like. It burns easily, so keep stirring.

Remove from heat and add sugar to your own taste.

Sprinkle with cinnamon and serve topped with warmed Half and Half.

Dec 1, 2019: TINKING IN DE DARK

Every night before I go to bed, I go in to check on my mother. Last night, I found her lying in bed, in the dark, wide awake. I turned on a little night light and said hi. She was excited.

"I've been tinking (sic)", she said, "and want to trow (sic) out an idea. Sit down for a moment." I did. "I'm tinking about trowing another birtday party for myself this Yuly and want to know how you feel about it."

"Great idea!" I said.

"I know it would mean a lot of work for you."

"No problem! I'd be happy to!"

"It would be at the Clubhouse again, and I would want to have this one catered."

"That's fine," I said, "so long as you understand it would probably cost $4,000—$5,000, maybe more."

"That's okay," she said, and she proceeded to describe the food, the crowd, the music. All perfectly Swedish.

Dec 6, 2019: BLAME GAME

When Mommy described her birthday celebration to Floyd's girlfriend Louise, she referred to the guests—several times—as 'Tony's friends,' insinuating that Tony threw the party to make himself look good, that he took advantage of her to throw a party for his friends.

I asked her later in private, "Why do you say 'his' friends? They're also my friends and your friends too." She's looking for ways to blame Tony, and makes faces, rolls her eyes and says passive-aggressive things like this business about Tony throwing the party for his friends.

"I don't feel well," she told me this morning. Aware that Tony has been under the weather as well, Asta said, "Tony should have gotten a flu shot."

"What are your symptoms?" I asked. She couldn't identify any. I offered to take her to the doctor, but she said she wasn't feeling sick enough for that. "Well, if you do have what he has, you may experience diarrhea for a day or two, so make sure you keep drinking so you don't get dehydrated."

"If Cary drops in, tell him I'm not feeling well. I don't want anybody but you telling him."

"Like who?" I asked. "Tony?"

"Yes, if you must know," she said.

Tony joined us in the kitchen and made some small talk. She rolled her eyes derisively and smirked.

"Slutta, va inte sont," (Swedish for 'stop, don't be like that') I said.

"Like what?" she asked innocently. But she assembled her face and added, "I'll say *nothing*." After breakfast, she returned to her room.

As usual, I checked on her at various intervals during the day to let her know when I'd be taking a walk, or running an errand and did she need anything, or letting her know I was home again and would be starting dinner soon.

"How are you feeling?" I asked later in the day.

"Fine," she answered.

"So you're not sick after all?" I asked.

"No, I'm not sick, why do you say that?" she asked.

"Because this morning you said you weren't feeling well," I said.

"Well, I can feel poorly without being sick."

"Okay, well I'm glad you're feeling better. Are you hungry?"

"Starving," she answered, blaming me with her narrowed eyes.

For dinner I had made 'garbage soup'—Asta's get-well chicken and vegetable soup recipe. It was tasty and she said so.

"Why isn't Tony eating with us?" she asked.

"Because he's watching a football game that started at 5 p.m."

"Doesn't he like this soup?"

"He likes it fine. He'll be having some later."

"It doesn't have pasta in it," she spat, insinuating that Tony needs pasta with meals, and pasta is inferior to potatoes. It's ridiculous.

Sticking to the subject of the soup, I said, "I've been making this soup for 40 years. It's my go-to get well soup when someone in the family isn't feeling well. Tony has always enjoyed it, and I made it for the both of you. Knock it off, Mommy. You don't have to be ignorant."

A few minutes later, after I served her seconds, she looked at me with teary doe-eyes. She didn't like being told she was rude. "Can I eat my soup in my room?"

She'll call Elsa and the two of them will bash Tony, this time because he likes pasta, doesn't feel well, and is having his meal in front of the TV, and they'll judge me for defending him. Then Asta will sulk until she's tired of sulking.

Dec 7, 2019: VICTIM

In addition to having a bad attitude towards my husband, Asta has a headful of medical anxiety. Currently, she's obsessing over her upcoming flu shot appointment.

- "The flu shot will put poison into my bloodstream, and my blood is already compromised."
- "I only go out once a week to my Spanish lesson, so if I get sick it will be because Tony didn't get a flu shot." Not because she didn't.
- "The potassium citrate that I take to prevent kidney stones is probably making me sick, given my low weight," and
- "There must be some *foods* that I should be eating that would *fix everything.*"

"We've asked the food question of the doctors multiple times, and there are no magic foods that will cure your leukemia (or foot neuropathy or glaucoma, etc.). And it's not Tony's fault if you catch the flu if you refuse the flu shot. We don't know if he had the flu this week. He had diarrhea, but no fever, and a fever is typically present with a flu." Too much to process.

"Don't talk back. Where did you come from? You've shanged. How could my own daughter be so insensitive? I'm your *mother*, not yust a *renter*," she said.

"You're not here because you're a renter. You're here because you're my mother." Today, I'm tired. Tired of having to cater, tired of putting my life on hold, and tired of catching baloney from her in thanks.

Tony and I ushered in the afternoon, and afterwards went out for dinner. We were going to be home a little later than planned so I texted Elsa and Chris.

"Could one of you please call Ma and distract her for a while so that I don't have to be put on the defensive or feel guilty for not being home 'on time'? Chris was busy, but Elsa called and conveyed my message to Asta. Then Elsa texted me:

"Ma is okay but she's *hungry*."

"Tell her to have a snack," I wrote back. I mean, duh. She's still capable of getting something for herself from her fridge. "And tell her we'll bring her a hot dog with sauerkraut and mustard." I appreciated that Elsa ran interference by calling Ma when I didn't want to, to make sure someone gave her the message. I needed a little space, just a little, with someone else in the middle for a minute.

When we got home, Asta's light was off, though I knew from communications with Elsa that they had been on the phone just moments ago. I went in and told her we brought her a hot dog. She wanted to eat in her room. I delivered the hot dog to her.

What do I want? I want to sit and knit without having to feel guilty for someone else's convenient reason. Asta knows I'm giving her all I've got, and all she needs. She knows we're taking excellent care of her here. I don't mean to sound like a victim.

I'm complaining. I'm tired. I'm sorry.

Dec 8, 2019: MORE REASSURANCE

Asta kept me company this afternoon while I sat sewing patches to Ronnie's and Angi's jeans.

"I want you to know," she said, "that if Tony or you ever felt like you couldn't handle having me here anymore, it would be okay if you moved me back east."

"That's not gonna happen, Mommy," I said. "If we need a break now and then or wanna go out of town for a night, we'll make arrangements and have someone come over to help out and make sure you eat, so that I don't worry. Your home is here and we're all fine. You can count on being here with us for the rest of your life."

Then I took her to Walmart because she wanted to buy a gray button-down sweater. Instead, she bought three bras, three pairs of briefs, lip liner, an eyebrow pencil and pet toys to send to Heidi and Elsa's two house cats. I bought shrimp for our party at work, some pet toys for Ronnie's cats and dog, an ingredient for tonight's dinner and a bottle of chocolate milk for Asta. It was a marathon three hour outing. Meanwhile, I got a nervous text from Elsa.

"*I couldn't reach Ma by phone,*" (OMG) "Could you check/see if it's off the hook?" I'm rolling my eyes. What's she worrying about? I'm right here.

Later, Asta asked me to help her go through a box of items she had set aside to maybe give as Christmas gifts. She gave me a few collectibles from her mother's house in southern Sweden. They felt like peace offerings. I placed them on display in our china cabinet.

Dec 11, 2019: WANT AND WASTE

Asta came over this morning in just her depends and a top, screwed up her face like she was going to cry, but refused to tell me what was going on, what she needed or why she was upset. Finally:

"I yust want French bread and a stick of butter so I can make myself something to eat, like I did in Woodstock," she said.

"We don't have any French bread today but Tony is going shopping today, we could ask him to pick some up," I said.

"No, no," she said, "he'd get the wrong thing."

"Well, I can certainly put a stick of butter in your fridge right now so you have it for whenever, and we have regular bread. Want some of that?" She did.

Of course she wants to maintain her independence. I almost always deliver *immediately* whatever she asks for, and try to anticipate her wants and needs, which change. One day she asked to have donut holes on hand, so I put a few snack size packages in her fridge. They sat untouched until she put them on her tray for disposal. Another day she wanted a quart of buttermilk, but once it was in her fridge worried that it was bad for her arteries. Today when I stocked her fridge with basics (e.g., yogurt, cheese, canned sausage, and almond toast cookies), I reminded her she had the store-bought chocolate milk.

"Take it into your fridge," Asta said, "because there's too much of it...."

Dec 13, 2019: SWEDISH DELIGHT

Tony and I were given free tickets to see the Palm Springs Symphony Orchestra. Tony had another commitment so I invited Asta to join me. After sleeping on it, she accepted. Why turn down an evening out, she reasoned.

Asta was dressed and ready when I got home from work at 6 p.m. We quickly ate the Subway sandwiches Tony brought home for us before heading over to the McCallum. I introduced her to some ushers I knew and we ogled the well-dressed patrons (men as well as women), with their face lifts and jewels.

We expected the show to be stuffy, but to our delight, they had a Special Guest: Gunhild Carling from Sweden. Gunhild played a kick-ass trombone, trumpet, pipe flute, regular flute, harp and bagpipes, sang and danced, and once even played for the King of Sweden. Any mention of royalty earns a star on Asta's scorecard. After the show, we nearly bumped into Gunhild in the lobby. In

Swedish, I praised her performance and introduced her to Asta. The two of them had a short but lovely chat in Swedish about Sweden—a cherry on the top of an ice-cream-Sunday event.

Dec 14, 2019: WEIGHT LOSS

Asta had a follow up appointment with her primary care doctor. She weighed only 107 pounds and asked the doctor for his advice.

"You are skinny but healthy, both in appearance and supported by the numbers in your blood work. Your weight loss," he explained, "is due to the leukemia. Your body has to work harder to produce blood cells, so you lose weight. But you don't need to worry about it. Your blood indicators show a good nutritional status. You can eat whatever you want, and you can even have up to three cups of coffee a day, so long as they're spread out over time."

We talked about her cardiologist, the medicine he prescribed, and its effect on her. "I'm not impressed with him," I said.

"I'm not either," the doctor admitted. "If you have a rapid heart-beat, massage the side of your neck or cough, or press down like you're going to the bathroom Number Two."

"You understand me," she said to him, happy to be offered natural remedies. She asked questions about the flu shot and agreed to accept the mild form, not the super flu shot which is otherwise recommended for the elderly.

At 9 p.m. she seemed fine, but two hours later, Asta woke me with a phone call. She wasn't feeling well. I measured a fever of 101 degrees. She was weak and needed help getting to the bathroom. I gave her a Tylenol and some juice and helped her back into bed. This morning, she feels fine and is looking forward to going to the Santa Lucia Festival tomorrow in Palm Desert.

Dec 15, 2019: SANTA LUCIA

"Elsa's more Swedish than Chris or you because Elsa was born in Sweden," Asta informed me over breakfast this morning. Elsa was three months old when they moved to America.

"Even though we are all three born to the same set of parents, you and Daddy?" I asked.

"Yes, if you put it that way," she said. Okay, that's interesting.

The Santa Lucia celebration at the Lutheran Church was supposed to start at 3 p.m. We arrived at 3:15 to an undecorated room containing five or six people doing who knows what. There was no merchandise to speak of and no music. Tony wandered around looking for the gathering, and asked twice to confirm we were at the right location. I helped a woman named Jenny dress the tables with packaged plastic tablecloths, and she became our friend for the evening. Jenny is half Swedish and lived in Sweden for two years after her parents' divorce. She was here to help the Swedish club with the event. I brought her over to Asta for conversation.

"The musician bailed and several of the girls who were supposed to be in the Lucia train didn't show up," Jenny informed us. "Would you join in?" she asked me. "You speak Swedish and can help sing the songs in Swedish." Uh-oh, they're desperate.

"Okay," I agreed, and went into another room to rehearse with two other girls: the daughter of a second or third generation Swede and her friend who was visiting from England. By tradition, Lucia girls are supposed to be teens and pre-teens. We put on wrinkled white Lucia gowns and practiced by singing along for a few minutes to a CD of Swedish Christmas songs, and soon we were standing in front of the audience of about 15-20 guests.

I had a hard time looking up from the words on the songbook, gagging as I was on swallowed pride. My effort to help rescue really wasn't helping matters. It was still a disaster of a performance. Nobody threw eggs or meatballs, but their palpable sympathy was equally dreadful.

After dinner, Asta and I were having a conversation at the merchandise table with a part-Swedish former school principal named Lotta who asked, "How long does it take to go by train from Stockholm to Skåne?" Ma and I answered at the same time.

"About an hour," Mommy said.

"About 12 hours," I said. I'm pretty sure Asta thought she was answering how long it takes to get by ferry from Skåne to Copenhagen.

Asta gave me the 'Don't contradict me,' look and the chat concluded without further incident.

"Sorry about that. I didn't mean to contradict you in front of Lotta," I acquiesced. "I thought you were answering a different question than the one she asked."

Asta gushed about the wonderful event and how proud she was of me for jumping in, participating, and singing harmony in Swedish. Tony, always the good sport when it comes to a disastrous performance, was in total agreement. "I think I'm gonna cry," he said.

As soon as we arrived home, Asta called Elsa and Chris to report. Both sent me texts complimenting me for making Asta proud and happy. Yes, I'm happy she's happy, of course. The things we do for love.

Dec 18, 2019: DEMANDS

The night before she has a blood draw, Asta likes to have a big steak dinner, like it's homework for a test on which she wants to do well. So last night we went out for steak. Over dinner I mentioned that since I had to work in the morning, Tony would take her for the blood draw, and out for breakfast after.

Asta met me in the hallway in the morning. "I want *you* to take me to doctor appointments," she demanded. "After all, you only work part time," Asta said.

"It's just a blood draw," I said. "You've been there before. It's easy. No worries."

She wanted me to feel guilty, and raised her voice so that Tony (in the next room) would hear it.

"Will he yust drop me off?" she asked. "Do I have to find something? Will they ask me questions?"

"He'll escort you in like he did before, and he'll help you check in. There are two of us, so Tony will take you to this one."

"I only want *one*. I could have had *one* if I had stayed in *Woodstock*," she said, and hobbled angrily back to her room. I went in a few minutes later and found her under the covers, pretending to be asleep.

"It's just a blood draw, Mommy. You won't even be seeing a doctor. And you won't have to give any information other than your birth date. You can handle that."

She refused to acknowledge my presence. I feel bad for Tony who is kind enough to escort her to the doctor and then take her out for breakfast when she's got such a lousy attitude towards him.

When I arrived home from work in the afternoon, she was in a foul mood, making snarky comments about Tony in every other breath.

"You seem angry," I said.

"I'm tired," she said.

"You didn't sleep well?"

"I slept okay."

I rolled my eyes and did what needed to be done: delivered her mail, brought her a glass of juice, helped wet her hair at the sink so she could wash it, and called Medicare for a duplicate card to replace the one she lost or misplaced.

I'm not a martyr or a saint, and I'm not perfect. Most of the time, rolling my eyes behind her back works as a valve. It lets some of the pressure escape.

Dec 19, 2019: THERMOSTAT

Most of the time, Asta chooses to sleep on top of the warm comforter on her bed rather than under it because she doesn't want to mess it up. She insists on wearing open-toe sandals without socks when it's 60 degrees out because the sandals go better with her outfits. She often refuses outerwear saying, "because I'm Swedish. Swedes love and are used to the cold."

We've had numerous discussions on each of these topics. The more I encourage, the more stubbornly she holds to her position. So when she's sitting there shivering—and I know she's cold—I insist on helping her put on a warm, light jacket. I take the socks off my feet and put them on hers, because my socks are already warm.

In spite of all this, Asta gripes to Elsa and Chris about how cold it is in the house. I swear she gets pleasure out of blaming Tony: "He won't turn up the heat because he's cheap."

I know she's 91 years old and skinny and needs to be warm, but I don't think it's too much to ask that she put on a sweater and socks, or crawl under the comforter at night. Tonight she was sitting on the edge of her bed, bundled in an old, worn, thin crocheted blanket, complaining about the cold but refusing to crawl under the covers. That her hair was wet and she was only wearing nylon stocking-type socks didn't help. I put a jacket on her and warm socks, and gave her a couple of warm corn bags.

She continued to complain, and I knew that my sisters—eager to problem-solve—are already talking about it. Bracing myself, I called Chris.

"Maybe we should get a space heater," Chris suggested.

"Not safe—too easy for her to put or drop something on top of it and cause a fire."

"Maybe we should increase her monthly contribution by $300," she said, "because money talks." Chris sends $1,000 a month to cover our mother's room and board.

I was kind of insulted by that. "We don't want any more money," I said. "We'll turn up the thermostat to 68." I already know that the house is rarely below 68.

Mommy's not suffering from anything other than her own stubbornness, and that's not something I can fix. Elsa and Chris aren't helping when—from 3,000 miles away—they react to half-facts and rumors. Arguing with them only makes me sound defensive. Mommy's fine. Sometimes she might need a sweater; other times just a distraction or project to occupy her hands and mind.

Dec 20, 2019: THERMOMETER

I'm sympathetic to the fact that with our thermostat set at 68, even I feel cold sometimes. I've looked into space heaters that plug in like night-lights, but all the electrical outlets in her room are behind furniture. She's not willing to rearrange her furniture and I'm not willing to put a space heater in her room that she can't see or operate safely.

"You can spend more time over here and sleep in Ronnie's room anytime you want," we've told her time and again. But Asta likes her apartment.

"Elsa has been pestering me lately," my mother said. "Has the package come yet? Has the package come yet?" Asta refused to say what was coming in it, but my guess is she knew very well.

I found a package addressed to Asta that I had put among the Christmas packages that were accumulating from all directions. "Could this be it?" I showed her.

"I don't want to wait until Christmas. Would you help me open it now?" she asked. It contained a set of thermal underwear (a nice gift) and a little indoor thermometer/humidity gauge. Objectively, this could be a handy device. My mother has the right to know how warm or cold her room is. Subjectively, I felt disrespected. I informally monitor the temperature in her room every time I go in there.

Tony entered the room as Asta gushed about her gift. "What did you get?" he asked.

"Thermal underwear," she said.

"And a thermometer," I added.

"Let us know if you're cold. We'll turn the thermostat up," he said.

"Oh, no, I'm fine," she answered. Which would have been true because she was wearing a sweater and socks, appropriate clothing for this time of year.

"I didn't complain to Elsa," Asta claimed to me, "but they were talking about how cold it is there and here, and so Elsa took it upon herself to send this thermometer." Maybe Elsa thought she'd gather some data.

"It's just more drama," I said. "Elsa being Elsa."

"Ja, drama, that's Elsa," she grinned.

Dec 21, 2019: POOR ELSA

At 11 p.m., I went in to check on my mother. She was laying on top of, not in, her bed. I brought in a warm blanket and put it on top of her. She wanted to talk about Poor Elsa.

"It's so unfair, after all the dinners she made for all those holidays, all the good she's done for everyone over the years, all those packages she sends, all the trouble she goes to... Marty, her ex, will have his brother visiting for Christmas. Her boyfriend, Tom, will be with his wife and family. Maybe she'll celebrate with Axel and Mallory..." Mommy often talks about what a hard life Elsa has had, how Elsa's not responsible for her troubles and doesn't deserve any of it.

"Yeah, her situation is pretty shitty," I agreed. I wouldn't want to be alone for Christmas either.

"And it's upsetting," she said, "that Elsa doesn't feel welcome here, while Tony pulls out the red carpet for *his* family."

"Ah, so that's where this is going," I said. Someone to blame. Why not Tony?

"Ja," she confirmed, "I feel so bad for her."

"You want us to invite her here for Christmas? Maybe she could fly out here real quick."

"No, no," she said.

"She made her choices," I said.

"What do you mean?" she asked.

"Well, you can't blame Tony for her divorce. And no one has said she can't come here."

"Well, that's what I'm laying here thinking about. It's yust not fair."

"I know, it sucks. Well, I just came in to check on you and encourage you to get under the covers. Want some help?"

"No, I'll go to bed in a little while."

"Okay. Good night, Mommy. I hope you sleep well. See you in the morning." I then brought in two warm corn bags—one for her feet, the other for her core—and made sure the thermostat was set on 68.

At 5:40 a.m. she was still laying on top of the covers, on her back in what she calls her 'yoga pose' (knees to chest). Her bedside light was on. She was sad, having probably been up all night thinking about Elsa's pitiful life and how Tony was to blame for all of it.

Dec 24, 2019: MY THOMAS THE TRAIN CHRISTMAS

Ronnie, Angi, Russell and Jack arrived and we celebrated Christmas last night. Tony and Angi were in charge of the turkey until I got home from work at 2:30.

Watching the meal preparations, Asta announced, "Elsa's cooking up a batch of Daddy's fish soup tonight…but," with a shrug and glancing at Tony added, "to each his own."

After an enjoyable dinner, the girls engaged us in board games, and gifts were exchanged with love and affection.

Elsa's gift to me was a potato-slicer with a recipe for Swedish Hasselback potatoes. No subtlety there.

"Oh, this is nice. I'll use it when I make this potato recipe," I managed to say politely, while thinking, 'probably never.'

Between Asta's digs and Elsa's intrusions, it's hard to keep smiling, hard to keep swallowing without choking. I coach myself to be bigger, more tolerant, more selfless. I remind myself that Asta is old and can't help it. I tell myself this is my job, I want no regrets, I can take it. I think I can, I think I can.

Dec 25, 2019: DATES AND TECHNOLOGY

Asta seems to be having difficulty grasping matters of date and time. She's having trouble wrapping her head around the fact that New Year's Day is not the day after Christmas. Our nephew's kids are visiting and I've recited Tony's itinerary for her 10 times (no exaggeration). He will be driving them to LA for a couple of days. He will not be flying with them to New York.

She tries hard to keep track of her appointments, has a calendar in her room for that purpose, and refers to it frequently: what's happening tomorrow, what's after that, what's coming up next week. I give her a lot of credit for her effort. I really don't mind repeating things (you get used to it), but it does seem to be getting harder for her to process information. Or maybe there's just been too much commotion around here lately.

She is also having trouble operating her phone, which is programmed with speed dial numbers (one for each of us). Sometimes she holds down the speed dial number for too long. When she fails to connect, she concludes her phone isn't working. I demonstrate that it is in fact working by (a) calling her phone from mine, (b) dialing my phone from hers, (c) calling Elsa or Chris on the speed-dial numbers we have set up on her phone, and (d) dialing a number for her because she has dialed the wrong number. Her vision impairment doesn't help.

Dec 26, 2019: COMPANIONSHIP

"Keep me company while I make marmalade, Mommy," I invited. "It should take two and a half to three hours." She did, and talked the entire time... reminiscing... the usual tapes... Tom, Elsa, Tony, Daddy, Sweden... funerals, Woodstock, Tom, Elsa... grudges, relatives, judgments...

It doesn't matter who she's talking to, she just likes to talk, and believes she should be able to say anything at all, even if it might be hurtful. "A mother should be able to talk to her own daughter," she rationalizes.

Today when she started going overboard, I turned to the stove and stirred the pot, let her talk to my back, and rolled my eyes when I had to. The marmalade turned out fabulous. Sweet with the tangy aftertaste of tangerine rind.

Dec 27, 2019: ARGUMENT

It's 62 degrees outside. Asta has had her door to the outside wide open for a couple of hours to let the fresh air in. She is happy and writing comfortably at her desk. Naturally, therefore, I turned down the heat, which had been set at 68. We don't need to let heat out the door if she's comfortable with the door open to 62 degrees. My sisters are not here to see.

During dinner this evening, after every sentence Tony uttered, Asta made a face, the one where her upper lip rises under her nose and the corners curl downward; where her ears pull her eyes back a little, drawing them further apart. It's the face that broadcasts her contempt. She makes these faces even when Tony is pleasantly agreeing with her.

Finally, I asked her to stop.

"Do I have to control my face?" she spat. "Would I have to wear a mask? What's wrong with you, Suey? What happened to you? I don't recognize you."

"All I'm asking is for you to be aware that you're making faces and it bothers me."

Asta went to her room.

"Just ignore her digs, her attacks, her eye rolling, and smirks," Tony said. "Don't let her push your buttons."

I went to Asta's room, turned on the light and apologized for losing my temper. I tried to communicate, without success, how the person she was hurting was me. I alerted Elsa and Chris.

"Just had an argument w/ Ma because of her constant smirking. Tired of the disrespect. She wants me to side with her against my husband. I don't expect either of you to change or fix anything, just see if maybe you can open her mind just a crack."

"When she and I fought with each other," Elsa wrote back, "I remember thinking that maybe a little vacation would be good for everyone. I still think that. She could come here for a while, or you and Tony could take a vacation while Chris and I are there in March." Elsa jumped at the chance to pursue her agenda.

"She's too frail to travel across country," I answered, not seeking a vacation.

Soon Chris called, having had a tearful call from Asta. "Why was Ma sobbing? Her only worry is the temperature in her room. I'm concerned that you're subjecting her to hypothermia."

I couldn't believe what I was hearing. My sister is accusing me of elder abuse. My mother acts like an asshole, and I'm the one on the defensive.

"Mommy is really confused about this temperature thing," I said. "She refuses to get under her warm bedspread, keeps the door or window open when it's cold out, and often refuses to put on socks or a sweater. She can sleep in Ronnie's room where it might be a little warmer anytime she likes, but she declines. A separate thermostat for her room would cost $2,000, and if we put in a separately-controlled heating/air conditioning unit in her room, she'd have no window, which she would never accept."

I can't dwell on it. I have a job to do. I brought Asta some corn bags and encouraged her to crawl under the covers. She refused, saying she's comfortable on top, covered by her green throw blanket. I'm not too worried. It's cool in her room, but not cold. She thanked me for the corn bags, however.

Dec 29, 2019: ELDER ABUSE

"What's the temperature in my room?" Asta asked when I went in to get her for breakfast.

"According to this thermometer Elsa sent you, it's 62 degrees. Are you cold?"

"No," she said, under her green throw. She was not under her warm comforter. Over breakfast, I opened the conversation.

"Let's talk about the temperature in your room," I said calmly. "Nobody wants you to be cold. You have options. You can sleep under your comforter, or in Ronnie's room."

"I'm fine," she said, "but Elsa is asking for temperature readings."

"I don't want my sisters thinking/talking about elder abuse. I don't want to think that social services might come and remove you because we don't keep the temperature in your room warm enough. Both Tony and I are happy to have you stay here with us, and we'll address any problems that come up as best we can. But I don't want them thinking you're being abused when you have options to keep you warm that you're refusing."

"Is it okay if I jump in?" Tony asked, coming into the room.

"Yes," my mother and I said.

"It's easy," he said. "You make your own decisions. Nobody can make you do anything. We'll just give you options."

"Maybe it was my fault for complaining about the temperature to Elsa," she said.

"Well, we've learned something from that thermostat," I said. "Your room is a degree or two off from the rest of the house, and we have to face the facts. Tony will talk to Chris."

"Yes," Ma said. "Please do that." A little later I heard from Chris.

"I just had a nice conversation with Tony about presenting Ma with alternatives," she said. "I know you already have. I know Tony already has. Now I will. I will also tell Elsa to back off and ask her to support the alternative of Ronnie's room on cold nights as needed. Sorry for all this."

"I've moved my sewing machine out of Ronnie's room and put a lamp on the desk for her. She's all set up, has two places she can use." I sent her a photo of the bed and desk in Ronnie's room. And then I took Ma to TJ Maxx, because when Tony and I were there together yesterday I saw a pair of yellow pants I thought she'd like, and had set the pants aside in two sizes. The size 8 fit her perfectly and looked beautiful on her. She also bought a warm, cozy pink sweater, a fashionable soft, long-sleeved top with a flounce (she loves flounces), and a long skirt, all for $80. We went for lunch at McDonalds.

"I'm sorry for all the drama over the temperature issue," she said. "It got blown way out of proportion."

"Yes, well, nobody wants you to be cold," I answered, "and they're 3,000 miles away. It's natural for them to worry."

Dec 30, 2019: BELIEVE IT OR NOT

"I tried to explain to Elsa that the temperature issue got blown out of proportion," Asta said, handing me a letter she had written to Elsa to put in the mail for her. I wondered why she couldn't just explain it over the phone since they talk on it daily. Maybe she was enclosing a check 'for the cats'. Doesn't matter.

After making and serving her brunch, I went on a shopping rendezvous with a friend. I was gone for several hours, but Tony was mostly home. When I got home at 5:30 p.m., Ma was sitting on the couch watching TV.

"That's an awfully long time to go shopping," she said. "Were you shopping the whole time?"

"Yes. Well, my friend and I had lunch first."

"Why is Tony already home?" she asked.

"The clubhouse was double booked so his HOA meeting was cancelled."

"I hate liars. I don't believe he had a meeting or that it was cancelled," she said.

"Well, that's what happened," I said. "If you choose not to believe it, Mommy, that's your business."

She didn't like the dinner I made, pushed the fish to the side of her plate, and ate only the potatoes, insisting she wasn't hungry. I prepared a second dinner for her, of which she ate every bite, of smoked salmon and sliced cucumber. Meanwhile, she complained about the weather and made false accusations about Tony. It's apparent that Elsa is wiggling her crooked witch index finger to coax Mommy back east, bribing her with promises of all the fun they will have.

"Yeah, well, I wish we could wave a magic wand and make it perfect for you, but that's just not within our power. Wherever you are—whether it's here or living with Elsa—there will be issues. That's just the way it is."

Dec 31, 2019: FINANCIAL BENEFIT

"Mommy told me firmly that she will not be moving back to the East Coast but has a hard time saying so to Elsa," Chris said. "I've told this to Elsa repeatedly, but she just can't let go. She says, 'We'd have so much *fun*'."

Right, for two weeks or until Asta's first unmet expectation. Maybe Elsa is looking for ways to defray the cost of groceries, utilities and home improvements.

"I just bought Elsa a Kindle," Chris said, "so she can talk about books with Mommy."

"Remember the bicycle-built-for-two she campaigned for a few years ago?" I asked. "How she pressured us to pay for it so that she, with her bad hip, could ride Ma, frail and nearly blind, around the neighborhood?" Chris had been willing to chip in, but I had refused on the grounds of it being unsafe. Mean, unreasonable sister that I am.

So, okay, having a Kindle isn't a bicycle built for two, but I believe this is how Elsa would operate if Asta were in her care: she'd buy things 'for Mommy's sake' that Chris wouldn't challenge. Elsa can be relentless when she wants something. Nobody says 'no' to Elsa.

New Year's Resolution: give Elsa less traction on the highway of my thoughts and feelings.

CHAPTER 4

DAILY MANAGEMENT

Jan 3, 2020: HIRING HELPERS

Tony and I are planning to be away overnight sometime soon and don't want to leave my mother alone in the house. She could fall or have some other emergency.

Asta herself has said, "I don't know what I'd do if something happened, like the power went out when I was home alone." Yet she is adamantly opposed to my hiring a 'caretaker'.

Nevertheless, we've been exploring all options, including:

(a) Hiring people we know:
- Eddie can barely cook an egg. Hiring him means more prep work for me.
- Our Buddhist friend was interested in the work, but she just moved to Arizona.
- Rosalva is willing, but her reliability remains a question mark.

(b) Entering into an agreement with an agency:
- $600 would buy 24 hours coverage.
- $300 would buy three 4-hour shifts: dinner, breakfast, dinner, but she'd be home alone overnight.

- Something less might be negotiable, but s/he would have to be here at mealtimes and overnight.

Whether or not Asta is willing to pay for a caregiver, whether or not she can choose her caregiver, and whether or not she is willing to accept a professional stranger as her occasional caregiver, I can't allow myself to be held hostage.

Jan 7, 2020: VENTURING OUT

We are still trying to find someone to take care of Mommy in our absence. Tony recommended a cleaning woman from the gym he attends and got defensive when I said I needed to meet her.

"She's doing us a favor," he said, "and if she can't do it, she said one of her friends could." Concerned I'd wear my assisted living administrator hat and scare her off, Tony wanted to be the middle-man.

"It's not about making the caregiver feel good, it's about taking care of my mother in our home. My mother needs someone who can speak English. Just any warm body won't do. I need to believe that the person we hire to care for my mother is capable, kind and trustworthy."

"Then *you* find the person," he said.

I reached out to a caregiver I'd met a few times who had been awarded the National Caregiver of the Year title at the agency for which I used to work. We talked on the phone, and with a week's notice she would come on any Friday night and stay for 24 hours for only $190. That's a great price, but more importantly, she has experience, is trustworthy, and I think Mommy will like her. It will be an easy job for her, and being a live-in is not new to her. I discussed with Chris that I intended to pay the caregiver out of Asta's funds, and she endorsed the expense.

"Tony said you may be going on a trip?" my mother asked at the dinner table.

"Yes, I've arranged for someone to stay over. Darla is very nice. I know her from my previous job. She also takes care of a retired doctor. I trust her. I'll show you her picture on Facebook."

"I wasn't expecting this trip to happen so soon. I thought you'd wait until Elsa and Chris were here at the end of March."

"No, but it is three weeks away. I'll arrange so you can meet her ahead of time." We sat in front of the computer and looked at Darla's Facebook page.

"What does she charge?" Asta asked.

"Well, it's an easy job for her, as all she needs to do is meals and take care of the dog. Otherwise, she can sleep and watch TV."

"Who's paying for it?" she asked.

"We'll split it," I said, which is what Chris and I had agreed to tell her.

"Of course you should be able to go away when you want to, but I'm not sick, so I don't feel I should have to pay for it," she said.

"No worries," I said. "We'll pay for it, because I won't be able to relax if you're home alone overnight. I need someone here in case of an emergency. And she'll take care of Dawson. You won't need to entertain her, and you might even like her. She is shy, but likes to talk."

At this time, the longest I'm comfortable leaving my mother home alone is four or five hours. I check on her before going to bed at night and first thing when I get up. When I wake up during the night (which is most nights), I peek in on her to monitor for falls or other medical emergency. I usually hear—and find it reassuring—when she comes in during the night to go to the bathroom. When she calls me in the middle of the night, whether it's because she's afraid or not feeling well, I am there in two seconds. It's just prudent to have someone available to help her out should she ever need it. She can preserve her savings for future medical care, but supervision (which includes meal preparation and companionship) comes at a cost as well.

So I'm not apologizing for having her pay for an occasional 24 hour shift. Had we gone through an agency, it would've cost three times as much. Tomorrow, I'll confirm the date with Darla and arrange a Meet-and-Greet.

Jan 11, 2020: MAKING FRIENDS

Asta got a phone call this morning from Leslie, a woman she met at the neighborhood New Year's Eve party we attended, and they made plans for Leslie to come over. At Asta's request, I picked up a cake, which Ma then ate half of that night. She asked that I squeeze some fresh orange juice to replace the four glasses that had been sitting in her fridge for a few days, which I did.

This afternoon, Eddie came over to visit her. I snapped a beautiful photo of the two of them sitting in the back yard talking by the pool and sent it to Elsa and Chris. Elsa lavished me with praise for enabling Ma to make friends. I get that she's patting me on the back, but she's dished out so much garbage, it's like pouring syrup on a turd. I'm not eating it.

Resentments aside, it is gratifying to see and help Asta develop outside relationships. Mutually beneficial all around.

Jan 12, 2020: FOOD PREFERENCES

For breakfast these days, Asta only wants soft boiled eggs and toast. No more cereal, no eggs sunny side up or over easy, no French toast, no omelets, no oatmeal. Soft boiled eggs only, she says.

When I served shrimp scampi the other night, she wrinkled her nose. "It's delicious, but I prefer bigger shrimp served with cocktail sauce."

Another potato recipe arrived in my email today from Elsa. This one was for Bacon Potato Corn Chowder. "I'm totally not being snarky, but...," she wrote. Edit out 'not' and 'but' to read her admission. I deleted her email.

Floyd and Louise came to visit and the five of us went out to a Vietnamese restaurant in downtown Palm Springs for dinner. It was an enjoyable evening and the food was delicious. Everyone ate every bite.

"I think my tummy is upset," Asta said. "Maybe the spices caused this sore inside my nose. I think I should stick with what I'm used to."

This evening I made Oboro, a Japanese dish that uses leftover meat—standard Costello fare. Asta pushed it around on her plate, ate only little pieces of the egg, and made a show of not liking the rice. She'd rather have potatoes.

"The Costellos sure like *different* foods," she said.

"Oboro is the Japanese version of putipanna," I said. "Putipanna is Oboro's Swedish sister." She wasn't buying it, so I made it easy for her. "I know you're not of fan of rice, so if you'd rather have leftovers, I could heat something up for you." I listed a few options from which she could choose.

"I don't want leftovers. I'm not hungry," she said.

I'm not worried. She won't starve. I put a nice-sized hunk of cooked kielbasa next to the jars of gourmet fruited yogurt in her fridge. She can eat whenever she wants. I try to accommodate her preferences without making myself their slave.

Oboro	*Puttipanna*
Cook leftover meat in a little bit of oil	Fry lots of onions in butter
Add equal parts soy sauce and sugar	Add potatoes, more butter if needed to help them brown
Dish meat into a hollow on top of a mound of hot cooked short white rice	Add cut-up leftover meat
Lay a thin egg omelet over top	Fry until a little crispy
Garnish with a side of green beans	Serve with a few slices of tomato

Jan 18, 2020: MEET AND GREET

Darla came over this evening for the Meet-and-Greet. I showed her around and introduced her to Asta. In Asta's presence, I emphasized to Darla that except for meals, Mommy is 'completely independent'.

"You're here for *my* benefit," I said, "because I worry and don't want to leave Ma home alone overnight. We have plenty of food for you to choose from to cook for the two of you. Just as a heads up, my mother really likes potatoes." I want her stay to be a success.

"We'll have a good time when Tony and Suey are gone," Asta said mischievously. "We'll turn on all the lights and leave the gas fireplace on. When that cat is away, the mice will play." Darla found her amusing.

Asta seemed to like Darla, Darla seemed to like her, and I'm giddy at the thought of getting away, worry-free, for a night with my husband.

Jan 20, 2020: NURSE RATCHETT

"I was in the bathroom for an hour with diarrhea," my mother informed me when I went in to escort her in for breakfast. She didn't want to eat, refused tea, and wanted to stay in bed. I cancelled her pedicure appointment. An hour later she called me on the phone.

"Could you put another blanket on me?" she asked. I did.

"Do you have a fever?"

"No, I don't think so."

"How do you feel?" I asked.

"Fantastic," she spat. I don't know why she had to snap at me like that. I kept an eye on her, and she seemed to feel better as the day went on.

Later, she was lying in bed with wet cotton balls on her eyes.

"One of my eyelids is swollen, but it doesn't hurt," she said. "It feels like maybe I have something scratchy in my eye."

"Want me to call the doctor?" I asked.

"No," she said, "not yet." Looking closely, I could see that one eyelid was a little bit swollen, but I saw no drainage, no eye crust, and her sclera were clear and white. I gave her a warm compress.

"I'll take you to the doctor if it doesn't resolve in a day or so. Meanwhile, we'll do warm compresses." I'll try a common sense remedy and err on the side of caution when it comes to taking her to see a doctor. When in doubt, have it checked out.

Jan 21, 2020: MISSING CDs

I had just come home from ushering after work and wanted to change my clothes and do gongyo (evening prayers) before making dinner.

"My CDs are missing," Asta said with her venomous snake eyes, "and I've looked everywhere for them."

"Well, I didn't take them, and neither did Tony. Let me help you look for them." We looked, but didn't find them.

"Where did they go?" she demanded. "They didn't walk away by themselves." This went on for a few minutes. I extracted myself.

Asta came into the living room where I was doing gongyo and started talking at me.

"Not now, Mommy, please. I'm doing gongyo," I said. She stood waiting, making a show of the fact that she has trouble standing. I tried again. "I'll come see you as soon as I'm done. We can talk then." She left indignantly. A few minutes later I joined her in her room.

"I have everything organized perfectly," she asserted. "I know where everything is."

"Let's try playing some of these unlabeled CDs in your CD player," I suggested. But then I failed to get her CD player to work.

"That's odd," she said, "that it would break *at the same time* that my CDs went missing."

"Unfortunately, Mommy, I can't make your CDs magically appear or fix your CD player with a snap of my fingers. I understand how frustrating it is when you can't find something. Really I do. But I assure you that neither of us has taken them, and I'd appreciate if you'd stop blaming us for their disappearance."

"I don't want to blame the people I live with when I can't find something I'm looking for," she said, with a hint of haughty. "Maybe I put it away somewhere when I was reorganizing." Yeah, that's most likely it. Asta is an intelligent woman. She rearranges her things all the time. It was refreshing to hear her *almost* confess in the Case of the Missing CDs.

"I completely understand how frustrating it is to not be able to find something," I said. "The CDs will probably show up when you're not looking for them. And if not, they can probably be replaced."

Jan 23, 2020: SOCIAL BUTTERFLY

It was time for Asta's Spanish lesson but my mother looked miserable.

"You'll probably enjoy yourself once you get there. But do you want me to cancel it? Because I will, if that's what you want," I said.

"I'll go, even though I don't really want to," she said.

Of course, she enjoyed her hour with Rosalva. We then had about an hour during which she could rest before we all headed over to Cary's house on his invitation to dinner. Another neighbor would also be there.

It was a lovely dinner party: wine and appetizers, pork roast and potatoes with peas on the side for dinner, and for dessert, home-made key lime pie. We were touched to see hanging on his kitchen wall a framed photo of him and Asta.

In the morning, Asta's friend Leslie paid Ma a short visit. Asta is basking in the attention.

Next week, we'll be joining our Scandinavian realtor and his spouse for dinner at a place in La Quinta.

Asta enjoys social settings, and easily captures people's attention. She handles herself well interpersonally and is genuinely fun to have along.

Jan 26, 2020: HIDDEN CAMERAS

In anticipation of hiring companions, I bought a trio of portable motion-detecting cameras. I positioned two in areas of the house where no guest should have reason to enter, and one in the corner of the garage so that I can see when the companion is coming and going and observe her escorting my mother from and to her room.

I can't tell Asta about the cameras because she would feel spied on. Furthermore, once the caregiver won her trust, my mother, embarrassed by my lack of it, would reveal the cameras' existence. I wouldn't want to work in an environment where cameras recorded my movement either, but as a homeowner and daughter, 'Sorry, not sorry'.

Interestingly, on their first deployment, the cameras revealed Darla entering and taking photos of the artwork in my office, but it seemed harmless. Darla didn't mention the motion detector (maybe she didn't notice it) and said she was willing to come back.

"I want Darla back next time you go away," Ma said "I don't want the caretaker to keep changing."

"That would be ideal," I agreed. "Since Darla prefers 12 or 24 hour shifts, we can ask her to be our overnight person." Photos aside, Darla's shift was a success.

Jan 29, 2020: PARTY PLANNING

"I'm tinking about trowing a party when Elsa and Chris are here at the end of March—only for my close friends—at the Clubhouse," Mommy said.

"How about at a restaurant instead?" I suggested, thinking the number of her close friends would be fairly few. "The clubhouse is too big for a small group of people, and costs money to rent." It also requires a considerable amount of effort on my part.

"No, I want to do it the Swedish way," she said. But I planted the seed with Chris, and soon it was Mommy's idea. Tony suggested a Japanese steakhouse where they prepare the food in front of you, a form of entertainment, and she was all-in. We spent time on the internet together gathering information, and she started putting together her guest list. Twenty-two names and she was just getting started.

"You might want to consider trimming it to just your closest friends," I suggested. "That would make the party more 'yours' and keep the cost closer to what you said you wanted to spend," which was $600-$800.

Difficult decisions to mull over.

Jan 30, 2020: INCONTINENCE

"Something doesn't smell too good in here," I said when I entered her room to bring her over for dinner. It smelled of urine.

"It couldn't be because, because, because..." Asta protested, and then her shoulders fell forward, heavily.

"It could be the sardines..." I offered. But we both knew what we were talking about.

She came to the dinner table and sat with her head in her hands until I served the meal. Tony and I carried on a normal conversation about my day, his day, her day, last night, etc., until she warmed up, forgot her misery, and got excited about the party she's planning. By the time we had dessert (lingon with half-and-half), party planning was moving full steam ahead and she was happily hashing out details. Next week we'll go to the Japanese steakhouse so she can see what it's like.

Jan 31, 2020: SQUAWK SQUAWK

"We're leaving the TV on for you while we go usher this afternoon so you can watch the news with Dawson if you'd like," I told her. "We expect to be home by 5 p.m."

Because of our assignment to 'outside' positions, Tony and I were able to leave after intermission. It was only 3:30 p.m., so we decided to go out for an early Mexican dinner. I'd make something for Ma when we got home.

We pulled in the driveway at 4:35 p.m. and I went directly to her room, as always. She was on the phone talking in hushed and anxious tones.

"Hi, we're home," I said.

"Oh, she's here," she said to the person on the other end of the line, and hung up. No good-bye or anything.

"What's wrong?" I asked.

"Where were you?" she questioned.

"Ushering, at the McCallum."

"For five hours?"

"Yes. Well, since we got out early, Tony and I had a bite to eat on our way home. I'll make dinner for you now."

"What did you have?"

"Mexican."

"I'll take care of myself," she said.

"Come on in, I'll fix you something."

"I was worried because you were gone so long," she said. Maybe she just wanted to complain about something to Elsa. Or maybe she fell asleep and lost track of time. Maybe she forgot that I told her to expect us around 5. Or maybe she felt hungry, and it became an 'issue'.

"Mommy," I said, "anytime you're wondering when I'll be home, before you get nervous, just call me. I'll tell you when I'll be home." I made dinner for her, made small talk, and put some kielbasa on the stove to put in her refrigerator later.

"I plan to be up writing later tonight, so I'm going to take a nap now," she said after dinner, and shuffled back to her room.

"Okay, I'm going to Walmart to pick up that movie gift card you asked me to get for Elsa for her birthday," I said, and left, completely forgetting about the kielbasa.

Five minutes later, she called me on the phone.

"My fire alarm is ringing!" she screamed. "What should I do?"

"Tony is home. I'll call him." I turned around and headed back home, calling Tony along the way until he answered.

"All the water had cooked off the pot of kielbasa and the smoke set off the fire alarm," he said. "I didn't answer your call because I was busy taking care of the stove and disarming the alarm."

He had everything under control so I continued running my errand, and ultimately delivered the movie gift card to her. That's when she presented an identical movie gift card and asked:

"What is dis?"

Feb 4, 2020: TRUMP DRUNK

After working from noon to 6 and then volunteering for a shift as an usher, I came home at 8:30 p.m. and was greeted with the equivalent of expletives.

"To tink dat anyone can support dose filty liar Democrats yust make me sick! I have not one ounce of respect for any of dem. Not even my own daughters!" she said emotionally, angrily. Asta had just witnessed Nancy Pelosi tear Donald Trump's State of the Union speech in half. "You!" she pointed at me.

I walked out of the room.

"What really makes me angry," she said, now directing her comments towards Tony, "is dat my own daughters are with *dem*!" She turned on her heel and marched back to her room. In a few minutes I'll bring in her medicine.

How did my mild-mannered, apolitical, diplomatic mother devolve into this angry, self-righteous, Trump-drunk fanatic? She's a victim of easy-to-remember catch phrases and gimmicks that she can parrot: 'Crooked Hillary,' 'Pocahontas,' 'Lock Her Up.' Once Daddy died, there was no one to tell her when she sounds ignorant to 'hol flabben' (Swedish for 'shut up'). Daddy would have been horrified by Trump's lies. All Asta knows is that Trump is a businessman, Daddy was a businessman. And that's why she likes Trump. Her logic.

You can't have a rational conversation with someone who thinks like that, so I did as she taught me, and turned the other cheek.

Feb 6, 2020: LESSONS

"What did I do," Asta said, as if pleading to God, "to cause my daughters to turn out this way?" referring to us with our spouses.

"What do you mean?" I asked.

"All those lessons you were given as children, you shouldn't be using those skills to benefit your men. They should take care of *themselves*."

"What would you do differently if you were any of *us*?" I asked.

"Well," she said, "I would stay home and be taken care of."

"That's fine and was normal for your generation," I said. "What you taught us, and what we learned as children through all those lessons and experiences you gave us, was to be independent and self-sufficient, and to have a good work ethic. Those are all good, right?" I was happy to give her credit.

She couldn't argue with that, so she came up with another angle, another reason to blame the men.

"It's because I complained about 'the men' (Tom) in Woodstock and Elsa couldn't take it that I'm here."

"Well, you're entitled to your opinion. But as long as *we're* happy with the men in our lives, what's there for you to worry about? Let's just appreciate them and what they do. A little appreciation is a good thing." Her complaining can be hard to take sometimes, but I don't want her to worry about being sent away.

And then I put in a load of her laundry.

Feb 7, 2020: REALITY CHECK

"I feel rushed," Asta groused at 10 a.m. She had a mani/pedi appointment scheduled for 12:30.

"You have over two hours. That's plenty of time. How much time do you need?"

"I'm always being pushed, pushed, pushed," she said.

"Let's see," I said, and checked the calendar, thinking maybe a little reality check might help. "On Monday you had Spanish. That's it. Today's Friday. If you don't want to go, I'll cancel."

"Then my toenails will grow into my feet," she said.

"I'm just pointing out that I'm not making you do anything. It's entirely up to you."

She gave me a dirty look.

"When you have things to do, you complain about being too busy. When you don't have anything to do, you complain about being bored," I said.

"I'm over 90. You don't understand."

"Nobody's forcing you to do anything," I said. "Maybe you could stop complaining."

"I'll yust say yes, no and amen."

"Whatever."

She refused to eat more than the bare minimum because she's afraid she'll have to go to the bathroom while getting her nails done. I managed to get her to eat an egg, 1/2 an English muffin, some orange juice and a few spoonfuls of yogurt. She swallowed her pill with a grimace.

Feb 8, 2020: HUMOR

When Asta and I arrived to the Clubhouse for the HOA Social last night, she put on her most winsome smile, and there was our friend, Cary. He made up our name tags and, peeling the backing off hers, turned to her and said:

"Now, if you'll allow me, I'll put this on your breast. It's the closest I've been to your breast in a long time, Dear."

She grinned, looked down at her chest and said, "Well, if you can find it."

∞

"It shows you never worked in a nursing home," she said, because I wasn't being sympathetic enough about her plight of our being out of applesauce with which to take her pills. Notes to reader:

(1) I worked for nursing homes for over 12 years, (2) she doesn't have any swallowing issues.

"Oh, we're in a nursing home now?" I asked with interest.

"I yust wish your attitude weren't so ... Democratic!" she scoffed.

I couldn't help but laugh. She huffed off with her cane to her room.

Feb 12, 2020: EATING IS POWER

Asta looked miserable last night when I came home from work. "What's going on? Why are you down?"

She refused to say, or couldn't say, but gave me the impression that it was because I'd been gone all day.

"Tony is out picking up a pizza for us to have for dinner," I said.

"I want to weigh myself before dinner," she said.

"Are you feeling skinnier or heavier?" I asked.

"Skinnier," she said. "I'm starving. Would you get my magnifying glass for me from my room?" I went and observed that she had only eaten one of the two eggs I'd made for her for breakfast, and only 1/2 of the sandwich I'd given her for her lunch. She could help herself by eating what I prepare for her, if not at once, then over the course of the day. She eats independently when she's awake at night. Why not during the day? Is she not eating to punish me for not being present at mealtime? Does she really need reminders and encouragement to eat when she is perfectly willing and able to eat at night?

Repeat performance today. Asta ate her breakfast toast, Greek yogurt with strawberry jam and swallowed her medicine with apple sauce, but left her sandwich, despite it being a BLT, her favorite. "I'm saving it to eat later tonight," she explained.

Feb 19, 2020: FOOD FIGHT

"Can't I have the red sauce?" Asta objected when I served linguini with clam sauce instead of tomato sauce for dinner.

"Well, this is what we're having for dinner tonight," I said.

"But I don't like it," she complained. "Why can't I have it with red sauce?"

"I didn't make red sauce tonight. This is what I made for tonight."

"I can't eat it. I'll have to force myself to eat it. I've never liked this dish. Can't I have ketchup?"

From a nutritional standpoint, that would be like giving her lollipops for dinner.

"I'm not serving you ketchup with pasta. You liked linguini with clam sauce the last time I made it," I said. "I don't run a restaurant. Sorry."

"I'll eat what you eat," she said, feigning resignation.

"Now you're talking," I said.

But she pushed it around on her plate and complained of being hungry.

"How could you be like that to your *92 year old mother*? How could you be so awful? Wait till I tell Elsa," she said.

"Go ahead and tell Elsa. Tell her I made clam sauce for dinner and how upset that made you."

"That's not the point."

"That's exactly the point. You're upset because I made something you don't want." And because I'm not jumping up to make a separate meal just for her.

"It's your attitude. I wish I could have a recording," she said.

"Me too. I wish we had a recording. I wish you could have heard yourself and seen your performance when I served dinner. You think I'm being rude? How about looking in the mirror?"

She's not the only one in this family. And no, I'm not sorry for making linguini with clam sauce for dinner, and I'm not sorry for not being sorry. She could be polite, show a little appreciation. She doesn't have to love it, but doesn't have the right to demand that I make something else. She's not allergic to it. It's not going to make her sick.

"I'll talk with the girls when they come here next month about going back to Woodstock."

"Because I served clam sauce for dinner. That's ridiculous," I said.

Tony neither sided with her nor came to my defense, changing the subject instead, bless his heart. She called on him to bring in her medications and had him set up the TV for her. She has no idea how lucky she is to have two people here to help her. When I'm the bad guy, she still has him.

Of course I'm not going to let her go hungry. I placed some leftover chicken in her fridge and poked my head in her room to let her know. She was on the phone talking with Elsa.

"Suey yust came in. She's been listening," she said in a whisper.

"I've not been listening," I said. "I'm just letting you know I put some chicken in your refrigerator in case you get hungry later. You can have your private conversation. I'm not interested in what you're telling Elsa."

I already knew enough. I knew she would bellyache, and I knew Elsa would sympathize with her. They'd talk about how hard-hearted I am, and how much better she would have it in Woodstock.

Feb 20, 2020: APOLOGY

Asta was lying on her bed facing the wall in the morning when I went in. She refused to acknowledge my presence.

"I'll be taking my walk and we'll have breakfast when I get back," I said. I went for my walk and called Chris, who had heard from Asta about our argument. They were circulating the word 'abuse' among themselves.

"I don't believe it," Chris said, "but Mommy can get very dramatic, and Elsa is buying into it."

When I went back to Asta's room an hour later, Asta was still on her bed in the same position. I sat down by her feet.

"Look, I'm sorry I got frustrated last night, and I'm sorry you got upset," I said. "But for what it's worth, if Tony had complained about dinner like you did, you would have ripped him a new asshole. I hope you'll think about that."

I made her two soft boiled eggs, toast, and fresh orange juice, and set up her meds with apple sauce. As per normal. I had a bowl of cereal. We ate in silence.

"Is there anything you want to say?" I asked.

"No, I yust got up."

"You might want to talk to Elsa and Chris today because they're afraid I'm abusing you."

"I don't feel you're abusing me, but I can't help what comes out of my mouth."

"Well, whatever it is, that's what they're hearing you say, and that's what they're talking about."

"I'll call them."

For dinner I made boiled—not fried—kielbasa and mashed potatoes. She ate her fill and updated me on her efforts.

"I talked to Elsa today," she said, "and told her that we could call it 'bad attitude' or 'personality crash', but not to throw around words like abuse."

"Whose bad attitude are we talking about?" I asked.

"It could be yours, could be mine," she said after thinking a bit. "I yust wanted you to know that I talked with her and told her not to use words like that."

"Thank you, Mommy," I said, "because they're so untrue and unfair."

Feb 21, 2020: INDIAN GIVER

"Do you still have that horseshoe that belonged to my father?" Asta asked while we were watching TV. "It's 100 years old and very valuable."

"Sure, I do. I have the replica on display in the dining room and the real one in the china cabinet among my valuables."

"Could I have it back?" she asked.

"Are you thinking of hanging it up? I could help you with that."

"Well, no..." she said. And then I understood.

"Has Elsa asked for it? Are you thinking of giving it to Elsa?"

"Maybe."

"So you want me to give it back to you so you can give it to her? I value the horseshoe too and don't really want to give it to Elsa," I said. "What's she going to do with it? Give it to Tom? Or one of her kids?" And then I felt guilty so I brought out the two horseshoes and offered, "You want to give her one of these?"

"No, forget it," she said. "I gave it to you, so I can't really take it back."

I ask myself:

- Did Elsa ask for it, or was it Mommy's idea?
- Should I be attached to something I don't need and am not using?
- Should I feel guilty that I didn't want to relinquish it to Elsa?
- Should I feel ashamed of myself?

It all makes me feel a little sad.

Feb 23, 2020: WHERE THERE'S A WILL, THERE'S AN ARGUMENT

"Elsa and I had an argument this weekend because I talked with her about my will," Asta said. "Elsa volunteered to look into it but didn't want me to discuss it with you or Chris until she had the answers."

"As I recall, your will says that anything that's left will be divided equally three ways," I said. "The only reason anyone would be upset would be if Elsa were trying to get more for herself. Maybe she feels she needs it more than Chris or I do. But you can do what you want with your money, of course." Asta likes to know she has money/power/control and the capacity to leverage it.

"She was only looking into it at my request," she said, shielding Elsa.

"That's possible. But why keep it secret?"

I want to believe Elsa's intentions are honorable, but in the past she has shown that she is quite willing to and capable of manipulating others for her own enrichment.

CHAPTER 5

CORONAVIRUS

The Coronavirus has been all over the news, and an epidemic seems to be in the making. The stock market took its worst tumble in years, and the clothing order I placed online is long delayed because factories in China have shut down. So far, few people in the US have been infected, but in the spirit of preparedness, I picked up some supplies. I gave Ma a bottle of hand sanitizer for her room and put a bottle by our front door. I gave a box of sanitizing wipes to Tony for his gym/volleyball bag, put a package in my car, a few packets into my pocketbook, and left a container in my office at work. And we've been hand washing. A lot.

Asta sat watching the news on TV while Tony and I ushered at the McCallum.

"I'm nervous about this virus," she said when we came home.

"Yes, it sounds pretty serious," I said.

"If I catch it, it's gotta be somebody's fault—somebody who goes out in the public among people." In other words, me and/or Tony.

"That may be true, but you have some power to help protect yourself," I said. "Tony and I are out—at work, at volleyball, at the gym, the McCallum—and may be exposed, so we're washing our hands often. Despite our best efforts, it may not be possible to avoid."

"I'm worried," she said.

"I understand. We all are," I said.

"How did it get started?" she wanted to know.

"It's my understanding that it crossed over to humans from bats in a certain cave in China," I said, "or it originated at some market. They're still trying to figure it out."

"I think it was developed in a lab in China and is being spread deliberately as a plot against America," she said. "Conspiracy theory."

"Is that what they're saying on Fox News?" I asked.

"The Democrats are saying it was Trump's fault," she scoffed. "Coronavirus is worse than AIDS. Where did AIDS come from?"

"That came from monkeys or chimpanzees," I explained. Or tried to explain. I looked it up on the internet and read it to her, describing how people hunted and consumed infected chimps in the Congo, and that's how it crossed over to humans.

"No, that was a plot too," she insisted. "They created it in a lab and deliberately spread it to punish gay men and drug addicts."

At this point I realized a conversation to educate was futile, so I steered the conversation to other things and soon she headed to the bathroom before going to bed. Leaving the bathroom, she summoned me into the hallway.

"I have something to say and I don't want you to interrupt me," she announced. "Don't blame the animals."

Mar 1, 2020: GEESE

"Let's take a ride over to the reservoir across the street and feed the geese," I invited. It was a beautiful day—windy, but sunny and 72 degrees. I gave her my new sunglasses from the 99 Cent Store and she looked like a Hollywood movie star. We packed three slices of bread, brought her red walker so she'd have something to sit on, drove over to the lake and parked close to the trail.

The trail was a little tricky with the walker, but we managed. Once situated, we tore the bread into pieces and threw it towards the geese. It didn't take long for them to approach and eat. It reminded us of Sweden and Selma Lagerlof's Goose Boy story. Asta felt a little cool so I got a towel from the car and draped it over her shoulders.

"Maybe we'll bring Dawson to the dog park there," she pointed, "or sit on the concrete bench by the road on a day when we wouldn't mind talking to people. Or maybe over there by the flowers, or there by the ducks, or there by the waterfall. Maybe we can make a routine of it, bring different treats for the geese and ducks."

"It might be easier to get to with a wheelchair," I said, planting a seed, "but this walker is good enough." She agreed.

I took a photo that she said I should post on Facebook so that her friends and family in Sweden could see how good and healthy she looks.

"I look so good," she said, "they might want to come and visit me here in California."

"That would be great," I said.

"We'll have to show this lake to Elsa and Chris when they come," she said. (We already have).

"Yes, we will," I said.

Mar 7, 2020: PRE-PANDEMIC

Coronavirus continues to be the talk of the nation. Like half the population, I have stocked up on disinfecting wipes, hand sanitizer, cold remedies, water with electrolytes, and food in case we go into isolation precautions.

We are discussing whether or not Elsa and Chris should follow through on their plans to come here in two weeks for a visit, when— according to the news—the virus is supposed to peak. Travelers are at high risk for exposure, and then they would bring it here, and catching it would likely kill Mommy. I have been discouraging—though not prohibiting—Elsa and Chris from coming by forwarding new articles about the risks to travelers and the elderly. All the experts are advising social distancing, even discouraging family get-togethers to reduce potential exposure.

We all know Asta could get it here even without their visit. We may not be able to prevent it with all our best efforts and intentions. But airplanes are a cauldron of germs that could put everyone at risk. Why chance it? I don't want to lose her to the virus.

Elsa and Chris are understandably reluctant to cancel their plans, as they've paid for the tickets and might not get a refund. And nobody wants to panic. But maybe they could postpone their visit for a couple of months and come in the summer instead.

I took Ma shopping to Revivals, Bed Bath & Beyond, Marshall's and Walmart because she was looking for a rug to go with the new bedspread I bought her. At each stop, I wiped down the cart handle with a disinfecting wipe, and we cleaned our hands when we got back in the car. We might have looked paranoid but I'm doing what I can to protect us.

"All this wiping makes me feel shildish," she said irritably. "You're being over-protective."

I normally hold onto the front of the cart to lead/ steer it, but trying to support her need for independence, I let go of the cart for a while. With her poor vision, she really couldn't navigate particularly well.

"You're misleading me," she accused.

I took hold of the cart, and returned her attention to her mission, which was to find a rug like the one she had in mind. "Boy, when you are determined to accomplish something, you don't give up. You have incredible stamina," I praised.

"Ja, if only I had my feet," she said.

"If you had your feet, you'd be running circles around me."

She loved hearing that and our shopping experience was salvaged. She found what she was looking for, and then some. Shopping is fun for her, and the walking is good exercise. We stopped at a fresh strawberry stand on our way home and enjoyed eating them in the car, tossing the green stems/crowns carefree over our shoulders into the back seat.

Mar 8, 2020: TRAVEL ADVISORY

"Nobody wants to say what we're all thinkin'…" I wrote in a text to Elsa and Chris after our local news reported that the Coronavirus had landed in Rancho Mirage. "…which is that your visit should be cancelled or postponed."

Chris called and we discussed the issues—losing money on the tickets, Mommy's disappointment vs. relief, and the risk of exposure.

"If she were to catch the flu and die from it, wouldn't you rather know that you weren't the source of the infection?" I asked.

"I understand and agree. I won't come," Chris said.

Asta brought it up at the dinner table for a family discussion. "Elsa called asking for advice," she said.

"It's not your decision to make, Mommy. It's theirs. I'm not stopping them from coming, but I am telling them I don't think now is the right time. I feel it would be irresponsible for them to come right now."

"I am 92," she said, fatalistically, as if Elsa's visit would be Asta's swan song.

"Yeah well, if we can reduce your risks, that's what I want to do. I don't want to lose you to the virus if it can be avoided."

Later, while I was ushering at the McCallum, Elsa left me a voicemail.

"I'm coming anyway. I'll spend a couple of days at Lisa's in self-quarantine, and if I don't have symptoms of a sore throat or anything, will come visit. I hope that puts your mind at ease."

I replied by forwarding a notice from the CDC (Center for Disease Control) stating that the incubation period for this flu is 14 days and that the flu can be transmitted before a person becomes symptomatic, so "No, your two or three day self-quarantine period does not ease my mind," I wrote.

Meanwhile, a state of emergency has been declared in our county and the BNP Paribas Open was cancelled. That's millions of dollars forfeited out of concern for people's lives. I forwarded a copy of that article too. In other words, Elsa, wake up. I may not be able to protect Mommy from the virus, but don't you come and deliver it to her on a silver tray.

When we got home from the McCallum, I went in to check on my mother. She was curled up on her bed in the dark under her green blanket, with her legs half off the bed.

"I yust want to sleep," she said. I saw a bloody napkin by her bed. She'd had another bloody nose. She seems to have them when she is upset or stressed. She's probably confused by Elsa's determination to come in spite of the risks in contrast to Chris's decision not to. I picked up the napkin, put it in her trash bin, and helped her move her legs more fully onto the bed.

"See you in the morning," I said. And then I sent a copy of each the quarantine and BNP Open cancellation articles to Lisa, my niece. Maybe Lisa can talk some sense into her mother.

Mar 9, 2020: BETTER NOT TO COME

Elsa posted an article on her Facebook page about a woman named Laura who flew to Italy despite a pandemic scare, got sick but was taken care of by angelic Italian women until she came to out of her coma, after which she returned to the US and her lovely life and could assure everyone that everything would be just fine! No worries!

I, who rarely post, replied, "She caught it, lucky she had no underlying conditions or they'd have buried her. Fear serves a purpose for survival. I'll listen to the experts." My mother's second cousin in Sweden posted a thumbs up to my response. I loved him for that. I called Chris.

"Elsa is trying to get Ma to sign a new will," Chris said.

Maybe that's why she's in such a hurry to come, I thought, but didn't say it.

When Ma and I talked about the dilemma of Elsa's coming or not coming, Asta said, "You and Tony could bring home germs from the McCallum, or work, or anywhere as easily as Elsa could by coming here."

"You might be right," I said, "but Elsa will be on a plane where exposure is increased, and she's disregarding and disrespecting our concerns. I'll ask for her itinerary and will pay for a hotel room so at least you won't have to share a bathroom. I've already talked it over with Chris, and she thought the hotel room was a good idea." Elsa would take offense, though, and there would be ramifications.

Tony and I went and ushered our shift at the McCallum. When we came home a few hours later, Asta was still in the living room watching Fox News. We'd been out in the public, but we're not ignoring or denying the dangers.

"We won't use your bathroom either," Tony offered, "to reduce the chance of introducing any germs we might bring home from wherever we go."

"Maybe now is the time for you to kick me back to the East Coast!" she spat, and huffed off to her room.

I went in to talk with her a few minutes later. She answered every question with sarcasm, bitterness and sneers until I was irritated. I don't know if she was upset because of (a) whatever Elsa's been telling her, (b) because I'd put Elsa up in a hotel, or (c) because she sat listening to the Fox News Trump propaganda for two hours and it made her hate me for being a Democrat.

"I don't want to talk about the Coronavirus or germs or Elsa's visit or anything," she said.

"Fine. I'll see you in the morning. Call me if you need me," I said. As I was exiting her room she made sarcastic remarks about calling me if she needed me. I closed the door (gently, in case you're wondering) behind me.

Elsa says "it's not like the plague," and I hope she's right, but I'm not going to discount authorities' warnings and recommendations, and I don't care if she ascribes to me a negative personality and attitude because of it. I'm doing what I can to take the best possible care of our mother. Elsa could stop being so selfish and help out instead by not coming.

Chris told me she had a dream that she knew a girl named Carina Varas (Coronavirus). I hope Carina doesn't visit our house. I don't like her. She makes me sick.

Mar 10, 2020: WHAT IF, HOW COME

What if Elsa were to come here and get sick? She'd be stuck at my house and I'd have to take care of her too. Or I'd have to ask Lisa to come get her. Would Lisa do it, or make an excuse—she has to work? What if the health department required Elsa to quarantine here at my house?

I forwarded another article to Elsa and Chris. Headlines: *"Everything travelers need to know about coronavirus. Coronavirus symptoms usually take five days to appear, study says."* It talked about flight cancellations, the need to be flexible, waived cancellation fees, and airline cleaning efforts (called 'defogging').

"Suey, you have made your wishes crystal clear," Elsa finally conceded with a text, "so I have postponed the trip and will reschedule when fear of the virus is over. That said, I hope you will practice what you preach and think about how you put Mommy at risk every time you come in contact with all those people at the theatre. Be happy. Be well. Hope to see you soon." Snarky.

"We are doing our best," I wrote back. "Thanks for helping."

"Is the best at this time," Chris chimed in. "Better safe than sorry."

"Took her long enough," I texted Chris privately. That drama's over and I only have to worry about Mommy and Tony and myself.

After dinner, Ma and I sat talking at the table. I wanted to address her fears and feelings and put things in perspective.

"First the international tennis tournament was cancelled, and now the Coachella festival has been postponed. There was a medic who caught coronavirus from his flight attendant girlfriend. New York subways are taking extraordinary measures. Schools have been or may be closed due to the coronavirus, and in spite of all our efforts, we could bring something home locally. We need to be social distancing—no handshakes, hugs or kisses. They're saying that transmission occurs through droplets or by touching something/someone contaminated and then touching our hands to our face. Tony and I wore gloves at the McCallum last night. The Department of Health is in charge of closures and cancellations of events. We're doing everything we can to minimize risk to you. Younger, healthier people like me and Tony are not at extreme risk but could still get sick or exposed, and we can't guarantee you won't get it."

"I think there's a double standard here in your discouraging Elsa from coming," she said.

"I'm not the one writing news articles warning people from traveling in airplanes," I said. "I'm not making it up." We weren't vacuum-tight sealed either, so maybe there was a bit of double standard. "Darla is coming on March 27th and will spend the night when Tony and I go visit Ronnie, *if* we go visit Ronnie."

"Is Darla taking care of sick people?" she asked.

"She's taking care of old people."

It all makes Asta so tired. All this thinking, thinking, thinking, talking, talking, talking. Evidently, she was on the phone all day.

"So, Elsa is mad at me?" I asked. I don't care if she's mad at me.

"She's disappointed," she said.

"I can understand that. How about you?"

"I'm disappointed."

"I can understand that too. I'm not trying to be a dick towards Elsa. I'm just doing the best that I can to reduce your risk of exposure. I also can't guarantee anything. All I can do is my best, and that's what I'm doing here."

Mar 14, 2020: WATERSHED

Elsa gave me a public middle finger by posting an article on my Facebook page about an usher who contracted the coronavirus.

Effective immediately, all shows at the McCallum are cancelled, and all classes at the College where I work are cancelled. We are still to report to work, but may soon be told to stay home.

Ronnie sent us some natural immune-enhancing supplements to help us all stay healthy during this crisis.

Extreme measures for extreme times. A Twilight Zone.

"We can still go to the park, can't we?" Asta asked.

"Absolutely!" I said. "We won't catch any germs there."

"Elsa was very glad to hear the McCallum closed," she said. Elsa would be damn-right giddy.

I saw a news clip in which the Coronavirus expert was asked if he would get on a plane. He said, "Only if I absolutely had to. Certainly not for pleasure." I couldn't resist, and sent it to Elsa and Chris with this text:

"Made the right call. It wasn't easy, but we did it. We still have no guarantees, but one thing is sure: we sing better in harmony," referencing our adolescent days as the singing Anderson Sisters.

We're more effective when we're facing the same direction than when we're pointing fingers at each other.

Meanwhile, I'm stocking up on disposable underwear for Asta. Preparing for the future. Planning ahead.

Mar 15, 2020: SNAP

News outlets are reporting that the highest number of coronavirus cases are occurring in New York. Elsa's Facebook posts have shifted to 'we-have-the-most-beautiful-parks,' still burying her head in the sand.

Yesterday was a good day. Asta and I spent a couple of hours at the computer finishing her book, and then celebrated with a visit to the neighborhood dog park.

Today was a bad day. Asta was up all night working on her book, comparing the old to the new drafts, mixed up the pages in the process and couldn't figure out which pages belonged to which draft. She was angry that I was getting her up breakfast, and blamed the mix-up of pages on me.

"You are so controlling," she began.

"How so?" I asked.

"Because you made me get up,' she said.

"I've been checking on you for two hours, and now it's 11:00. Time to get up for breakfast." I said.

"You deliberately ruined my book. You should have let me read it to you," she insisted.

It's true that I refused to type her book one word at a time as she read it to me. She's almost blind and it would have taken forever. I admit, I don't have the patience to sit and type at that speed. Instead, I retyped her manuscript following her marked-up draft that sat in front of us, with her sitting next to me.

"Elsa would have let me sleep. Elsa wouldn't have ruined my book. Elsa would have let me read it to her one word at a time while she typed," Asta said, inventorying how Elsa would have done it right.

I snapped. "Stop being such a bitch." I'm not proud of myself, but there it is.

"Elsa would NEVER say that to me," she said.

"Actually, Elsa would and did. She said bad things about you to people all over Woodstock," I said. Tony came out and intervened.

"Asta," he said, "it's wrong for you to compare Suey negatively to Elsa. Elsa couldn't wait for you to move so she could screw Tom without you looking over her shoulder. Suey here has been doing a great job taking care of you and meeting your needs. People who live together are going to argue sometimes, and it's okay. We're happy to have you and will take care of you for the rest of your life."

Asta, unable to process anything after the words, 'screw Tom,' sat at the counter with her head in her hands, and then retreated to her room.

Ma looks forward to her daily calls with Elsa—the gossip and companionship—and I wouldn't deprive her of that. But it's utterly disrespectful that they whisper about me behind my back and plot whatever they plot, while I'm here responsibly taking care of Mommy 24/7/365, trying to keep her safe and happy. I'm fighting an octopus, and the octopus has the advantage.

Mar 16, 2020: GOING THROUGH MOTIONS

"Poor you," Asta said to me in the kitchen while I was putting dinner on the table. "Now you have two of us to take care of," meaning herself and Tony, who's been in avoidance mode *and* under the weather.

"Yup," I answered, with my back to her.

"I wish I could take you and Ronnie away from here," she said. "Away from him."

I served, assisted, went through the motions, politely took care of business, and allowed the distance between us to be bridged by the tasks that needed to be done.

"Tell Tony I hope he feels better," she said on her way back to her room.

"You can tell him yourself," I said. I then texted Chris, who rules the Go-Between role. "If she is wondering what she should/could do to mend fences, you could suggest that she not to put a halo on Elsa's head and horns on mine. You could tell her that a little appreciation—not only towards me, but towards Tony as well—would go a long way."

I admit I wasn't innocent in the latest interaction, but would it be too much to ask a 92 year old to take some responsibility for her words and actions? I'm tired of being blamed, tired of how rudely she speaks of Tony, and tired from knowing she's playing the role of victim exceedingly well to an especially eager audience of Elsa.

Mar 17, 2020: BULLETS

"When I spoke to Ma, I reiterated that I didn't think Elsa was prepared to take good care of her in the long run," Chris wrote. "Ma asked again why she left Woodstock, and why you and Tony wanted her there so badly. I reminded her of some of the things Elsa couldn't handle or didn't handle well, and reassured her she is better off staying where she is. I also told her that you are not the enemy. You are there every day, doing your best. And then Mommy wanted to get off the phone to call Elsa to thank her for the Goodie Box she sent."

"What happened when you talked to Elsa?" I asked, knowing that Chris would have called Elsa before calling to speak with Ma.

"Elsa is pushing to get her back to Woodstock," she confirmed. "If Ma goes to Woodstock, I know we're looking at a repeat of the old scenario after about 10 days. But Ma is of sound enough mind that she is allowed to make her own choices."

I'd like to see research on soundness of mind when it comes to a phenomenon I've noticed. I'd call it the Arrogance of Age: when older people think they're just as good at solving problems in their 80s and 90s as they were in their 40s-50s-60s-and even 70s. The kind of arrogance that makes someone say to the person helping them to their feet after a fall: "I've been walking all my life. Who are you to tell me I need a cane?" They make decisions based on past experience, not current circumstances. They're not able to see the full picture, and that's why adult children step in.

My mother may be able to make effective choices about some things, but moving back to Woodstock would not be one of them. In senior care, the POA makes the decision, not the person whose judgement is clouded or impaired.

It was morning, and I went in to check on Asta as usual.

"Do you really want to live 'like this'?" she asked, meaning with her in her room and Tony in avoidance mode.

"No," I said. "I want this to blow over and have everything go back to normal."

"After what he said to me? Are you okay with what he said?" she asked.

"Yes. He stood up for me when you were criticizing me and calling me controlling, because you were mad at me over how I typed your book," I said.

"And then there was that word you said: bitch."

"Well, your blaming me about the book was unfair. And then it was all about how Elsa would never talk to you that way."

"Not to my face," she said.

"Maybe not, but to everybody else and all of Woodstock," I said. "It's not right for you to try to drive a wedge between me and Tony."

"Is it right for him to drive a wedge between you and your mother?"

"He came to my defense."

"After what he said to me about Elsa? He should apologize."

"Or you should."

"Me?" she shrieked, "he's the devil."

"Is this about your going back east?"

"Well, yes, I've never been happy here."

"I need to hear it from Chris." I started to place a call to Chris.

"Call Elsa" Asta said. Stupidly, I did.

"We all feel sorry for you," Elsa said, full of pity and full of herself. "We all know how he is. I would *love* to have her here," she gushed.

There sat Elsa, teetering on the edge of climax in her angel suit. You could almost hear the heavenly choir in the background. I started to interrupt her.

"You called me, and now you won't listen," she said.

"I'm not going to listen to *that*," I snapped back.

Elsa and I then you-you-you'd for a minute. The same words were coming out of Elsa's mouth that had earlier come out of Mommy's, confirming their collaboration on the narrative, turning real life into bullets for gossip's sake. The bullets are:

- Mommy has never been happy here, because of the weather, or anything and everything else.
- Everyone in the family agrees: Everyone is against Tony.
- Poor Suey, Victim of Emotional abuse.

These are the cards they have in their hands, and they're playing them like their lives depend on it. Their chat sessions fuel Asta's tantrums. She feels like she has to take sides. Elsa, meanwhile, is squashing Tony and I with her boot and pissing on us for good measure. This is what I visualized as Elsa talked at me through the phone.

I held the phone as far away from my ear as possible, looked at my mother, raised my shoulders and mouthed "WTF?" Why should I have to put up with such garbage from anyone, much less my sister? All I want to do is take good care of my mother and treat her with respect no matter what. I ended the phone call with my finger.

"I'm going for a walk and will make our breakfast when I get back," I said to my mother. "Today's a new day. Let's start fresh. No more talk about you moving back east, okay?" I asked. She agreed. I left for my walk and called Chris.

"Mommy's not going to move," Chris assured me. "That's just who Elsa is. She's going to do what she does, and I'm going to run interference." By the time I returned to the house, civility had been restored, and we were able to conduct breakfast absent the company of Evil Eye and Sharp Tongue at the table.

Mar 18, 2020: QUIET AFTER THE STORM

Each of us is doing his/her own thing today: Ma is resting or napping, except when I go in to visit. Tony is working out and watching TV in our bedroom. I'm organizing my clothes closet and reorganizing the drawers in my office.

I made Mommy's favorite meal for dinner: kielbasa with tater tots and a side of Brussel sprouts. We ran out of apple sauce so I made chocolate pudding to help her swallow her pill.

I called Chris today to celebrate her retirement which became effective today. For once, we didn't talk about Mommy.

Mar 20, 2020: COVID ANXIETY

I worry about every little cough or sneeze, whether it's mine, Tony's or my mother's. Except for essential workers, the whole country has been sent home from work. Floating hospitals are being delivered to California, and New York is adding hospital beds for the nightmare ahead in the next few weeks... or months. When hospitals are adding beds in anticipation of an onslaught, you know it's coordinated between agencies, and you know it's serious. I texted Chris.

"Remind Ma that she has a Lifeline button she can push in an emergency. She doesn't want me to remind her because it would scare her."

I have to keep a calm face for both Ma and Tony, and I don't want to dump my anxiety on Ronnie. I chant every day to differentiate anxiety from reality.

Asta likes having me home again all day and enjoys having all three meals together. She loves that we're using the tincture that Ronnie gave us, eating Cold Eeze throat lozenges prophylactically, and introducing silver lotion into our noses. She's thanking me more than ever these days. Chris must have encouraged her to do that.

Mar 22, 2020: QUARANTINE

Here's how I'm an old Girl Scout:

- I sent an email to our HOA representative asking if the gate security staff could call each household weekly (safety check) and coordinate a food delivery.
- I'm distributing my homemade fabric face masks by mail to family and friends.
- I upcycled a pair of denim loafers into a pair of sandals for Ma. She'll be able to wear them even if her feet swell up a little, or if she wants to wear socks.

I took Asta to our neighborhood reservoir. She seemed okay walking in her new denim sandals. She sat on her seated walker tossing bread bits to the ducks and geese, and I sat next to her on the hillside overlooking the lake, listening to the cascading water. We talked about the occasional passerby and I took a picture of her with the flowers in the background and the mountains in the distance. Texted the photo to Chris with this message:

"Our quarantine. Not too shabby."

Right about then, our friend Cary came walking his dog. We visited, awkwardly maintaining the recommended six feet distance between us. Asta and Cary cheerfully assured each other (and themselves) they're not ready to say good-bye yet.

Mar 23, 2020: STRAWBERRY PRESERVES

Tony and I had already gone to bed. Lights were out. We were sleeping.

"Suey, Suey, are you awake?" Asta called urgently from the hallway. I jumped out of bed and ran into the hall to meet her.

"What is it? What is it? What's wrong?" I asked.

"I can't find my yar of strawberry preserves."

"Where was it?"

"In my drawer."

"Did you check your fridge? Maybe you didn't see it? Can I look for you?"

"It's not there. I already looked. Where could it have gone?" she said, giving me the 'look,' accusing me or Tony of taking it. I didn't bite.

"We have strawberry preserves in our fridge. I'll get that jar for you."

"I don't want that one. I want the one Elsa sent me."

"Well, nobody took it out of your drawer or out of your fridge, so it must be in there somewhere," I said, "But we have strawberry preserves that you can keep in your fridge."

"Forget it," she said, huffing her way back to her room. That was her midnight emergency.

In the morning, she said, "Maybe I misplaced it."

"Or maybe you gave it to me because you had no room in your fridge. I don't know. I'll check the pantry and show you the several jars of strawberry jam we have, and you can tell me if any one of those is the one you're looking for."

But by then she had talked herself out of wanting it, and didn't want to see what we had in our cupboard.

Mar 24, 2020: THIRD WHEEL

Tony and I typically watch Andy of Mayberry and Gomer Pyle in bed, but last night, for something different, we watched a TV movie in the living room. We watched, of all things, the movie 'Outbreak.' Very relatable, obviously. Best of all was the happy ending, where the married but separated scientists reconciled and fell in love again after he saved her life by getting the medicine to her at the last possible, most crucial moment. Ma would have been welcome to join us, but I had not specifically invited her. After the movie, I went in to check on her before I went to bed.

"You look depressed," I said.

"Bored," she said.

"Would you like to listen to your Kindle? How about putting on the radio? Wanna play a game of cards?" I made a bunch of suggestions.

"No, no, no, no, no," she answered.

"Even though we're in the same house, maybe you feel alone in your apartment. It's hard living alone after having lived with somebody else all those years," I said. She's been alone in that sense since Daddy died five years ago.

"I'll be alright," she sniffed, and turned over in her bed to face the wall.

"Okay, see you in the morning," I said.

Mar 27, 2020: HOME RUN FISH STEW

For tonight's dinner I made Daddy's famous fish soup:

- Cut up a pound of salmon (skin on) into 1 inch pieces. Boil in lightly salted water and drain.
- Boil together till tender: 1 cup leeks (I used scallions and red onion), 1 cup potatoes, 1 cup carrots. Drain.
- Combine all ingredients into one pot. Add three cups milk, three tablespoons butter. Add salt and a generous sprinkling of dill (I used dried, but fresh would be better).
- Heat through. Serve with cucumber/tomato salad, and Rye Crisp bread or dinner rolls.

Our lives revolve around our meals these days more than ever. Tonight, Tony asked 101 questions about Uncle Andy, and Asta had all the answers. After dinner, she and I watched TV together for a while. I couldn't change the channel from FOX because she fell asleep with the remote in her hand.

Mar 28, 2020: ROSE GARDEN

(cue the song, 'I Never Promised You a…')

Tony suggested we take Asta to Frank Sinatra Park. "It has a nice walking path. It would be easy for Asta and isn't far from here. It would get us all out of the house, and show her something beautiful and new. It would be safe in terms of social distancing."

I extended the invitation to Ma on several consecutive days. She repeatedly refused.

"I hate to say it," Asta said, "but I thought the park was yust mother-daughter time."

"The park in our development has been that, but going to Frank Sinatra Park would be a family outing," I said.

"No, I don't want to go," she said. "I'm waiting for an apology from Tony over the 'screwing her boyfriend' comment."

"It would mean a lot to me if you would come with us to the park," I said. "It would also mean a lot to Tony, whose idea it was to show it to you."

"For your sake," she granted, grimacing.

We went, stayed six feet away from everyone we saw, sat on a park bench, talked about the beautiful landscaping and its maintenance, and appreciated the picturesque fountain. Asta talked about Sweden. I picked a flower in honor of her mother's birthday, which is tomorrow, while Tony walked Dawson around the park. On the way home, we stopped at the drug store to pick up Asta's prescription eye drops. While inside, I picked up some drawing paper and pencils because Mommy had mentioned wanting to do some drawing.

Mar 29, 2020: SAFETY TRUMPS RESIDENTS RIGHTS

Asta asked me for a candle to light in her room in honor of her mother's birthday. I gave her an artificial one like the one we have on our altar. She wasn't happy about the fake candle, but as they say in assisted living, 'safety trumps residents' rights.'

Apr 1, 2020: UNCLE ANDY'S PAINTING

Asta pointed to Uncle Andy's painting that I had hanging in the garage.

"That painting came from Uncle Andy's house," she said. "I want to give it to Axel. I wrote his name on the back of it."

I took it off the wall, and on the back it read "from Uncle Andy's house," but Axel's name wasn't on it.

"Well, I want to write it there now," she said.

What could I say? It was only hanging in the garage. So I handed it to her and she wrote "to Axel" on the frame at my urging in an effort to protect the canvas.

Apr 2, 2020: PLANNING AHEAD

My mother is planning to throw another party as soon as we no longer need to fear this virus, perhaps this upcoming July.

"We may want to wait a few more months," I suggested, "since we may still be social distancing then. How about in October? By then the virus will have had six months to wind down and maybe we'll be getting back to normal."

"October would be doable, as long as people can still swim at that time," she said.

"Yes, they can," I said, "at the Clubhouse," which is where I knew she wanted the party to take place. "They keep the water temperature at 84 degrees all year."

"I want a sit-down buffet dinner with at least 20 people. We will serve some kind of roast, but no music this time. I don't care what the party costs. I'm only spending your inheritance anyway, so what do I care?"

"Go for it," I encouraged.

"Guess what Elsa told me," she said.

"What did Elsa tell you?" I asked.

"That when she retires, she'll sell her house and move to California near where Lars lives. I'd love that. I'm planning on living to 100."

"Now that's what I like to hear!" I said, referring to her plan to live to 100. That she has something to plan for and/or look forward to is the best medicine her immune system could ask for.

Apr 3, 2020: EARTHQUAKE

The house shook and the air sounded like thunder. We had an earthquake, 4.9 on the Richter scale. It lasted long enough to make you say 'Wow'. I immediately went to check on Ma. She was in the garage futzing around in her corner.

"Did you feel that?" I asked.

"I did, but thought it was the garage door being put up or down," she said. She couldn't wait to get on the phone to tell Elsa and Chris. An earthquake. How exciting.

"We may have aftershocks, and the best thing to do if you feel one is to stay in bed and cover your head," I told her. Another takeaway from my nursing home days.

Apr 5, 2020: THE LIST

"How late were you up last night? What were you doing?" I asked Asta in the morning, making small talk.

"I was up very late," she paused, "writing."

"Oh yeah? What are you working on?" I asked, curious. I support her creative endeavors.

Another pause. "A letter... I didn't want to tell you, but it's to you girls... in light of the coronavirus and the earthquake."

"Oh." I didn't want to invade her privacy by asking for details.

"Who gets what..." she volunteered. Last will and testament stuff. It could be coming from genuine fear of pandemics and natural disasters.

"You've done that already. I have a copy, if you want me to dig it up. You don't have to start from scratch."

"No, I haven't done it before. Not like this."

"Did Elsa suggest you do that?" Was Elsa persuading Asta to modify her will?

If looks could slice, I'd have been shredded. "If I said 'Chris,' would you be uncomfortable with it?" she asked.

"You can do whatever you want. I just ask that you don't add things to your list that you've already given to me."

"Do you think that little of me?" she asked.

"Well, you wanted the horseshoe back, and then Uncle Andy's painting."

"The painting was always mine and it had always been intended for Axel."

"That's fine," I said, "and now it's got his name on it." I was tying my sneakers and getting ready to leave for my walk.

"Help me bring my juice and pills to my room. I'll finish my breakfast in there. I don't want to eat alone."

I brought her juice to her room and she carried her pill cups.

On my walk, I called Chris. "I think Elsa is encouraging Ma to write a new list to distribute her belongings."

"Remember not to get hung up on the stuff," she said.

"The only thing I want is the dove painting, which has been promised to me since forever." There, I said it. Made it known.

"By the way, I've been monitoring the checks Mommy writes to Elsa," Chris said.

"For the cats?" I asked. "Fifty dollars here and fifty dollars there?"

"More like $200," she said.

"Well, Elsa's got a lot of cats," I feigned.

"Not that many," she acknowledged.

I got home from my walk, defrosted Asta's fridge and went around disinfecting high touch surfaces. I stopped in to let her know what I was doing and to clean her doorknobs. She was sitting at her desk, writing. Quickly, she covered the paper with her magnifying glass and curved her arm around it, like a school girl preventing me from peeking over her shoulder to cheat.

"I'm sorry about earlier," I said. "Sorry that I was in a hurry to get moving when you hadn't yet finished your breakfast, and sorry that I brought up the thing about the horseshoe and Uncle Andy's painting."

She was mad at me for asking about the will and Elsa's involvement in it, and mad at me for airing my concerns. I exited her room and went about my business. When I later stopped in, she was lying in bed facing the wall.

"Tony and I are going for a short bike ride," I informed her.

"Enyoy Yourself," she said sarcastically, "and make sure you wear masks," she said, drawing a long downward curve with her upper lip when saying the word 'masks'.

"Okay," I said.

"Practice what you preach," she said, sounding just like Elsa, her coach on the opposite coast.

Apr 7, 2020: UNDERDOG

Over dinner, the three of us were discussing the stimulus payment the government is sending: $1,200 per person.

"Maybe you'd like to rent a place on the beach for a couple of weeks and your family could all come and go," Tony suggested.

"No way. I would hate being stuck in a house looking out the window as my family came and went," she said. "I've been thinking I might give it to Elsa. She really needs it. She can't retire because she can't afford to."

"Great idea," Tony said. "Elsa could use the help and I'm sure she'd appreciate it."

I'm less gracious and suspect Elsa of soliciting gifts with 'poor me' statements. She can put on a good show. Complete with costumes, makeup, animals and clowns. People buy tickets for that stuff and reward the performance with applause. Asta wouldn't be able to resist *The Underdog*.

Apr 9, 2020: QUALITY TIME

Asta enjoys helping me 'steal' pink grapefruits from the trees in our neighborhood. They're on community property and we're welcome to help ourselves, but we treat it like mischief when we bring home fresh fruit for free. It's fun, an easy outing, and it's Grapefruit Season.

We went picking today. As per routine, Asta sat in the car while I picked and handed grapefruits to her through the open car window. She kept count and put them in the bag.

We prolonged today's outing with a slow drive around the neighborhood to see if anyone was out, and we came prepared for a stop at the reservoir/lake with slices of bread for the ducks. We pulled up along the curb next to the lake, car windows still open. Asta rubbed the slices of bread between her palms and threw handfuls of breadcrumbs out the car window. I kept quiet as equal quantities fell onto the floor of my newly vacuumed car.

"Want to help me make some face masks?" I asked her when we got home.

"No, I want to nap," she said, and went to her room. Forty-five minutes later, she came back. "Maybe I could help for a little while."

"Here's what I need you to do. First, turn in the seams, right side out. Then insert pipe cleaners for the bridge of the nose," I demonstrated. While we worked, she talked and told her stories. I am impressed by her fine motor skills. In spite of her severe vision impairment, she can still thread the pipe cleaners into the narrow seams and bend the ends in perfectly.

"How about if I get us a snack?" I suggested, and brought in a container of yogurt for each of us.

While she ate and continued to talk, I discretely took a snapshot of her in her colorful clothes, with a project on her lap, something to eat in her hands, a story on her lips, and red-slippered feet that weren't touching the floor. The camera angle made her feet look cartoonish, but that only added to her charm.

Apr 13, 2020: SILVER LININGS

At Asta's request, I provided yellow craft paint and paintbrushes for a project she had in mind. She painted the 6" diameter wooden star that hangs in her window and the flames of the candles on her ceramic Lucia statuette's crown. Otherwise, she's been occupying herself listening to 'The Witching Hour' on her Kindle. This morning, she gave me a 45 minute speech about witches and yoga and cults and Reiki while I prepared breakfast, cleaned up and set tonight's dinner up in the crock pot. A pleasant morning.

After breakfast, she sat outdoors in her alley in the sun for a while, then puttered around her room organizing her music tapes and CDs.

"How about if we order you a new CD/tape player?" I suggested. "They're only 30-40 bucks and we could get it delivered."

"No," she said. "I don't want to. I'm happy with yust my tapes. Maybe Chris can fix the machine when she comes."

"She's not coming till maybe October. Are you sure?"

"Yes," she said.

"Okay." If she doesn't want it, I'm not going to push it.

"One good thing about the Coronavirus," she said, "is I don't feel I have to get dressed up or put on my eyebrows."

"That's for sure. I'm still in my pajamas from a couple of days ago," I admitted.

"We have an excuse, a silver lining," she said. "And I always have my Spanish lessons if I'm looking for something to do."

Tony and I are always here, so she feels comfortable and secure even though we may be in separate rooms. We see each other at and between meals, once or twice before bed, and I usually peek in overnight. Nobody's underfoot, nobody's hovering, and nobody feels like a burden.

Apr 15, 2020: LUXURY CAR

Today while Asta napped, Tony and I bought a gray-blue 2017 Toyota Corolla sedan with leather seats, alloy wheels, low mileage and a sunroof for $14,000 through Shift, an online used-car service. We didn't have to leave the house. After dinner, the three of us drove in it to Palm Desert and back.

"You have rich tastes," Asta said in her flattering way.

"Champagne on a beer budget," Tony boasted.

"Daddy would call it 'riding in style'," I said, because we had the windows down.

"Next time, I'll wear my sunglasses and hat," she said.

"And a valet will come and open your door, and you'll give away autographed copies of your books," Tony said.

At home, I put on Andrea Bocelli's Easter concert at the Duomo, as recommended to us by Chris and Elsa, and then she wanted to lay down. I'll check on her before I go to bed and help her put a story on her Kindle. I've already put a sandwich in her fridge for tonight.

Apr 18, 2020: SUPERVISION

I've been bringing buckets of salt water from the pool to Asta in her alley, where she likes to sit soaking her feet.

"It's good for my neuropathy," she says.

"I don't think you should keep your feet in the sun so much," I said. "They're getting dark." Privately, I worry that a tan could obscure a circulatory issue, or that she'd fall asleep in the sun and get burned.

"You're being overprotective," she said.

But I keep an eye on her because the weather is beautiful this time of year, and it would be easy to stay too long in the sun.

Apr 19, 2020: ASKS AND MEANING

"Come join me in the back yard while I read this afternoon," I invited. Asta accepted and laid down next to me on the two-person chaise lounge... and started talking... about Sweden, an old friend from grammar school and recollections from eighty years ago. She was getting louder and louder. It was fraying my nerves.

"Ma, could you just lower the volume a little?" I asked. "I'm right here, next to you."

Instead, she shut up completely. Five minutes later she was sound asleep. I stayed outside for another 15 minutes, then went inside and about my business. When I brought her in for dinner, she looked at the ramen noodles dish and frowned.

"Where's the red sauce?" she asked accusingly.

"We're not having red sauce tonight," I said. "If you don't like this, I'll make you a little pizza like the ones we had for lunch yesterday and you liked."

"I don't want pizza," she said. She ate a bite or two of the Ramen noodles dish and pushed the rest around on her plate, throwing eye daggers at Tony. "It's Italian," she said with contempt.

"It's not Italian, Mommy," I said. "It's Ramen noodles." In truth, I don't know what national heritage Ramen noodles could claim. But to make matters worse, I was out of applesauce and had served coconut cream pudding with her medicine instead. She spat out her pill and threw it onto the plate in front of her.

"I know this wasn't the greatest dinner," I admitted. "I'll make you a sandwich or something later."

"Don't bodder. I'm yust not hungry," she said, and with her signature downward curl of the lips, removed herself from the table and headed to her room, tossing over her shoulder, "After all, you told me to be quiet."

"I just asked you to lower the volume," I defended. "I didn't tell you to stop talking."

Apr 20, 2020: FOOD CHEER

Tonight's menu of 'food that she's used to' was intended to coax Asta out of her funk:

- Fried chicken livers (enough to put leftovers in her fridge that she can nibble on at night)
- Boiled potatoes
- a side of spinach (from frozen)

I had her instruct me on how to make gravy her way. Despite having had diarrhea today and not feeling well in her stomach, she ate with a ravenous appetite, and drank the bit of gravy that was left over.

For tomorrow night's dinner, I made homemade wonton skins and filled them with leftover roast pork, Brussel sprouts, scallions, ginger, soy sauce, and smoked sesame oil. I also made a homemade wonton soup broth. Tony has requested a sweet and sour shrimp dish to go with it. I have all the necessary ingredients and will name (with a wink) tomorrow night's dinner 'The Wuhan Special'. Daddy, who used to make menus featuring dishes he creatively named, would have approved.

Apr 22, 2020: SORE GUMS

"My gums are bothering me a little," Asta said. "I do not want to talk to a doctor about it. I do not want Anbesol. I will rinse my mouth with salt water and Listerine."

"I'll pick up some Listerine tomorrow," I said. "What do you want for a snack tonight?"

"Nothing. I don't want to irritate my gums."

"You're too skinny, Mommy. How about an Ensure? Here are Stella Doro almond toast cookies to dip in your coffee, and there are glasses of red juice in your fridge." If her gums are still bothering her in a couple of days, I'll take her to the doctor. Meanwhile, I'll prepare common sense soft food meals and offer alternate nourishment options.

Apr 23, 2020: INFORMATION MANAGEMENT

"My phone isn't working," Asta announced, presenting me with both of her phone handsets. "*Somebody* must have messed with it."

"Let me take a look," I said. I verified that her phone works fine, and then observed her press the speed dial number for too long. "Hold the speed dial button to the count of two (count: one, two), until you can see the name of the person you're calling on the screen, like this," I demonstrated.

"How does your air conditioner work?" she asked, presenting her little thermostat from Elsa.

"If the temperature in the house goes above 80 degrees, the air conditioner turns on and cools the air," I explained. "Here is the vent that brings cool air into you room. You also have a ceiling fan that circulates the air in your room. The temperature in here shouldn't vary from the rest of the house by more than 2 or 3 degrees, but if you feel too warm at night, you can sleep in Ronnie's room." I repeat, restate, and breathe.

"How did I spend the cash I took out of the bank last time?" she asked.

"First let's see how much you took out," I said, and pulled up her bank account on my computer. "Okay, so you withdrew $200 cash in January. You spent about $80 on your mani/pedi appointment, and $20 here and there, I'm sure," I explained. "The best thing would be to use your debit card, not cash, so you can monitor where your money goes. I send Chris a receipt for every transaction we make on your card. Cash is harder to track."

"I think I should be saving money out of my pension," she said, "even after giving you $1,000/month."

"Don't forget that some medical expenses also come out of your income. Talk to Chris." I give her credit for trying to grasp her finances, for trying to stay informed and involved.

Apr 25, 2020: APPRECIATION

"Join us in the pool when you're ready," I said to Asta.

She, Tony, and I spent an hour together in the pool, talking and paddling about, enjoying the sun and water and environment.

"Yours really is a beautiful yard," she raved, "and this pool is really nice." She wasn't criticizing, for a change, the privacy that our high hedges and gated community provide.

"Daddy would have loved it here," I said. "Had Tony and I already been here when Daddy retired, the two of you might have moved here instead of Woodstock."

"I would love it here if I had my feet, if I was able to get around," she said. "Take a picture of me in the pool in my inner tube. I want to send it to Elsa & Chris, Ronnie & Angi, Lisa and Jane. And print a copy that I can send to my friend Hilda in Sweden so she can see me looking good and having fun in my sunny back yard pool in Palm Springs." I took a few pictures from which she'll be able to choose.

May 2, 2020: DREAMS AND REMENISCINGS

"It was a good dream, for a change, about decorating..." Asta gave as her story starter, and then described at length how she decorated each house she's lived in over the past 60 years. She remembered the furniture, the colors she painted the walls, and detailed what she would do differently today. Meanwhile, I made a scrambled eggs/ English muffin/juice breakfast for the two of us.

"Remember the hot pink room on the third floor of the New Jersey house?" I asked.

"No, we didn't have a hot pink room. I don't remember it. It's not possible. I have an excellent memory. Your memory is wrong." But I remember the hot pink room.

I nodded intermittently, dropping a word here and there to participate, and after an hour of this got up and put the dishes into the dishwasher. She didn't get the hint until I excused myself to go brush my teeth.

Offended, she said, "I want to talk. There's no one else to talk to and I want to talk. There's nothing else to do here. But you're too busy. What do you have to do today?"

"Let me see, what's on the list?" I said, taking her question literally. "I'm going to spot clean—"

"Spot clean," she spat. "Didn't you do that yesterday?"

"No."

"Then the day before, and the day before that?"

"I can clean if I want to."

"Of course you can. So I won't talk. I'll go back to my room without music, alone, so you can clean or do whatever you want."

"I'm sorry, Mommy. I'm sorry I'm not everything," I said, knowing full well that I am enough, and that we are providing her excellent care and support.

"No, you're not," she said.

"I'm sorry I'm not more patient," I added.

"No, you're not patient. Yust stop talking," she said.

Speaking of dreams, I had one about Elsa the night before last: You know how when you lay next to someone and they drape their leg over you? Well, she had her leg on me and it was too, too heavy. I needed her to move so I tried to pinch her, hard, but she didn't move. I tried again and again, but to no avail. Finally, I yanked myself away and was free of the weight of her.

I returned to my mother's room at 1 p.m. to remind her we'd meet for a dip in the pool at 3:00 p.m. as usual.

"I think I'll pass," she said.

"I'll come back at 3:00 in case you change your mind."

Over the next hour, Elsa cheered Mommy over the phone with news about an old artist friend of Asta's. Elsa sent me copies of the news clipping by email, which I printed off and gave to Ma. Again, I tried to coax her out to the pool.

"Ja, I think I will. I'm feeling better now," she said.

So, as much as I groan at the quantity of Elsa's social media crap, I'm glad she was able to pull something from it to cheer our mother. I'm glad she can be another set of ears for Asta's never-ending reminiscing. Reminiscing is a great activity for many elders. Personally, I've never been big on nostalgia. I can only stomach so much of it, and then I want to shoot myself.

May 6, 2020: TO PLEASE OR NOT TO PLEASE

For dinner tonight I made shrimp fried rice. Knowing Asta doesn't like rice, I offered to heat up one of the Hungry Man frozen dinners she enjoys that we keep on hand for her, but she refused.

"I'll have what you're having," she said, and proceeded to push the rice around on her plate, looking disgruntled. "I have a bit of a headache. I've had it all day, probably because I don't eat enough."

I thought back. For breakfast, she had her usual breakfast of two extra-large soft-boiled eggs, buttered toast, a half grapefruit and juice, and a dish of applesauce with which to take her pill.

"I'll bring you an egg salad sandwich that you can eat whenever you want," I offered.

"Usch," (Swedish for 'ugh') she said, wrinkling her nose.

"You don't want egg salad? I'll make something else."

"I don't want to cause any trouble," she claimed, still showing her disgust at the dinner in front of her.

I stocked her fridge with fresh salami, juices, skorpor, and cans of Vienna sausage to join the bottles of Ensure, yogurt cups, chocolate bar and 1/2 grapefruit, then brought in a ham and cheese sandwich.

"Is that better?" I asked. Maybe my words came a little too loudly or too quickly for her capacity or emotional state. Maybe they sounded harsh because I was standing in the doorway, or maybe because I'm just tired.

"Why do you have to say it like that?" she winced, scrunching her face to produce tears.

"I'm sorry. I'm doing the best that I can," I said.

May 8, 2020: DISCRETE SERVICE

I heard an unusual mechanical pulsing and followed it to Mommy's bathroom. Asta was fiddling with the new Water-Pik Elsa sent her, not in the least bit aware that she was spraying water all over the mirror. So as not to embarrass her, I waited across the hall in the den until she was done. We said our good nights and she headed to her room for the night.

We take little assists for granted, picking things up that she drops, adjusting her shoes or slippers before they fall off while she's walking, turning off the water she's left running in the bathroom, and fetching whatever she asks for. I've discovered that I rather enjoy my caregiver role.

Tony, ever the conversationalist, gets her talking with questions about Sweden and her youth, for which I'm grateful, because I've run out of things to ask and say.

May 10, 2020: MOTHER'S DAY GIFTS

Elsa put a video on Facebook and asked me to show it to Ma. "It'll make her cry, but that's okay," Elsa said. It was a made-for-Mother's-Day sentimental video. Hallmark Greeting tears.

I forewarned Ma that Elsa said the video would make her cry, and asked her if she wanted to see it anyway.

"Ja, yust so I can tell Elsa I saw it." After listening to it in its entirety she gave her assessment. "It's bullshit."

Asta gave *me* a Mother's Day gift—the photo of a little Yorkie she'd cut from a magazine and put into one of her old picture frames.

"It's from me and Dawson," she said. "You can replace the cut-out picture with a real one of him." I appreciated the effort she had put into it and put it on display.

The shoes I ordered for her haven't yet arrived, so I spent several hours with her going through my digital photos so she could select the ones she wanted me to print, and then I went and printed them at Walgreens.

"I dropped some water bottles behind the dresser in the garage," she said that evening.

On recovering them, I found another ship painting. On close comparison, she confirmed that the one she had hidden was the one she wanted Axel to have, vindication that I hadn't taken her painting for myself. We placed it back in its secure hiding spot, and returned mine to its proper place on the garage wall.

May 15, 2020: DOG HOUSE

"Quiet!" Tony commanded Dawson, who was barking, barking, barking during dinner last night.

"Don't yell at the dog," Asta scolded Tony.

"I've heard you do the same thing when Dawson's been noisy," I said. Asta often claps her hands and loudly tells Dawson to be quiet.

"It's mean and rotten to tell a dog not to bark," she lectured.

"Sluta," ('stop' in Swedish) I said, but she continued to scold him. Tony put his head down and kept quiet.

This morning, Dawson was barking again. Asta caught herself before clapping.

"I guess I overreacted yesterday," she said.

"Yes, you did," I said. "It was hypocritical of you to criticize Tony for doing exactly what you do."

"Here you go making excuses, defending him," she said, contorting her face in an effort to spill tears. Tony entered the room. She lashed out at both of us.

"I don't know who's more henpecked—you or him!"

"You said yourself that you overreacted. Well, I agree," I said, thinking maybe I shouldn't have to *always* eat shit without protest.

"I was *starting* to say I'm sorry," she spat. "Well, I'm taking it back!" She finished her breakfast in silence and excused herself to go to her room, as if that's a punishment that I am imposing.

Tony, who stayed out of this nobody-wins conversation, took the high road and said, "We're taking care of your mom because it's the right thing to do." He's a good man.

At 2:15 p.m. I went to see Asta. "I'm sorry for upsetting you earlier," I said. "Want to come out for our 3:00 swim?"

"No," she said. "I'm tired."

"Well, come out if you change your mind." Whether she's in a good mood or a bad mood, healthy or sick, I'm going to continue to take good care of her.

May 15, 2020: CARE PLAN

It's time to implement a care plan and see what there is to see. A care plan will:

- Help me monitor when Asta takes a shower and how often she refuses them,
- Document the activities we engage her in or that she refuses,
- Keep track of what she eats and refuses to eat,

- Monitor her weight,
- Remind me to look at her feet, and
- Help highlight the emergence of a change in condition.

She is relatively easy to care for in the sense that she joins us for meals, takes care of her own toileting, dresses herself, walks short distances (between rooms) with just her Winnie Walker or cane, sees well enough to pursue her hobbies, and manages to keep herself somewhat occupied. She does not yet need a wheelchair (although she'd benefit from one for long distances), doesn't need help keeping herself clean (other than set up for the shower and assistance with washing her hair) and doesn't need any skilled medical care.

But she's getting harder to please.

"It's a beautiful day," Tony said. "Let's all go for to ride in the car with the windows down."

I handed her a scarf for her hair.

The three of us got in the car and took a ride with the wind in our hair. When we pulled into the driveway afterwards, she thanked us with dripping sarcasm. That evening, she refused to eat the nachos I made for dinner because they're Mexican (not what she's 'used to'). I heated up a Marie Callendar frozen dinner for her instead, and she objected because it wasn't the Hungry Man brand that she favors.

"I'm yust not hungry," she said, dropping the saucy meat onto the dining room rug for Dawson.

I'm not going to change her behavior. I don't know how to care plan for attitude. I bit my bloody tongue.

May 16, 2020: CORNERS

As usual, last night I checked on Asta before I went to bed. She looked like hell.

"Are you okay?" I asked, and sat down on her bed by her feet.

"Ja, I'm okay," she said. I looked her in the eye, said nothing, and waited. "What?" she asked.

"Nothing, just checking," I said, maintaining eye contact while she sat up, not sure what I was looking for, but unable to tear my eyes away. Maybe something medical was going on.

"It'll blow over," she said with a grin, taking responsibility for her negativity, perhaps, and assuring me her attitude would improve.

"I know," I said, believing.

I stocked her fridge with halved cherry tomatoes (I'm afraid she might choke on whole ones), juices, cut-up watermelon, and a BLT. I'm concerned about her appetite and weight loss.

In the morning, I served two eggs easy over, toast, juice and a half grapefruit. She spat out the egg, and only ate half of one piece of toast and a few wedges of grapefruit. I coax, but I can't force feed her.

I set up her shower and washed her hair. She agreed to join us in the pool this afternoon, so maybe we're turning the corner. Happy to welcome her back.

May 18, 2020: WANT AND NOT WANT

"When I die, I want my ashes to go to New York quickly," she said. "I don't want my ashes to get stuck here."

"We'll get you to New York quickly," I promised. "Airlines do it all the time. They have procedures and protocols."

"I don't want to be alone when I die," she said.

"I will make sure you're not alone when you die," I reassured her. "When it comes time for that, I'll take time off from work. And Chris said she would come and stay for as long as needed to help out. We have a plan, and that is to take care of you here at home, and inter your remains next to Daddy's ASAP."

Pivoting, Tony urged, "Come with us for a day trip to the ocean."

"What if I had to go to the bathroom? I can't walk on the beach with these feet. Besides, if I went with you, how would I be able to refuse going with Elsa? She's been trying to talk me into renting a house on the ocean 'for the family'."

"With us it would just be a day trip," I said. "With Elsa, it would be for days or a week, depending on Elsa's vacation plans." Asta grew up on the ocean. We can justify disappointing Elsa if Asta would like to see it again.

"I would rather have people come visit me here in the comfort of my own home. As far as I'm concerned, the community pool across the street is as good as the ocean—and less effort—and it wouldn't be at my expense."

"That's true. Anyone who wants to see you can come visit you here. We could still take you for a day trip, though, if you'd like. Where we go, it would be easy. There are little patios with tables and chairs close to the restrooms. If you have any interest in spending a few hours on the beach, we could easily pull it off and still be home in time for dinner that night."

"No, I don't want to," she said. Period. End of discussion.

May 19, 2020: PLANNING AHEAD

"Your mother is going to live to be 100," Tony said, "and I'm okay with keeping the status quo until you turn 65. But then I'd like us to have some freedom to come and go. By then she'll have lived with us for five years. Maybe then Chris should have a turn at taking care of your mother."

I don't expect Ma to live two more years, but you never know.

"I'm not going to be okay with shipping her across the country at 94 years old," I said. "You criticized Elsa for making Asta move at age 89. How would it be okay for us to move her back at 94?"

I understand his wanting us to have some freedom. Asta makes it difficult by trying to dictate who can take care of her in our absence. It may be easier if we make it routine and hire someone to come over every week for a few hours so that Tony and I can have a little time to ourselves.

I went for an afternoon walk and called Chris. "I'd like you to think about moving out here in two years," I said. "When I turn 65, Tony will expect us to have a little bit of freedom. Hiring anyone will be problematic. You know how resistant Ma is. That's when we'll need your help."

"I don't think I can make Paul move with me," she said, "but I'll come out and live there for as long as needed." She could rent an apartment nearby at Asta's expense. Chris could have a life of her own here, and by relieving us now and then, allow us have a life as well. "You can count on it," Chris said.

I believed her.

"Elsa told Ma that we, collectively, failed her," Chris said, by keeping her in my house, allowing or causing her to be unhappy.

"That's bullshit," I said. "For $1,000 a month she gets meals, 24/hr. supervision, laundry, housekeeping, shower assistance, assistance with ambulation as needed, reminders as needed, her fridge stocked; support in things like the use of her phone, the TV, her kindle. She gets escorts to medical appointments; has a private room, a swimming pool, goes on outings, has activities and companionship, and all her errands run.

"We share our supplies with her freely, and sometimes my clothes. We didn't take her in for the money, Chris, but her contribution does offset the costs. It's only fair that she contribute financially to the household. She'd pay a lot more in an assisted living facility. So no, 'we' haven't failed her. All her needs—and then some—are being met."

"Elsa should consider reframing, like I do, when Ma complains," Chris said, "by suggesting that maybe she ought to appreciate how good she has it with you. I'm on her shit list for days when I say things like that, but those kinds of things need to be said."

"Yes, they do," I agreed.

May 20, 2020: LIVING THE DREAM

Last night I dreamt that I was in the kitchen cooking for my family. A group of five men arrived, guests of the house, and I was to prepare them a meal. I don't know what happened to the meal I had planned, but it fell by the wayside and was forgotten because I had been too busy.

I looked in the fridge to see what we had, what I could put together. There wasn't much for these unexpected guests. Chris approved my decision to make grilled cheese sandwiches. They are easy to make, people generally like them, and I had the ingredients needed. I set about making them.

While my back was turned, someone put a wooden cutting board between the frying pan and the flame on the gas stove—a major fire hazard. I managed to prevent that catastrophe, but then I turned and saw the bread had been thrown into the wet sink. Now I wouldn't have enough to feed everyone. When I then turned back to the stove, I found that soapy water had been thrown into the frying pan, and the sandwiches I was cooking were ruined. I hollered to everyone, making them listen.

"Who put the cutting board under the frying pan on the stove?"

"I did," a little girl said. Mommy started scolding her, but I told her to stop. I had more questions to ask.

"Who threw the bread into the sink?" I asked.

"I did that," said Elsa.

"And who poured soapy water over the sandwiches?" I asked.

"That was me," Mommy said.

My point was made. No sense in singling out and scolding any one person. Multiple people were interfering, making my task impossible. Extremely frustrating.

I woke up with a twitching left eyelid.

May 22, 2020: MINE

During family swim time today, Asta dipped her head under the water, proud of herself for being so bold and daring. We came into the house refreshed.

"I left my sunglasses outside," she said.

"I'll get them for you," I said, and retrieved her sunglasses from the patio table. I'm constantly fetching her sunglasses. She has several pairs and they follow her around the house and yard.

"These aren't mine," she said, trying them on.

"Sure they are. These were sitting on the table out there."

"No, I left my sunglasses by the pool," she said. I went out to look and came back.

"Those were the only ones out there."

"No, I brought out a different pair."

"When I came out to the pool today, you said you had forgotten your sunglasses and asked me to get them from your room. I didn't see any on your desk so I went into your alley and found these and another pair on the table."

"Let's not argue. I know what I know. And these aren't the ones I had out there today," she said.

"Let's go look in your room," I said, thinking it would put her mind at ease if we found the sunglasses she was looking for.

"Why?"

"I want to show you where I found the ones I brought out to you and show you the other pair out there," I said. "And you can show me where you usually keep your sunglasses." Tony offered to get the other ones from her alley, but I didn't want Asta blaming Tony for returning the pair of sunglasses she had convinced herself had been moved or stolen. Reluctantly, she followed me to her room.

"Where do you keep your sunglasses?" I asked.

"In this drawer," she said. She opened the drawer, and there they were. She picked them up and examined them. In all seriousness, she asked, "How did these get here?"

"I'm just glad we found them," I said.

Having found the missing sunglasses, she cheerfully treated me to a monologue about her various pairs: her favorite ones (the ones we just found) that I'd recently gotten at the dollar store, the pair that I just brought in from outside by the pool, the ones with the wide side pieces still outside on her table in the alley, the blue ones, the pink ones...

I then set up her shower and helped her wash her hair. After dinner, we went grapefruit-stealing and drove around the neighborhood, dropping grapefruits off at friends' doors. A lovely outing.

Soon after returning home, Asta came looking for me. The tablecloth was missing from the table outside her door.

"Suey," she called out, "ask Tony if he moved it." She can't ask him? He was no further from where she was standing than I was. I asked.

"The wind blew it off the table so I picked it up off the ground and put it in your laundry basket," he explained. I opened her laundry basket and there it was.

"It's *my* alley and I don't want anyone touching my stuff," she scowled.

May 26, 2020: VENTURING OUT

As we floated around in the pool, Asta enjoyed talking about her book(s), and how/where she gets her inspiration, how she comes up with the context in which she develops her characters. She claims to not want anyone to feel she is writing about *them*. She described, at length, the writing process she used for her latest book. I sat back and took pleasure in watching and listening to her. Tony's occasional probing question or comment kept her going. We usually get out of the pool when the fountain turns off at 4 p.m. but today we were too absorbed in her story-telling to notice.

Over dinner, Tony broached the subject that I had been dreading.

"There's something I want from you, Asta" he said. "It's really hard for me to get Suey to agree to get away because she is so concerned with taking care of you, but we need to go out now and then. I'd like you to try not to make her feel guilty. We'll have Rosalva come over to make sure you're safe. We'll continue to wash our hands and practice social distancing to reduce the risk of bringing home the virus, but we need to get away to the ocean over the summer."

"I'll ask Rosalva to wear a mask, and you should also wear one," I said.

In truth, we had already arranged for Rosalva to be here from 3-7 p.m. while we're in LA this Saturday. We'll be home by 8 p.m.

"Oh, sure," she said, pleased at the thought of hanging out with Rosalva. Not as difficult as I was expecting.

May 29, 2020: COMPETITION

Ronnie asked me to send her a picture of each of her sets of grandparents—Ma & Pa and Nan (Marie) & Pop. Asta asked to see the pictures I selected. The photo of Marie showed her leaning on her elbow on a boat hull in a fetching white bathing suit.

Promptly, Asta called Elsa and asked her to find a certain photo of her in her 40s wearing a white bathing suit.

"I looked great in that photo," she said. "But I don't think Elsa will find it, or maybe she won't send it because she didn't look so good in that photo."

I am fascinated by Asta's drive to compete: Which of the two grandmothers was better looking in their white bathing suits? My mother has always been a very attractive woman. I never realized how competitive she was. Daddy knew, and found it attractive in her. Her Leo-ness.

May 31, 2020: PROMISES, PROMISES

Tony and I were preparing to leave at noon for our errand to LA.

"Jag mår illa," (I feel sick) Asta said over breakfast. Maybe this was a test and she wanted to keep me home or make me feel guilty. Maybe she was nervous about my leaving. But she couldn't have been feeling too sick because she ate a hearty breakfast of eggs & toast with jam, and a side of fresh blueberries with cream.

"Rosalva will be here from 3—7," I assured her.

I put on a crockpot and communicated all my preparations to Chris: emergency contacts, emergency information location, back-up caregiver contact information, spare key location... It's hard to relax/enjoy and not worry/feel guilty.

During the drive, I revealed to Tony how Chris agreed to come live here to share the job of taking care of Ma once I turned 65.

"That's a good plan," he said. "I don't want to have to be the bad guy. We need to be able to enjoy our retirement some. She'd come?"

"She said she would," I said.

We stopped for dinner at the Vietnamese restaurant in downtown Palm Springs and brought home an eggroll for Ma. We were home by 7:30 PM.

When I could speak with Rosalva in private, I asked her to come over for four hour shifts every weekend moving forward. If we make it routine, maybe Asta will be less inclined to protest.

June 3, 2020: MONOTONY

People are rioting within a mile of Ronnie's apartment in LA. "Come home," I urged her and Angi. "Bring the Pets."

"We're on our way," Ronnie replied. They were already in the car and on the road. Ronnie and Angi have been at least as diligent in their quarantining as have we, so we agreed to not wear masks.

We visited, had dinner and wine, talked, watched the news together and were grateful to have them here instead of there. Ma was happy for the "break from the monotony," as she put it.

During pool time the next day, Ma described for Ronnie and Angi a 'funny conversation' she just had on the phone with Elsa.

"Elsa ran into a nun that we know, and Elsa said to me, 'If you don't want to live with me, wouldn't it be fun to live with the nuns?' I laughed. 'No way, I'm not religious,' I said."

Asta doesn't realize that Elsa is trying to sell her on moving into a convent with ill, frail and elderly nuns. I shake my head in disbelief.

Things calmed down in LA so the girls headed home, and everything reverted to the monotony of long luxurious soaks in our lush, private, park-like back-yard pool setting.

June 6, 2020: EXPECTATIONS

"Ma is refusing to come out for breakfast, so I'm bringing in her breakfast on the tray," I alerted Chris by phone.

"That's rough," Chris said. "Download the new books to her Kindle. Might be a diversion." Stories on her Kindle might distract her, but Mommy is losing weight and my sisters have expectations.

"Yesterday she told me she wants six small meals a day, as she's probably already told you and Elsa. Just for the record, I'm not going to cook and serve all day long. I make two full meals a day—breakfast and dinner—and bring her a fresh sandwich or snack every night. Despite her insistence that she'll eat six meals a day, it's just not true. She has snacks in her fridge that she could help herself to but doesn't. She says she gets absorbed in what she's doing and doesn't think to go get it herself. I've offered to give her reminders, but she doesn't want them.

"I've also been encouraging her to exercise her legs. The only walking she does is from her room to the bathroom or kitchen. I've offered to walk with her to the corner and back, or from her door outside to the backyard along her alley. 'My yoga stretches are enough exercise,' she says. 'They're not weight bearing, though,' I told her. She wants to remain independent, but she's clearly getting weaker. Could you please encourage her to let us bring back Jenna, the physical therapist, to work with her on strengthening?"

"I will," Chris committed. "And maybe you could make her 2 sandwiches... one for the evening, and one for lunchtime, along with a reminder that she has it." Maybe Chris hadn't been listening, or didn't grasp the futility of encouraging Asta to eat. Nevertheless, I brought Ma a sandwich for lunch, and in the early afternoon reminded her to eat it. At 3 PM, when I went in to get her for pool time, it was still sitting on her bedside table, untouched.

"I'm yust not hungry," Asta said. "And I don't want to eat it now because it would spoil my appetite for dinner. Put it in my fridge for tonight," she said.

June 5, 2020: MISSING LETTERS

Asta stayed in bed all day, and as far as I could tell, sat up only long enough to eat breakfast. She refused to join us for pool hour, but did come out for dinner. It wasn't long before she launched her accusation.

"Who gave me my childhood friend Hilda's address? Hilda hasn't gotten either of the letters I wrote her."

Upon inquiry, Asta produced a letter that Elsa had sent her. In the letter Elsa has written, in large dark typescript, an address 'proving' that I, Suey, had given Asta the wrong address.

"It wasn't important enough to get the address right," Asta spat, venom coming at me from her eyes. She had spent a lot of time writing those letters.

"Well, let's take a look after dinner," I said.

After dinner, she showed me the address she had copied onto the envelopes to Hilda.

"That's my handwriting," I agreed. And then I opened the message in which Hilda's daughter had provided her mother's address. I compared it to what I had written. "They match. Now let's take a look at what Elsa sent you." Reluctantly, she complied.

The numbers in the address Elsa sent didn't match the numbers in the address Hilda's daughter sent.

"So," I interpreted, "either Elsa made a mistake or Hilda's daughter made a mistake. But you mailed it to the address her daughter sent us."

"Then why didn't she get my letters?" she demanded.

"That, I can't answer. But it certainly looks like you sent them to the address her daughter provided."

June 7, 2020: ELSA, ELSA, ELSA

"Elsa's had a hard life," Asta began after breakfast. "She's a good girl with a huge heart and she's extremely generous. Nothing is her fault. She does not deserve to be the black sheep." Her monologue went on for 30 minutes easily, without my adding a word.

"Okay, okay, that's enough," I said, finally. "Can we please not talk about Elsa?"

"We're *family*," she protested. "I should be able to *talk*, and I want to have it *out*." Her point was that that *we*—me and Tony—are not treating Elsa fairly, and it's *our fault* Elsa doesn't feel welcome.

"Again? We had this very conversation last week," I said. "I'm just asking for a little respect, Mommy. More than that, I'm begging. Please let's not talk about Elsa."

"*Elsa* would *never* talk to me like that," she said. "*Elsa* would *never* talk back, *Elsa* would take me back in a heartbeat."

"And *Elsa* would put you in a nursing home lickety-split," I predicted. I texted Chris and asked for a favor.

"Not my finest moment," I admitted, "but I get so sick of hearing about how perfect Elsa is. I said it the way I saw it, and now she's upset with me. Could you please call her on the phone and talk her off the cliff?" An hour later, Chris texted back.

"All better," she wrote. But of course, when I went into Ma's room, she was lying in her fetal position with her face to the wall.

"Mommy?" No answer. "Mommy?" Silence. "Mama?"

"What?!" she spat.

"All right then, never mind," I said. "I'll come back later." I returned at 2:15 p.m. "We're going swimming at 3 p.m. as usual. Why don't you join us? Let's cool off with a dip."

"I'm tired. I don't feel like going swimming, I yust want to rest."

"Well, come on out if you change your mind," I said. I went back in at 3 p.m. "We're going for a dip now, in case you want to join us."

"No," she said. At 4:15 p.m. I went in again.

"We'll be having dinner in about an hour," I said.

"I'm not hungry," she said. "What are you making?"

"Meat loaf and carrot fries."

"Bring it to my room," she said.

"You're refusing to come out because you're upset with me?"

"I'm very upset," she said.

"So you're going to hold yourself prisoner in your room all day? I think you should come out, but I'll bring it in if you insist. Dinner will be ready in 45 minutes. Come out if you change your mind."

A little while later, Ma entered the kitchen.

"I'll yoin you at the table for dinner," she said, "so der won't be talk in de neighborhood."

We do not talk about Asta among our friends and neighbors the way Elsa used to do. All people around here have heard about her from us is that she is wonderful, funny, delightful, perfect, no trouble at all. Period. A goddess, an author, a beauty, a Swede, for God's sake, and 'almost completely independent.' That's the portrait we put on display.

Tony kept a light dinner conversation going about this little and that little thing. Times like these I appreciate him more than ever. Later in bed, he whispered a request.

"If they make a movie about us, I don't want to be seen working out in my boxer shorts," he said.

"Who would you like to play you in the movie?" I asked.

"Brad Pitt," he answered.

"Good choice," I said, and fell asleep smiling.

June 10, 2020: INHERITANCE

"Let's talk about money," Asta said from her inner tube in the shallow end. "Whatever's left at my death, that is, and how I want to distribute it. As I recall, Daddy put something in the will for the grandchildren, like $1,000 each," she said.

"As I recall," I said, "the two of you put the will together, and it said that whatever was left would be divided equally among the three daughters. Giving something to each grandchild came up more recently and it's a great idea. I'm sure we all expect that to happen."

"Well, I've been tinking," she said. "Maybe I'll divide what's left equally among my grandchildren."

"You could do that," I said, "but Chris has no kids. She might feel hurt."

"Oh, I've taken that into consideration," she said. "I promised Chris that any money that's made from my books, or from the sale of the new screenplay I'm working on, will go to her." Asta's books are very valuable to her.

"Yeah, well, any surprise windfall would be nice for anyone," I said, happy to be supportive. I'm not counting on any inheritance. End of life care could gobble that up a flash.

"I'm thinking I should talk to a lawyer so all three of you would know." This was her punchline, the fire for which had probably been built in Woodstock and fanned over the telephone wires.

"You have the right to change it," I said.

"All three of you are secure. You don't need anything."

"That may be true, but Elsa has three kids, so three quarters would go to them. I have one kid, so one quarter would go to her. Chris has no kids, so nothing would go in her direction. Have you thought about it that way?" I asked. "When it comes to money, talk to Chris. She's your POA. She'll make sure that your wishes, whatever they are, are followed."

June 11, 2020: ETHICAL DECISION MAKING

Asta worries, understandably, about Covid-19 and is having a hard time deciding whether or not to go to her next scheduled oncology appointment. She has leukemia and doesn't want to risk exposure. I'm letting the decision be hers. One minute she wants to keep the appointment; the next, she doesn't. One minute she wants me to schedule a haircut for her, then she changes her mind. She doesn't want me or Tony going anywhere. She wants the fortress to be impenetrable.

So when Tony and I informed her we'd be going to San Diego this weekend to ride our bikes in a park wearing masks, Asta became indignant.

"What's good for the goose is good for the gander," she said, using a phrase she likely picked up from Elsa. If Suey can run errands or ride a bike in San Diego, then Elsa should be able to travel across country on a plane.

"I'm not stopping Elsa from travelling," I said. "Elsa can do whatever she wants, go wherever she wants, and visit you here at our house whenever she wants. She can take you to Lisa's house for a visit or to a beach house on the ocean, if that's what the two of you arrange. I just don't want her or you getting on a plane with all those people breathing each other's air."

We all make choices. Hopefully responsible ones.

June 12, 2020: REMAINDER

"Elsa retyped Daddy and Mommy's will in its entirety and sent it to me in an email 'for clarification'," Chris wrote in an email. Specifically:

- Elsa thought Mommy's address needed to be changed.
- She wanted to add language gifting $1,000 to each grandchild at her death, and
- The paperwork identified Elsa as health care proxy (I had that updated when Ma moved in with us two years ago).

"She's obsessing over trying to make sure each grandchild receives $1,000, which is no big deal," Chris said.

We talked about the possibility that Elsa could be planning a trip to California with a new will in hand with the intention of getting Ma in front of an attorney to sign it, or persuading her to make Elsa the new POA.

"I've asked her to please stop harping to Ma about it," she said. "It causes Mommy anxiety. I'll write a response to her email tonight and send it to both of you."

"By the way, Chris," I said, "the time is coming that Ma will need help ambulating or need a wheelchair. She'll need help getting to the bathroom or transferring onto a commode. We may need to hire helpers. Ma's savings will diminish rapidly then."

"Honestly, what would make me happiest," Chris said, "is if we spent Ma's remaining 125k on making her comfortable and safe and as happy as can be so that there is nothing left to quibble about."

I agreed.

June 13, 2020: NO FILTER

"Now I get you two," Asta announced from her inner tube in the shallow end of the pool. We waited for her to finish her thought. She was quiet.

"Did you change your mind about saying whatever you were going to say?" Tony asked.

"Ja," she said, and then—because she couldn't resist—she said with a sideways grin, "Some women marry beneath them." I shook my head in disbelief.

"So you think that's what Suey did?" Tony asked with a chuckle, letting it roll off his back.

Backpedaling, Asta tried to deny her rude assessment.

"He's always been generous and handsome," I said. "He used to get up at 4 in the morning to snow-blow the driveway, and then would snow-blow it again at 10 p.m. after coming home from refereeing in the evening after teaching during the day."

"I'm an ex-hard worker," he said.

June 15, 2020: DAY TRIPPING

"We're leaving soon," I said when I brought breakfast in to my mother. "Rosalva will be here later this morning. She'll bring in and unpack our food order, and then she'll come back and stay from 3-7 p.m." I helped her put on her Lifeline emergency call button necklace.

At the horror of having a caregiver (who she likes), Ma raised her hands to heaven and cried, "Is dis what my life is going to be?"

"You've got the emergency call button in case of an emergency, and Rosalva will be here to keep you company. You'll be fine." Tony and I left. I texted Chris to let her know that Ma was anxious about our leaving. Chris said she'd call in 30 minutes.

Tony thinks 'Never Went Anywhere Ever' would be a great country music song title. I took a picture of him wearing sunglasses at the window of a Greek restaurant in Ocean Beach, with his uncut coronavirus hair, as handsome as Anthony Bourdain.

When we got home at 9 p.m., Ma pretended to be asleep and did not respond to my greeting. I let her sleep.

In the morning, she was cooperative, issuing no complaints. I went about my business, as normal. No digging or prying, just living and doing what we do. Later in the day, I called Chris. "How was your phone call with Mommy this weekend?"

"It was tough," Chris said. "She was manic. I was on the phone with her for an hour and a half! Who knows how long she was on the phone with Elsa. I think we need to increase Rosalva's hours to keep Ma calm and distracted, because I can't do that again."

"Don't go there, Chris," I snapped. "Don't tell me you can't talk to her on the phone for an hour and a half once a week. Try having her live in your house. But yes, I'll ask Rosalva if she could stay for more hours."

"I'd be surprised if Mommy lived another six months," Chris said. I don't know what crystal ball she's looking into.

I brought Ma a cup of tea for her constipation and sat down on the edge of her bed. Change is hard, and Asta has to get used to a 'new normal' which includes hired help.

"We're going away this weekend on another day trip," I informed her gently.

"Yust don't bring it (the virus) home with you," she frowned.

"I'll do my best not to," I promised. "We avoid crowds and closed-in places, and we'll continue to wear masks and wash our hands often. And we're chanting every day to all stay healthy."

June 16, 2020: TO GO, OR NOT TO GO

"I like Rosalva a lot," Mommy said, "but I don't want her as my babysitter or even as a paid friend."

"The word for someone who takes care of an older adult is 'companion', not 'babysitter'," I said. Words have meaning.

I drove Ma to the post office to drop off two of her letters in the mail. It's good for her to get out of the house, if only for a few minutes, and it reassures her to witness her letters being deposited in the mailbox outside the post office. We talked about the virus in the car.

"The world should yust slow down and not open up until it's over," she said.

"People have to work to pay their rent, their bills, their medical expenses, and put food on their tables," I said.

"Well, at the very least, no one should be going anywhere for *fun*," she said. "I don't like that you're risking my health by going away and mingling with people," she said.

"We spend most of the day in the car, visit only open-air stores and bring a picnic lunch so as not to eat inside a restaurant," I said.

Then Eddie called and told her he had been exposed to Covid.

"It's everywhere, Ma," I said. It's tiring trying to reassure her that our hand washing, mask wearing and crowd avoiding are going to keep her safe, because the truth is they might not be enough. We're looking down the barrel of an ethical dilemma:

1. Are we obligated—because of her age and leukemia and because we can't guarantee she won't catch it—to forfeit the few freedoms we have?
2. Is it defensible that we would try to enjoy an occasional outing while observing safety protocols?

Elsa couldn't handle taking care of Asta, and Chris has been clear from the get-go that she wouldn't take her in. Yet they'd be the first to judge me if Ma were to get sick from Covid. Even though we may go on a day trip once a week, and may occasionally go to grocery stores and other places of business, she is frankly, truly, safer living here in our house than anywhere else.

June 20, 2020: PHYSICAL THERAPY

"Let me arrange some physical therapy home visits for you," I begged.

"Absolutely not," she proclaimed.

"How come?" I asked. "You liked Jenna."

"It's nothing against Jenna," she said. "The reason I don't want physical therapy is because I can't feel my feet. She can't do anything about that. The reason I have trouble with balance is because I'm blind. It's useless."

"I just think it would be good for you to move around more, get some exercise," I said.

"I get enough exercise in bed with yoga stretches," she said, demonstrating how she lays on her back and pulls her knees to her chest. At least in the pool she moves her legs a little. Yesterday she refused our daily dip. I hope to persuade her to get in the pool today.

June 24, 2020: ZOOM

"How about if we Anderson Girls connect on Zoom once a week or every two weeks?" Elsa suggested by text. I assumed she meant us three sisters and instantly had agita. I'll gladly set Ma up on a Zoom call with one or both my sisters, but I can't see any joy in a three-way video phone call with just me, Chris and Elsa.

"A regular phone call would also be an option," I answered, thinking that if Elsa wanted to talk to me, she could call me on the phone. We don't need a video conference to say hello. I called Chris.

"Elsa wants to talk to Ma face to face," Chris explained.

"That's not how I read 'how about if we Anderson girls connect'," I objected.

A few minutes later Chris wrote, "I just confirmed with Elsa that she means to talk with Ma on Zoom."

Soon, Asta and Tony and I were in the pool.

"Elsa wants to talk with you on Zoom," I told Ma. "You'll be able to see each other on the computer screen. Chris can join in too. Anytime they set it up, I'll set you up on this end, okay?"

"I dread it," Ma said.

"I'll stay out of the way so you girls can talk," Tony offered.

"You most certainly ought to be on the call," Asta said. "I think the purpose of the call is to make peace."

"Oh, I'd be happy to sit in, if you want me to," he said, riding the wave, bless his heart.

I texted this exchange to Chris, who wrote back "The more, the merrier."

But there are too many contradictions in the messaging re: who is supposed to be on the call and why. If it smells like fish, it's probably fish.

Asta stressed all night about the scheduled Zoom call, and by morning was crying about it. "Elsa's going to make me see Heidi on the computer screen. I don't want to see Heidi and I don't want Heidi to see me."

"You don't have to be on the call if you don't want to be. I'm not going to force you, and I'm not going to let anyone else force you. I've got your back. It's up to you."

Asta spent the afternoon dressing up and making herself look good for the camera.

The call began at 6 p.m. We talked about hair and makeup, girly things, safe things, dumb things. Tony made an appearance, waved and said "Hi, Love you guys," and we returned to our familiar, familial banter. The call lasted half an hour.

June 28, 2020: AT WHOSE EXPENSE

"When are you going away next?" Asta asked the morning after Rosalva had been here again.

"Possibly Friday, if Rosalva's available. We're planning a day at the beach," I said.

"Who's paying for Rosalva?" she asked, looking bitter, preparing for battle.

"We're splitting it," I said, as Chris and I had agreed I'd say.

"Who's splitting it?" she asked.

"You and I."

"I'm not asking for a sitter," she protested.

"Well, I'm not going to stay home all the time, and someone needs to be here for your safety."

"Why wasn't I consulted?" she demanded.

"Chris and I discussed it. Chris wants someone here too while we are gone. But even if we have to pay for it, we're going to go places from time to time." She continued to protest until Tony came into the kitchen.

"Did you and Ragnar go places when you were in your 60's?" he asked, although they didn't have an elderly dependent parent restricting their activities.

"What does he have to do with it?" she asked. "I shouldn't have to pay for your fun."

"We'd like to go out more often," Tony said, "but right now we can't." It didn't have to be said that 'we can't' because she lives with us and needs supervision, and because of the coronavirus. "You're always welcome to come with us. It's not the money. We can handle that. Not a problem."

This issue keeps repeating and is giving me indigestion. I alerted Chris. "Who's paying for the caregiver continues to be an issue. Tony and I don't need a caregiver. Mommy does. We're paying for our fun. She says she's saving her money for when she needs a 'real nurse,' but she needs to spend money on the companion caregivers she needs now."

"I'll pay for it out of my own pocket," Chris said. Anything to avoid an argument. Buying peace.

"That's ridiculous, but do what you want," I said, "and this is how it's going to work: I'll pay Rosalva out of Mommy's local account, and you keep that account funded. As POA, it's your responsibility to release her funds for her care needs. If you'd rather pay for them out of your own pocket, that's your business."

I respect that Mommy wants to have some control over her finances, but she doesn't comprehend that meeting her supervision needs costs money. Nor does she appreciate the financial value of living with us in our home.

June 30, 2020: FAMOUS LAST WORDS

"Elsa's trying to talk me into moving back to Woodstock," Asta revealed while we paddled around in the pool. As if this were something new.

Straight from the hip I told her, "Elsa won't be able to handle it as soon as it's no longer a party, when you get sick and need help."

Elsa thinks she's being compassionate in telling our mother she has 'options' when Ma complains to her over the phone about me and/or Tony. Elsa from La-La Land is brainwashing our mother.

"It was really great living on my own in Woodstock." Ma reminisced through rose-colored glasses. "I called in food deliveries from Tops, and Elsa was right next door in case of emergency."

"Well, no 90-year old should live alone," I said.

"I bet you didn't expect to have me still living here after two years," she said, fishing.

"Mommy, you're doing great," I said, "and we're happy for that. Let's keep it that way."

"Yes," she agreed, "I'm good. It took me a year to adjust to the heat and the gated community, but I'm doing very well. Poor Elsa was struggling when I lived next door to her. It's very different there now, though. Tom doesn't come around much because his wife is home..." This must be part of Elsa's sales-pitch. Ma turned away from me and spoke to the pool wall. "And yust to have da last word, it's always de men's fault."

Ugh. Whenever she insists on having the last word, you can count on it being mean-spirited. I could only turn away and shake my head.

July 1, 2020: VASES, VAHZES

Over dinner, Tony and I were discussing buying new vases for the altar. We agreed that they should meet certain criteria in terms of height and color, and that they should be simple rather than ornate. I might prefer them to be able to hold water for real flowers and be washable. He might rather they have skinny necks. Asta's opinion and experience informs her that the freedom to decorate the home belongs exclusively to the woman.

Asta addressed me, like any mother might or would: "You should get whatever you want," and tried to produce a few tears of pity for me. When that didn't elicit a response, she sprang her 'meaningful eye contact' on me. She wanted a showdown. Instead of looking away, I held her gaze, with eyebrows up, as if to say, 'You've got to be kidding me.' A stare down. I waited. She blinked.

Tony and I coaxed her into my office to look at some of the alternatives we had been considering, and we showed her where on the altar they'll be placed. Tony encouraged her to voice her opinion. She blossomed at the invitation to contribute her expertise.

July 2, 2020: NAME THE PROBLEM

"What's the temperature outside?" Asta asked as the three of us paddled around in the pool.

"About 100," Tony said.

"Ja, my room is 104," Mommy said.

"Your room is not 104," I said. "We keep the thermostat at 80 and the air conditioning system feeds your room."

"My little thermostat says 104," she insisted. This is what she's telling my sisters, I'm sure.

"It's not possible. I've been in your room," I said. "It could be 84, but there's no way it's 104."

"Oh, that's what it was! 84!"

Later in the afternoon, I got an email from Chris. "Elsa, Lisa and I are talking about buying an air conditioner for Ma for her birthday. Elsa did a lot of research," Chris wrote. "You can pitch in too if you want."

"She won't want to lose her window," I answered.

"We're concerned about heat-related illness, and it's gonna get hotter. Watch this video of the air conditioner," she directed. I didn't.

"Her room is air conditioned along with the house. We keep the thermostat at 80 degrees. I am in her room several times a day."

"I'm confused. I thought Ma's room only had a fan," she wrote. "I want to avoid a repeat of last year's headache."

"Her room has had air conditioning since day one. Last year's headache was in winter, so we turned on the heat." I'd bang my head against the wall if I had time for it. I went and invited Ma over for breakfast.

"Just so you know," I told Asta, who doesn't like surprises, "Chris, Elsa and Lisa are talking about getting you an air conditioner."

"I don't *want* an air conditioner," she hollered. "Why won't anyone *listen* to *me*?" She launched into a ten minute speech, and concluded with a vengeance. "While we're at it," she said, "I want to talk about the vases again, because Tony is controlling and you need to find your voice." 'Finding your voice' is a popular-culture expression that she probably picked up from conversations with Elsa.

"Mommy, that's enough. Just stop. I don't want to hear it," I begged. She kept going. I tried changing the subject, to no avail. And then I looked at her objectively. Suey on duty, here.

"Is there something wrong with your nose?" I asked.

"No," she answered.

"Why are you pinching your nostril like that? Did you have a bloody nose this morning?" No answer. "Well, I guess I'll take my walk now. We'll have breakfast when I come home."

I called Chris while out on my walk. Ma had already gotten a hold of her first and given her an earful about the air conditioner.

"What's frustrates me," I told Chris, "is that you guys don't trust that I'll make sure Ma is cool enough or warm enough, or that I'll keep her fridge stocked with snacks and juice." It's one crisis following another, most of them manufactured by phone. "Tony and I are willing to take care of her for the rest of her life. If the three of you believe we're not doing a good enough job, she can move anywhere except in with Elsa. It may interest you to know that yesterday Ma said that she was thinking how nice it would be to live with you."

"It's not gonna happen," Chris said.

"Moving in with Elsa or moving in with you?" I asked.

"Either," she said. Then pivoting, "I wonder when Ma would be appropriate for placement. I wonder when she'll become a danger to herself and/or others." Standard elder-care speak.

"If she were to leave the house unescorted and get lost; if she were to light real candles; if she came at someone with a knife; if she were to become a frequent faller, that kind of thing. She's still self-managing her incontinence, feeds herself, and has no skilled nursing needs. By no stretch of the imagination is she a danger to herself or anyone else at this time."

"Well, you need to take care of yourself and your marriage," Chris said.

Wait, I thought we were talking about what's in our mother's best interest and where she should live.

"I am taking care of my marriage, by hiring Rosalva once a week so that Tony and I can get away for a few hours," I said. My marriage is not the problem. The problem is talking on the phone.

"I'm urging Ma to back off on trying to make you feel guilty for that," Chris said, sounding supportive but bouncing all over the board. I want to believe she has my back.

"Thanks," I said. "I'm counting on you to move here when I turn 65 to help us take care of Ma for however long she has left." I downloaded and shared a countdown app: 820 days till Chris moves to Palm Springs, California.

July 5, 2020: TALK, TALK, TALK

"Would you like me to help with your hearing aids, see if we can get them to work?" I offered gently after breakfast, after having had to repeat something three times.

"No, I hear fine," she said. She hears fine on Planet Asta, just fine in Asta Land. She hears herself talking very well.

Asta expects me to sit with her and listen at length, and sulks when I disappoint her. I've run out of things to talk about, and I don't want to trigger an hour-long monologue about Elsa, Sweden, or her books. So after serving breakfast and keeping her company while she ate, I went around the corner into my office to do some business. Twenty minutes later, she was still sitting at the counter, waiting for me to notice her there.

"Wanna watch some TV in the living room and catch up on the day's news?" I invited.

"No," she said, "but could you give me a Band-Aid?" She'd been picking at a mosquito bite on her upper arm and had scraped it open. I washed the area and applied some healing ointment and a Band-Aid.

During pool time in the afternoon, Ma listed why she doesn't like California. "Pot is legal, and smoking pot leads to hard drugs. I don't like how houses are in gated neighborhoods. You never see anybody. California might be a good place to live for a younger person who can walk..." but not for her, who can't.

I drifted away on my pool float and closed my eyes—she was talking to the wall anyway, not to me. I contributed an occasional sentence—two, maybe three, during that hour—to be polite. It doesn't matter what anyone else says. She can't hear, and doesn't mind that she can't. In fact, it works to her advantage because she doesn't want to be interrupted. Dialogue breaks her concentration, nudges her off the track of whatever train of thought she's riding.

Asta wasn't always this way. She used to love to talk *with*, as opposed to *at*, people. I loved talking with and to her. She used to be interested in hearing what other people had to say. Now it's like her hearing deficit and mild cognitive deficit have joined forces to dominate the conversation.

July 9, 2020: THE FOOTBALL AFFAIR

Asta had me drive her to the post office so she could, once again, witness me drop her letters, unmolested, into the Post Office mailbox. It's a sad state of distrust, but I don't want to challenge her thinking. Instead, I help her into the car, call it an outing, and try to keep things pleasant.

"I've been listening to the Stormy Daniels book about Trump and am learning what a pig he is. If you want the truth, 95% of men are pigs," she said, itching to criticize Tony, or Paul or Tom. She has opinions and was eager to let them out.

"Let's not go there, Mommy," I said. She held her tongue until we returned home, had gotten into the pool and she was comfortable in her inner tube.

"Like I said, 95%," she said, needing to have the last word. All I could do was shake my head.

Tony soon joined us in the pool. The three of us were floating, conversing and having a leisurely time. Tony and I started tossing one of those kiddie-sized plastic footballs back and forth. And then a toss of Tony's went off-course and hit Asta in the back of her head.

She hadn't seen it coming. It surprised her. Her face screamed hate, not hurt.

"I'm soooo sorry," Tony said.

"That's called elder abuse," she snapped.

"Mama, it was an accident," I jumped to his defense.

"Was it?" she asked, determined to make an ugly accusation. Material for her phone calls with Elsa and Chris. Material to turn into a Scandal.

"Sjems du inte?" (Aren't you ashamed?) I asked her in Swedish. The little tap on her head by the pool toy didn't warrant an accusation of elder abuse. "To throw those words around when you're living in our house and all we do for you?" I'm horrified that she would even suggest it. I too have pride.

"Me sjems? It should be him! Of course you have to protect *him*. Typical," she spat.

"Yes, *you* should sjems. You were wrong to make that accusation. Look in the mirror for a change."

The party was over. Tony went inside. I got out of the pool and set up her chair the way she likes for sitting and drying off after a swim. I changed into dry clothes, sat on the lounger across from her and texted Chris and Elsa.

"Heads up," I wrote, "Tony mis-threw a light pool toy today that hit Ma in the head and she accused him of elder abuse. Tony apologized, but that wasn't good enough for her. I'm not happy, she's not happy, and Tony's not happy." I brought my phone over to Ma.

"I just sent a text to Elsa and Chris," I said, "so they know what's going on before you call them, which I know you will. And just so you know what I'm telling them and there's nothing going on behind your back, I'll read it to you."

Asta didn't want to join us at the dinner table. She wasn't hungry, she said. So I brought her dinner to her room on the silver tray. When I returned at 8:15 p.m., I saw that she had picked at her dinner and was laying down. I sat at the foot of her bed.

"Can I tell you why I'm upset?" I asked. "Because if anyone heard you claim elder abuse, like Lisa or Rosalva, or if Elsa or Chris were to believe you, they would be obligated to notify social services or the police and there'd be an investigation. That's how the system works, and an investigation would be deeply humiliating to me."

"Anyone who knows me knows that I would not talk outside the family," she said, on the defensive now.

"Even talking inside the family, I am deeply, deeply offended by your accusation today."

"Well, I was deeply offended by getting hit in the head with a ball," she said.

"It was a very light ball and accidental, and you know it. Think about it, Mommy. I'll be back to check on you before I go to bed."

July 10, 2020: OPTIONS

To what rights does being 92 years old entitle one?

- The rights to be loved and assisted—yes.
- The right to insult and accuse those who do everything they can to take care of you, who make sure all your needs are met—no.

I called Chris. "She can't live here if she's going to accuse either one of us of abuse," I said. "That's my line in the sand."

"I talked to Ma last night," Chris said, "and scolded her in no uncertain terms about the unacceptability of using those words and leveling false accusations of abuse. I told her she could be removed from the house by authorities whose intentions would be to ensure her safety, all because of her choice of words. Elsa is suggesting having Asta live with her six months of the year, and with you six months of the year. I said, 'No, that's not in Ma's best interest.'" Speaking to me now, Chris said, "After all, I don't think Ma is going to live another year. You should look at this as a narrow window of time." Suddenly, she was selling me on keeping our mother at my house.

"You might be right, but she could also live several more years."

"What about her dementia?" she asked.

"Once she is given a diagnosis, assisted living facilities—if she needed one—could charge a lot more per month for their services. Securing a diagnosis of dementia wouldn't be doing her any financial favors. She's not an elopement risk. We're not planning on placing her, but maybe we need to keep our options open, because the words she lets escape her mouth may turn into Cinderella's horses that come and take her away."

"What can I do for you?" Chris asked, recognizing that taking care of Asta is hard.

"I'm thinking of taking 100 days off the countdown till you move out here," I said.

"Deal," she said. We laughed. I moved the date up from Sept 30, 2022 to June 30, 2022.

July 11, 2020: THREATS

Everyone's walking on eggshells. Tony is avoiding being in the same room with Asta, and Asta is refusing pool time. She is thanking me more than usual for little things, and I—frostily—am going about my business, making sure she has what she needs, offering choices, and trying to invite her back into the daily routine. Civil and business-like. On Thursday, she wanted to have dinner in her room so Tony and I ate together. Last night, Tony wanted to have dinner on his own in our bedroom, so Asta joined me for dinner in the dining room. If the three of us meet at the table tonight, it will be miserably quiet.

"I don't feel comfortable being left alone with her," Tony said, "for fear she'll make another accusation. I want you there as a witness."

He worries what Elsa is saying about him and us behind our backs. Meanwhile, the three of us in *this* household have to navigate the elephant in the room. It ties a knot in my stomach. I don't know how to steer this family to the other side of the chasm. Maybe another conversation, head on.

"I'm worried because Rosalva is coming tomorrow," I told Asta. "If you cry 'elder abuse', she will have to report it."

"I yust said that as a warning to Tony," she said.

"A warning?" I got mad. "That's the problem! You're still blaming him. The issue isn't the ball, it's the accusation. I want you to understand that."

"You tell him I won't blab," she said.

"No, you tell him," I insisted.

"It was Tony's fault and you're yust chasing after him, defending him," she said. "I shouldn't be here. I'll have to leave. I would never blab outside the family." The drama was building.

"Well, you've already told Elsa and Chris, and Elsa has surely told Lisa." I mimicked how she would have told Elsa. My bad behavior.

"Get out of my room! I paid for it and I pay rent. Get out!!! I don't want to take this abuse from you!"

"There you go again! Abuse. You love that word!" I yelled back. "Let's call Chris." We did.

"She's been screaming at me for an hour," Asta claimed. "I can't breathe." I had been in her room for ten minutes.

"Handle it, Suey," Chris said. We hung up.

"I'm sorry, I was out of line by yelling at you," I said. "Can you forgive me?"

"Yes, I forgive you."

"I just don't want you making false accusations."

"And I forgive Tony and I forgive everybody for everything, including myself for moving here," she sobbed.

She may move back to Woodstock once the pandemic is over, but there are better options. I called Chris again.

"I'm not pushing for this, but if she wants to move and is willing to stay in the Desert, I'm familiar with the assisted living homes in this area." I sent her links to the websites of two facilities I think Asta would like.

I went in and told Asta that dinner would be ready in half an hour.

"Send Tony in so I can have a *private* conversation with him," she said. I sent him in and I took the dog for a walk. He filled me in when I got home.

"She started by saying she would never use the word 'abuse' outside the family, and I explained to her the problem with saying it at all. Everything was fine until she started criticizing you, saying Elsa would *never* talk to her like that, how you're not the daughter she raised, Elsa this and Elsa that, how Elsa would have handled the situation so much better. And that," Tony said, "is when I lost it and said, 'For two years Suey's been bending over backwards to make sure you've had everything you needed and wanted. She's been available day and night, supporting you in every way. It was Elsa who demanded you come here and told everyone in Woodstock you were crazy and impossible to deal with.'"

I came home and Asta was in tears, mad at me for hollering at her and upset with Tony for taking my side and telling the truth.

I'm tired of the negativity, tired of having to defend Tony, tired of being angry with Elsa. I'd like to return to the place where I can regard Mommy as the beautiful, charming, funny, creative and diplomatic person that she is—and not the miserable, blaming, judging, critical and accusing person she appears to have become. I'd like to remember Elsa as the generous big-sister comedienne. I'm tired of the drama and the division the two of them have been stoking in my household. I'm tired of the suspicion and distrust Ma feels towards me and us because of it, and I'm sad we are here now, struggling with these issues, all of us angry and upset with each other.

July 12, 2020: IF WISHES WERE FISHES

"I wish you could curb the knee jerk reactions, although I completely understand them," Chris wrote, straddling the extremes, covering all bases. "I should have taught you my methods years ago, I guess."

"Maybe you could do this better than me...," I answered carefully. "I wish a lot of things. Doing my best here."

"I didn't mean that. I couldn't do it *at all*!"

So if, despite her 'methods', she couldn't do it *at all*, how could those methods be useful at all for me? I could teach a course on Chris's methods, by the way. I'd call it 'How to Avoid Conflict in the Home.' Students would learn how to:

- Swallow their thoughts and feelings
- Bite their lips or tongues
- Buy their way out, maybe
- Juggle, play cards (distract, entertain)
- Play music

Presently, I'm all out of methods. I can't make Asta happy, I'm not allowed to get angry, and no matter what I do, it's never enough. Here are some wishes of my own:

- I wish Elsa wouldn't play perpetual tug of war, as if Ma would be happier, safer there than here.
- I wish Mommy would be more accepting and less critical of Tony.
- I wish Ma could hear better so we wouldn't have to repeat *everything* two or three times.

- I wish Ma could see better and walk better so she would be able to visit her new friends in the neighborhood independently.
- I wish I didn't have to worry about Mommy's happiness every single day.
- I wish there were no Covid-19.
- I wish Tony and I could have a little more spontaneity in our lives. I wish we could go out to dinner without her, without feeling guilty and without having to prepare a meal anyway.
- I wish I didn't have to deal daily with experiences capable of triggering knee jerk reactions.
- I wish everyone had perfect control over their reflexes.

July 20, 2020: BALLOON POPPING

We are planning a little dinner party to celebrate Asta's 92nd birthday and proposed inviting our friend, Cary, and possibly Rosalva over for dinner.

"I don't want a party," Asta said. "I don't even want you to stay home. Go on your usual day trip Sunday. I'll celebrate my birthday with Rosalva."

"I don't feel comfortable going away on your birthday. We'd like to celebrate your birthday with you. Tony suggested that after dinner we show the video of you acting in your nun role. I've already called Elsa and asked her to send me the DVD. We wanted it to be a surprise."

"I don't want to show the video," she said. "Tony yust wants to show off and you have to go along with it. Do whatever you want. I don't want a celebration this year because Elsa and Chris won't be here. But if you do have them over, I'll fake it."

I felt completely deflated. Later she called me into her room.

"I've shanged my mind," she said in an about-face. "I'd like to have Cary and Rosalva over."

I'm glad, as this little celebration is all we can realistically do—in the middle of a pandemic—to honor her on her birthday. No one is pretending they don't recognize that this could be her last.

July 26, 2020: PARTY PANDEMIC STYLE

"Let's drive over to Eddie's house for a gift exchange," I suggested. Eddie had written a touching poem for her that I printed and framed for him to give her. Masked, we visited him in his apartment parking lot for a few minutes, then drove to the 99 Cents store.

It was the first time in four months (due to Covid) she'd gone out shopping. I brought along her seated walker. Going up and down the aisles was good exercise and she enjoyed picking up thank you cards, birthday cards, socks, hair things, beverages, cookies and a cake that she can offer when Rosalva comes over tomorrow.

A few neighbors remembered Asta for her birthday: June called on the phone, Marie stopped by with a card and gift, and Cary dropped off a card. We ordered a take-out dinner from Babe's, had a little cake and gave her a few gifts: a pair of the slipper shoes she likes, and two pairs of soft jersey pants that Tony bought for her on our day trip last weekend. We put together and delivered a dinner container to Cary, our way of including him in her birthday celebration without risking anyone's exposure to Covid. We then put a movie on the TV, most of which she slept through. All things considered, it was a perfectly satisfactory birthday.

CHAPTER 6
ENGAGING HELPERS

"Rosalva won't be coming this weekend," I informed Asta. "She's sick."

"So it wasn't convenient for you or Tony?" she spat.

"Mommy, she's sick."

"Or didn't Tony want her to come because Rosalva and I had *plans*!"

"Mommy, Rosalva is sick and said she can't come this weekend."

"So you talked to her?" she asked, indignant that I had talked with Rosalva behind her back.

"I'll read you the text messages," I said, and did. "Rosalva doesn't want to risk bringing germs here to you."

"Who's coming then?" she asked.

"We're going to ask Eddie," I said.

"Why can't I yust wear that thing around my neck?" she asked, referring to her Life Alert necklace. "Where is my independence? I have no independence. Nobody cares what I want."

"I'd feel better if you had someone here in case of emergency," I said, "and Chris would feel better too. It's a win-win for everyone. You'll have someone here in case of emergency, Eddie can go swimming, and I won't have to worry. Rosalva offered to send a friend of hers. Would you rather we do that and have someone over that we don't know?"

"No, I know Eddie," she said, adding bitterly, "You go with Tony. I know it's important to you."

"And I know it's important to you to have someone here." I just can't let her dictate whether I can leave the house or on what terms. Eddie is a reasonable companion for when Rosalva's not available.

July 31, 2020: IMPULSE CONTROL

I've asked Asta a dozen or more times to please use the plate I set out for the dog when giving him table scraps.

"He needs to know he's a member of the family," she said, preparing to drop a piece of meat onto the new area rug we'd recently placed under the dining room table. She saw me looking her way. Reluctantly, she deposited the scrap onto her empty dinner plate.

Impulse control takes self-discipline. Asta would rather rebel.

Aug 2, 2020: SITTER

"We're picking up Eddie this morning," I said. Eddie doesn't drive and we didn't want him to have to take public transportation during Covid and in this heat.

Ma counted on her fingers the number of hours that Eddie would be here, compared to Rosalva's four or five.

"I suppose he's not being paid because he's a friend," she said, fishing.

"He is a good friend to the family," I said, neither confirming nor denying her suspicion. Tony and I went ahead with our plans.

On our return, and after ferrying Eddie back to his apartment, we brought home pizza for dinner. Asta, exhausted, was in no mood to talk, having forced herself to entertain for all those hours.

Aug 4, 2020: THE EVERYTHING LIST

"Hi Suey," Elsa texted. "Just want you to know that I know what it feels like to be the daughter who is on call 24-7... *doing everything* ... while the two sisters who live so far away get waaaaaay too much credit for the little they can do. Thanks for all you do for Mommy."

(a) No, she doesn't know what it feels like to do everything;
(b) Doing 'everything' must mean something very different to her than to me. Asta is still independent with dressing, transferring, eating, toileting and ambulating short distances;
(c) I'm not doing this for credit.

I'm not going to brave a discussion or enter into any debate. I replied with a thumbs-up emoji.

Aug 7, 2020: RESISTANCE

"What are your plans for the weekend?" Asta asked. "Who's coming while you're away?"

"Eddie," I answered. "Rosalva may have been exposed to the Coronavirus at work and that's why she didn't come last weekend. She's still self-quarantining through the weekend."

"How long will this be going on, where you go every weekend?" Ma challenged, giving Tony and me horrible, angry, suspicious looks.

"We're going to do something fun together once a week," Tony answered. "You can come anytime you want."

She folded her hands across her forehead for a bit, then raised her head and announced in her most accusatory tone, "Elsa would *never* go away for eight hours and leave me with a babysitter."

"Companion," I corrected. Terminology wasn't the issue, but that was the end of any argument she was going to get from me. It's just not negotiable. We will not be held prisoner.

Aug 8, 2020: PHONE STRESS

Last night, Asta retreated to her room, turned out the lights and talked on the phone at length to Elsa. (I know it was Elsa thanks to caller ID on our cable TV). This morning, she said, "I'm extremely tired due to stress."

I went about my day, but stopped in at various intervals to (a) encourage her to come over for breakfast, (b) collect and return her laundry, and (c) offer to pick up anything she needs/wants from the store. I helped her re-hang a picture, encouraged her to drink an Ensure, and invited her outside for our 3:00 swim. After dinner, we sat and chatted at the table for a while.

"I don't know if you've talked with the girls," Asta said, "but there's talk about my being a snow bird." Pause.

"What do *you* want?" I asked.

"Well, I don't know. The summers are so hot here. What's your opinion?" she asked.

"Travelling is hard for someone who's 92 years old. I wouldn't do it if I were you, and I don't think it's in your best interest. But if that's what you guys decide, do what you need to do. I've made my opinion clear."

"But then Tony would have you to himself," she said.

"Tony and I like to get away one day a week. That's enough."

"It's yust sitting on a plane," she said.

"Yeah, but the last time you flew you got cellulitis in your legs. Your doctor said that with your leukemia, flying would be risky because of the germs on planes." The discussion that never ends. Until I change the subject. So I changed the subject.

We called her hairdresser and scheduled a home visit for Wednesday.

Aug 10, 2020: REMUNERATION

"Call me," Chris texted. I called her when I got off work. "Eddie emailed Elsa that he had a bad feeling about Ma's finances. He wrote that you and I are in cahoots. Elsa called him and recorded their phone call, then called me and said, 'We have to *do something* and *take back control* of the *money*.' What did Tony say to Eddie about money?"

"Tony said that when he drove Eddie home, Eddie said he wanted to be Ma's regular companion but was uncomfortable taking payment from us. Tony told him not to worry, there's money set aside for her care—but she doesn't know it's coming out of her account, so asked Eddie to please not mention it to her."

"Eddie told Elsa you paid him $80, or $10 an hour, whereas Rosalva gets $20/hour," she said.

"We paid him $80 for the shift. Had he been able to get here and home on his own, we'd have hired him to work for four hours, which is all we needed him for, and he'd have earned $20/hour, same as Rosalva."

"Well, Eddie told Elsa he suspects financial abuse. I think you should repay Ma's account for whatever has been paid to Rosalva and other caregivers."

"No," I said. "Better to come clean and acknowledge who's paying for it. The cost of her caregivers is her expense, not mine and Tony's. She can't take care of herself, doesn't want to be alone, and benefits from having someone nearby in case of emergency. We will continue our once-a-week day trips, and will continue to arrange for a companion or caregiver at her expense."

"Do you think it was legal for Elsa to record the phone call?" Chris asked. "If we could listen to it, maybe we could maybe defend ourselves."

"Tony and I have done nothing wrong. I'm not in the least bit worried," I said. "I've accounted for every penny of hers that's we've spent, and every cent is legit."

"Elsa wants 'transparency' in Ma's finances. She thinks you should inventory what you're doing for Ma that would justify $1,000/month," Chris said. "I told her that as POA, I don't need her permission to make financial decisions on Mommy's behalf, but in the interest of transparency, I'd do a full accounting."

Chris reminded Elsa that Elsa had been collecting $800-$900 per month when Mommy lived next door in Woodstock: a $500 a month stipend *plus* reimbursement for food, an hourly wage for services like mowing Mommy's lawn, and so forth. Elsa is still receiving checks from Ma for as much as $200 per month—i.e., a full 20% of what Ma pays us for her room and board, supervision and etc.—'for cat food.'

In response to Elsa's hysteria, my mother questions our integrity and insists we shouldn't be spending her money on services she hasn't approved. Chris tried to reason with her.

"I told Mommy that you have every right to a life of your own," Chris said, "and that she has no right telling you how to live your lives; that being under your roof and in your care doesn't give her the right to tell you whether or when you can go anywhere; that you don't owe her your in-home presence 24/7; that her care is not your financial responsibility, and that she needs to wrap her head around that and come to terms with it. I also told her I wanted to hear the tape, but Ma said she doesn't want to get you and Tony in trouble. I assured her that you won't get in trouble because you haven't done anything wrong. I even told her how I used to pay Elsa out of her money when she lived next door. Ma thought everything Elsa did for her then was entirely out of Elsa's own pocket and solely out of the goodness of Elsa's heart."

That we're even having this conversation is exhausting. It's like Eddie pulled the pin on a hand grenade (that wasn't even real) and threw it onto the field, Elsa caught it and ran like her hair was on fire, while Chris stood on the fifty yard line looking back and forth, trying to figure out which team she was playing for. And I'm in the locker room, cleaning toilets, not questioning my minimum wage.

Aug 13, 2020: GOOD BYE, EDDIE

"We won't be bringing Eddie back, Ma" I told Asta in the pool when we talked about the upcoming weekend.

"Why not?" she asked innocently, as if she couldn't guess why.

I answered her literally and directly. "Because he had no business emailing Elsa and getting in the middle of things he knows nothing about. And then he refused to talk with me when I called. Therefore, I will not be hiring him again as a companion, and I will not be inviting him over as a friend."

"How did you hear?" she asked.

"Chris told me," I said.

"Surely Tony must have said something that alarmed Eddie enough to notify Elsa," she demurred.

"Tony told me what he and Eddie talked about, and I have no problem with any of it," I said. "I've sent Chris a receipt for every penny I've spent from your account, and we don't have access to your savings. Chris is in control of your purse strings. We have done nothing wrong."

Asta listed the issues. "Elsa wants me to be a snow bird. She's lonely. It was a bad time for her back then. Tom is the love of her life. And now Eddie is in the middle and Chris is in trouble too. I yust wish you girls would patch it up and get along. I yust want peace."

At 92 years old and frail, she should have peace. "Everything will be fine. It'll all work out," I assured. "Meanwhile, you don't have to worry about anything. I'll do the worrying for you."

Aug 14, 2020: MENU SERVICE

"I eat what you eat," Asta said at the breakfast table. "You don't have to do anything special for me."

"Okay. How about cereal or oatmeal this morning?" I offered, taking her statement at face value.

"Nah," she said, wrinkling her nose, "I'd rather have an egg—sunny side up—with bacon." So I made her a sunny side up egg, bacon and toast breakfast. I had a bowl of cereal.

Later in the day she reported, "I have a sore throat." I prepared a cup of chamomile tea with honey for her and took her temperature. No fever.

"Wanna join me in the pool?" I invited, thinking maybe a distraction would help.

"No. For dinner I yust want chicken noodle soup. I'm not hungry," she said.

So for dinner I heated up a can of chicken noodle soup and made her a large grilled cheese sandwich to go with it. She ate it all. I don't think she's sick. I blame her sore throat on the dry heat and the fact that she sleeps with her mouth open under the ceiling fan.

Aug 16, 2020: INNUENDO CHESS

"Dawson seems sad," Asta said when we were out floating in the pool. "Why is Tony keeping him hostage inside? Why doesn't he let him out?"

"Dawson can come out if he wants, but it's 100 degrees out, so he'd probably rather lay inside on the cool tile floor. He was peppy when I took him for his walk this morning, and he had a good dump. He's fine."

She questions Tony's whereabouts with his new job as a census enumerator. "Tony works on Sundays? That's odd," she said, looking down to her left, testing the taste of her words.

"Census workers choose the hours they are available. Sundays are good because working people are more likely to be home, so Tony's helping his employer by working on Sundays," I explained.

"Are you driving him around?" she asked, not looking me in the eye. Surely, I'm doing his job with or for him, enabling him in ways she disapproves.

"No, but I will be running some errands today. Is there anything you need while I'm out?"

Aug 17, 2020: TALK ABOUT MOVING

"Elsa called and told me all the neighborhood gossip," Asta reported gleefully as we floated in the pool. "She gave me an update on the status of the sale of my old house and the people who have come to see it." I listened closely for what she might be saying between the lines. It came out after dinner.

"I've been tinking," she announced, all smiles. "I really would like to go back to see the house and stay for a couple of months."

We've had this conversation, or something like it, a hundred, a thousand times. It's the Elsa-the-horse-whisperer effect, and it's tiresome beyond measure.

"Maybe you should check with your doctor," Tony said. "See what he says about travelling."

"Maybe it doesn't matter what he says," Ma said.

"You would want to go *now*? During the pandemic?" I asked in disbelief, incredulous that my sister would dangle the danger like a treat.

"Of course not," she said.

"If you go, you might not want to come back, or might not be able to," Tony said.

"Thank you for making the decision for me," Asta glared with a 'smile' at Tony. "I'll take it under advisement."

I called Chris to fill her in.

"If she can have *a day* of happiness in Elsa's care, let her have it," Chris said. A stunningly unambitious goal.

"Elsa *should* be capable of making sure Mommy's care needs are met, and if Elsa were to squander Mommy's money, so be it," I said. "What *would* bother me, however, are …" and I listed my concerns:

1. It won't take long, after having relentlessly campaigned to get her back, for Elsa to complain how hard it is taking care of Asta;

2. Elsa will resume talking negatively about Ma behind her back, causing Ma embarrassment and unhappiness;

3. The stairs at Elsa's house will trap Ma inside all year. Here we have no steps and she can access the outdoors independently simply by opening her door. And when it's too hot for that, we've got the pool;

4. How profoundly disappointed Ma will be when she realizes Elsa's not up to the task, or when Elsa dispatches her to congregate care.

"I share the same concerns," Chris said. "But if Ma *does* decide to make the trip, I'd insist that it be for no longer than three months. After that, she'd go back to California with a better attitude, and God willing, have a little more time to appreciate and enjoy your good care."

"Well, I'm not drinking the Kool Aid," I said, "that seeing her old house from Elsa's window or reuniting with Heidi, or being dependent on Elsa instead of us is going to make her one iota happier. For *her* sake, I hope she stays here."

Sept 1, 2020: NAPKINS

When Covid-19 broke out, there was a rush on paper products at the stores. Toilet paper was the rage, and paper towels were hard to come by. We were well stocked on toilet paper, but I realized that by switching to cloth napkins, we could not only conserve on paper towels but could add a touch of elegance to our table. I upcycled an old cotton sheet into a set of cloth napkins and we reduced our paper towel consumption dramatically. The switchover was a success.

A package came today for Asta from Elsa.

"What did she send you today?" I asked, curious.

"Paper napkins," Asta answered. "I must have talked about it when you switched to cloth ones."

Elsa has to stick her nose in everything.

Sept 4, 2020: SPLISH SPLASH

"Elsa read me the terrible weather report for today in Palm Springs," Asta said as we floated comfortably in the pool. "Heat wave, worse than ever."

"Yes, this is as bad as it gets," I acknowledged, spreading my hands to embrace the setting. Horrible, right?

"Yes, the heat is horrible," she insisted. "I just can't get used to it." Splish, splash.

"I was reading in an old diary," I said, "about when I visited our family in Sweden in my early 20s and I met your half-sister."

"No, you didn't. Impossible. I know better," she said, expounding first on how what I wrote in my diary in the summer of '78 couldn't possibly be true, and next why California really doesn't suit her. After forty-five minutes of speaking, she reached her conclusion: "Elsa wants me there. She is lonely and could use the financial help if I were there instead of here. If I listen to my heart, I would do one thing, but if I listen to my head, I'd do another, and I know I'm better off here."

Her negative stream of consciousness and hearing her say that her heart was in Woodstock with Elsa sent burning acid into my stomach. I answered simply, "I agree, you're better off here."

Asta then started criticizing Tony for not liking Elsa, regurgitating how Elsa doesn't feel welcome here. I made my way to the shallow end and got out of the pool.

"Time for me to call and order dinner. We're bringing Chinese home tonight."

Sept 5, 2020: SNOW BIRDING

"Elsa told me my old house sold for $225,000. The older couple who bought it plan to use it as snowbirds. See, snow-birding is an option," she said with a smirk.

"It's probably medically safe for them to travel," I said.

Sept 8, 2020: RETURN TO WORK

"My employer has asked us to volunteer to work in the office, and I'll be going in two days a week." I informed my mother.

"I'm underfoot. I think I'll move back to Woodstock," Asta said.

"Tony will be home, so you won't be alone," I said.

"I don't want him to be my caretaker," she balked.

"You don't need a caretaker. You pretty much take care of yourself. Do you want me to hire someone to keep you company while I'm at work?" I asked.

"No, no," she said.

"Well, if you need a companion on those two days a week that I'm at the office, I'll make it happen."

"No, I don't want that," she repeated.

"Do you think Elsa will stay home 24/7?" I asked.

"Of course not. Elsa would go on day trips, but not as often," she said. "What if I had a stroke?"

"If you ever need more care than I can provide, I'll make sure you get it." I'm not going to say 'I'll quit my job.'

"Well, the heat of the summer is over, so I'll think about it over the winter. Who knows what'll happen between now and next summer?"

"Well, you'll be another year older, that much we can predict."

Sept 11, 2020: MEANINGFUL ACTIVITY

Before our daily dip in the pool, I asked Mommy to trim my hair. She brought out her old hairdresser's suitcase. I washed my hair so it was clean and wet, and set up the chairs outside so that she wouldn't have the glare of the sun in her eyes, and so that when I was seated, the bottom of my long hair would be easy for her to reach. She had me take my top off so she could trim against my bare skin. Despite being legally blind, she did a good job.

Sept 15, 2020: SUBSTITUTE

Rosalva has to leave town for a few weeks so she introduced us to her friend Merana who would serve as her backup. Merana seemed quiet, but nice enough. I trusted Rosalva's referral.

I gave Merana a brief tour, showed her where we keep the emergency paperwork, and told her that Ma is independent with her ADLs, just needs meals provided, safety checks and companionship. The four of us women sat in the living room so Asta and Merana could get to know each other a little.

"I don't want to be underfoot," Asta told me after they left.

"I don't want to have this conversation again, Mommy," I said.

"I have to have it out," she insisted. She's upset that I go on a day trip once a week, that I have a part time job and that I will be returning to the office.

"No matter who you live with, that person won't be staying home all the time," I said.

"I feel guilty that you're paying for a companion for me, but I'm determined to save my own money until sometime in the future when I might need to pay for a real nurse."

"I'll work something out with her. No problem."

"Well, the weather is getting cooler," she said. "Things will stay as they are... *for now*."

I'll leave the game "Judge for Yourself" out on the dining room table for them to play and encourage Merana to read and discuss the situations with Ma. I'll also put out a deck of cards and suggest nail care. Activities they might enjoy together.

Sept 17, 2020: CALCIUM SUPPLEMENTS

"I read this article to Mommy," Elsa's email began, "and she has decided she wants to take some control of her health by getting more calcium in her diet naturally rather than taking her OsCal pill every day. She developed an aversion to milk after she found a cotton ball in it some time ago. I was thinking that we could support her desire if you buy small, individual cartons of whole milk *and* chocolate milk that could be stocked in her fridge."

Ma uses cotton balls daily to clean her eyes at her desk, and once dropped a cotton ball into her glass of milk. She has not wanted to drink milk since. The rest is bullshit. Here's why:

1. Small milk containers are not economical.
   a. We use 2% milk, which has more calcium than whole milk.
   b. I offer fresh milk with every meal (she chooses juice)

   c. I keep her fridge stocked with 6 oz. lidded glasses of 2% milk. We/she could add powdered chocolate anytime (she declines).
2. Her fridge is stocked at all times with, but she rarely consumes, calcium-fortified strawberry-flavored (her choice) Ensure.
3. Asta has been taking OsCal for years at her doctor's recommendation.
   a. She self-manages her OsCal and can discontinue it any time at her discretion.
   b. We have an appointment with the doctor for a flu shot on Monday and will ask the doctor about OsCal at that time.

Elsa's intentions may be good, but 'we' can support Asta by not frightening her with articles from the 'People's Pharmacy' about over-the-counter supplements that her doctor has recommended she take for bone health. 'We' can ask her doctor if there's any merit to the article's warnings. The real question is whether or not Asta needs supplemental calcium and how to safely get it in proper quantity and form.

I'm not going to quibble with Elsa over the merits of milk vs. dietary supplements. I will help our mother get educated answers for her questions and let her decide for herself.

I didn't write back.

Sept 28, 2020: MEDICAL ADVICE

Asta's appointment with her oncologist went well. Her blood counts remain stable. The doctor wants her continue taking OsCal for bone health. We went to Elmer's for a celebratory breakfast. She practically licked the plate.

I'm more concerned about falls than I am about her leukemia. When walking towards a target, like a curb, car door, or pool railing, she tends to lean forward or reach out way too soon, putting herself at risk of falling flat on her face. I remind her constantly to take another step or two before reaching for whatever it is. She gets super annoyed with me.

Asta is frail, unsteady, and consistently refuses my encouragement to exercise. I tell her she needs weight bearing exercise, such as walking, to strengthen her legs. She insists the 'yoga stretches' she does on her back in bed and her walks to and from the bathroom and dining room are all the exercise she needs. At the doctor's office, I suggested another round of physical therapy, but in front of the doctor she refused, explaining that the last physical therapist had her 'running up and down steps.' She promises she will exercise by walking with her walker up and back on the brick walk outside her door once the weather cools down a bit.

Meanwhile, I texted Elsa: "The doctor told Ma to avoid whole milk. He acknowledged that she is skinny but said her blood chemistry indicates she is well nourished. He encouraged her to drink Ensure, and said that skim milk would also be okay." I'd love for Elsa to get the message that she can stop with the medical and dietary advice.

Today we are getting our flu shots, so tomorrow Asta will have a fever.

Sept 29, 2020: AGING IN PLACE

My mother's room didn't smell fresh today. She wasn't feeling well and didn't want the breakfast burrito and cut up apples I served.

"Yesterday's breakfast was better," she sniffed, so I made her a second breakfast of potato cakes and an English muffin/egg sandwich, which she ate.

I washed her bedspread and gave her a shower.

Oct 6, 2020: GRANDFATHER'S ACCORDION

My mother's father (Morfar) was a popular accordion player in his hometown in Sweden. I played accordion as a child so I was the beneficiary of his. I've long understood that Asta would like it thrown into the ocean, like a burial at sea, after her death.

"You wouldn't mind giving back Morfar's accordion that I gave you years ago," she stated as a matter of fact. "I want Axel to take Elsa out on a sailboat and throw it in Lake Ontario. Elsa will perform a ceremony. After all, Axel is the first grandchild and Morfar liked him." Axel is Morfar's great-grandchild and Morfar never met him.

"How about if Tony and I take you out on the ocean on a charter boat and you can throw it in yourself?"

"I'm afraid of being out on a boat. I can't swim anymore," she said.

"You would wear a life jacket and you could sit the whole time," I said. "I thought you wanted to throw it in the ocean. Lake Ontario's not an ocean."

"Well, the ocean waves will push it to shore." Clearly, she's rationalizing. "And furthermore, Tony is Italian." I'm not going to argue about the accordion. Or Tony's ancestry.

"Okay, you can take it back and give it to Elsa to dispose of in Lake Ontario," I said. "I'll take it down from the shelf now and we'll put it in your room. How does that sound?"

"No, no. It can stay there for the time being," she said.

I can practically hear the conversation between Asta and Elsa. Asta is talking about throwing the accordion into the ocean and how maybe the three of us sisters could do that together someday, and Elsa counters with the suggestion that Axel could take her out on his boat and throw it into Lake Ontario. Elsa would gush, "I would *love* to do that for you, Mommy," and the two of them would start planning. Taking the accordion back from me would be preferable to disappointing Elsa.

In the morning, I again offered to bring the accordion to her room so she would know it's hers to do with as she wants. She didn't want to do that, she said, until she "talked with the girls."

"Want me to text them and let them know?" I asked. I wanted this to be over.

"No, I'll tell them," she said.

Later, Asta asked me to join her on her 'strip' to discuss the accordion. "I yust want to make sure it doesn't end up in a landfill somewhere," she said.

"It will not end up in a landfill. I understand its meaning to you. I admit I felt hurt that you were taking back something else you'd given me, but you can have it back if you want. If there's anything else you want back, though, I wish you'd let me know now so we could be done with it."

"You misunderstood," she said.

"I don't think I did," I said. We put the issue to rest, and the accordion will remain on display on our living room shelf, for now.

Oct 12, 2020: SWOLLEN FEET

At 5:00 a.m. Asta called me on the phone, afraid because her feet were swollen. One had a painful reddened area that she kept rubbing. I'm not medically trained, but I've worked among nurses for years and am aware that the swelling could be heart related and the reddened area could be cellulitis.

I tended to her calmly. No alarms, no drama. Gave her a Tylenol, a cold compress, and some pillows on which to elevate her feet.

"We'll keep an eye on it, and if it gets worse I'll take you to the doctor. But it doesn't seem like an emergency right now," I said.

"But I feel dizzy," she said.

"I'm going to bet that's fear. Understandable, but I don't think we have an emergency here. Let's elevate your legs and I bet you'll be better later today," I said.

I texted Chris and Elsa to let them know I was monitoring. Walking was harder for Asta than usual, but she got better as the day went on. Until she spoke with Elsa, that is. Then, she became so anxious and weepy that Elsa texted me.

"I could be there tomorrow," she said. (Drama!)

"Yes, I know, but that's not necessary," I replied. "She'll be fine, and she'll be seeing a nurse tomorrow anyway when I take her for her scheduled ear lavage."

At Asta's request, I brought in her meals on a tray, checked on her frequently throughout the day, and escorted her to the bathroom as needed. Now it's the end of the day. Her feet look much better, she's smiling and is in pretty good spirits.

Oct 14, 2020: EARS, SKIN AND BROWS

Today was Asta's ear lavage appointment. On the car ride over, she expelled a lot of air blaming others for 'Daddy's miserable death because he didn't die at home', but it was good to get her out of the house.

The ear lavage procedure was interesting to observe. By the look on her face, you would have thought it was very painful. I couldn't resist sneaking a photo. Drama at its finest.

"Did it hurt?" I asked afterwards.

"No, not really," she said, making me laugh. And then I noticed a 1/2 inch skin tear on her arm with a little pool of blood underneath. I asked her about it and she started attacking it with her fingers.

"Stop, stop, stop!" I begged her. "Stop scratching it! Stop touching it! Let's clean it and apply a Band-Aid." Once that was done, she complained that I hadn't put the Band-Aid on to her liking. I promised we'd change it later today so she could look at the area she had been scratching.

Another thing she 'worries' is her eyebrows. She used to scratch and pull at them until they bled and formed scabs. Now she lets me pluck them for her once or twice a week. She likes her eyebrow area bare and smooth, and puts a lot of energy into replacing them with brown shadow or eyebrow pencil.

Oct 22, 2020: FAIR SHARE

Tony and I were talking about how bored Asta must be since Covid. Although she declines invitations to go out on errands and outings, she might enjoy going out to eat on a regular basis. It would give her something to look forward to, something to think and talk about, and a reason to take a shower and wash her hair. She often offers to treat when we go out to eat but we don't want to take advantage. We presented her with an idea.

"Tony will pay for one week, I'll pay for the next, and you can pay for the third," I suggested.

"And when it's your turn to pay," Tony joked, "we'll be sure to go someplace expensive." He's been making this wise-crack for as long as I've known him. She's heard it many times in the two and a half years that she's lived with us.

When I later went in to check on her she was waiting for me, fretting over what her turn of paying for dinner will cost. "After all," she reasoned, "I don't eat much, and I don't want to have to pay for your drinks. I think we should all go Dutch."

There's no way I'll ask for a separate check for my mother. That would just be too weird. Nothing's easy.

Oct 30, 2020: EMERGENCY CALL SUPPORT

Asta called me into her room at 8 p.m. to show me her wastebasket, half-filled with bloody paper towels from a nosebleed.

"Tip your head forward, and pinch your nose," I said, reading instructions online for stopping nosebleeds. She was anxious, so we talked about going to the emergency room.

"I don't think we're looking at an emergency here. I don't know what they'd do for you there that you aren't already doing here now. They'd probably do a bunch of tests and tell you what you already know—that you have leukemia. Maybe they'd keep you overnight for observation. Again, I don't *think* we're facing an emergency at this moment, but if you want to go, of course I'll take you. Let's wait a little while and see if it stops by following the instructions."

The nosebleed subsided. I brought her a cup of tea and a banana. Ten or fifteen minutes later she called me back in. Her nosebleed had started again so she had pulled out some 'going to the hospital' clothes and was shaking with fear.

"Maybe fear is causing it to bleed more. Let's do some yoga breathing to calm your nerves," I said. Again, I didn't believe we were looking at an emergency room visit. She just needed to be patient and pinch her nose, no cheating. While she did that, I picked up her ukulele and song book and played one short familiar tune after another. Soon she was tapping her feet and singing along. The nosebleed stopped. I had her lay down, tucked her in, turned down the lights, promised to check on her during the night, and asked her to call me if it started up again. She slept well.

"If something were to happen before Rosalva arrived or after she left, and I was alone and afraid, what should I do?" she asked. She knows we don't leave her alone for more than four hours at a time.

"You have an emergency call button. If you're alone and it's an emergency, just push that button. Someone will talk to you through the pendant, and the paramedics will come." We periodically test the pendant so she knows how it works were she ever to press it on her own.

"And if I didn't think I needed to go to the hospital, who would I call?" she asked.

"You'd call me," I said. "We'll turn around from wherever we are and head home right away, and if I think we need an ambulance, I'll call one."

Nov 1, 2020: WHEELCHAIR READY

Yesterday morning, our neighbor June held a Covid-safe Halloween party, of sorts, at the end of her driveway and we'd been invited to drop by for a glass of cider, cupcake and candy. I escorted Mommy to the party at 8 a.m. before Tony and I left for our day trip. We brought her seated walker as she can no longer stand for any meaningful length of time. Because of the slight pitch to the driveway and the wheels on Ma's walker, June offered a chair, which she accepted. When it was time to transfer back to her seated walker, Asta quipped:

"And here I thought you were going to spoil me," meaning push her home in the seated walker. I'd love to have a wheelchair as an option, but for vanity's sake, she's resistant. Wanting her to keep walking for as long as possible, I haven't pushed the issue.

Nov 9, 2020: RESTAURANT FOR ONE

Asta was so weak yesterday morning that she needed my help to climb onto the bar stool at the kitchen counter. Her temperature was normal. Blood pressure, normal. No cough, no shortness of breath, no swollen extremities, no facial droop, no nothing that I could observe, but we were concerned nonetheless. She did not want to go to the ER.

"I'm going for my walk," I said.

Asta rolled her eyes and made a snarky remark, implying that I didn't care enough to stay home when she was ill.

"Do you need me to stay here with you at bedside?" I asked.

"No," she said.

"Okay. Tony is home, but you can call me if you need me. I could be home within minutes. Later, I'll be running an errand, so think about if there's anything you might want or need."

"Can't Tony go for you?" she asked.

"No, he can't," I said. I was planning to get my hair cut.

"I'll yust call de girls," she said, looking defeated.

"That's fine. I'll be back in 45 minutes." I sent a heads-up text to Elsa and Chris and within minutes received an answer from Elsa.

"Just spoke to Ma and asked her if she could have *anything in the world*, what would it be.... and she said, 'Steakad korv with potatoes and cream sås' (Fried sausage with potatoes and milk gravy)." As if I run a restaurant whose menu includes 'anything in the world.'

Her intentions might have been good, but how rude. "Tonight I'm making Uncle Andy's beef stew," I replied. Now the special dinner I had planned would disappoint Asta, because it wasn't her 'anything in the world.'

Ma stayed in bed until late afternoon, then ate a healthy helping of beef stew. After dinner I extended an invitation. "You're welcome to watch TV with me, but we'll be watching something other than politics," I said. I cannot stomach Fox News. She scowled at not having her way and her channel.

"Don't bodder to check on me tonight," she threw over her shoulder on her way back to her room. I will check on her anyway, of course.

In the morning, Asta was fine. Over breakfast she asked slyly, "Are you making kielbasa for dinner tonight?"

"We don't have kielbasa. I'm making steak on the grill tonight." She rolled her eyes and frowned. "Rolling your eyes?" I asked.

"No, no," she denied. "Could you make me cabbage soup?"

"Yes, I can make that today..."

Nov 26, 2020: INCIDENT REPORT

We finally replaced my mother's dorm-sized refrigerator in the garage with a full sized refrigerator. It provides more shelf space for her and allows us to store beverages in it.

2:30 a.m. Phone call. I went running.

"I hit my head on the door of the new refrigerator," Asta said.

"What happened?" I asked. Something about her explanation didn't make sense, but she grew annoyed when I asked for clarification. She seemed okay. I got her an ice bag and went back to bed.

3:30 a.m. Another call. I went running.

"I'd like another ice bag," she said. I provided it to her. She still seemed okay. "I'm going to tell you the trut. I went to the refrigerator for something and stumbled on the threshold in my doorway. I fell forward slowly and hit my head on the coffee table. I don't want to go to the emergency room. I'm okay."

"Ah, that makes more sense," I said. "You seem okay now, but we'll see how you are in the morning and I'll take you to a doctor."

"Did you raise the threshold in my doorway when the refrigerator was delivered?" she asked.

"No, we didn't," I said.

"I fell because it was dark," she said.

"That's very possible. Make sure you turn your light on when you're moving around in your room," I said.

At 6:30 a.m. she called me again. This time she was fully dressed.

"I'd like to go to the ER."

"Urgent Care opens at 7 a.m. I'll take you there then." Once we got there, we found that due to Covid, the hours had been changed. We waited outside. She sat in her seated walker.

"When they let us in, do you want to push me in on this?" she asked hopefully, indicating her walker.

"You probably want to show them you can walk. But we probably should be getting a wheelchair soon if you think you'd prefer to ride."

"I don't want a wheelchair because that would make me look sick."

"I understand, but a seated walker is not a wheelchair," I said. "We can postpone it for now."

She was evaluated and sent home with instructions to continue ice packs 3x/day and take Tylenol if desired. At home, I created a simple 'Incident Report' to track events, and notified Elsa and Chris.

Dec 1, 2020: MEDICAL UPDATE

"Ma's doctor called with the results of the tests she just underwent," I wrote in an email to Chris and Elsa, "and here are the findings:

- "Her heart is good, but she does have a narrowing of the aortic valve and a slight leakage that causes her to be tired. The other valve is also narrowed, which causes some pressure on the lungs. That's why she gets short of breath, which she hasn't noticed because but she doesn't move around very much. He said that's why her ankles swell up. She can/ should elevate her feet.
- "The arteries leading to her brain are 50% occluded on one side and 40% occluded on the other. Could lead to a stroke.
- "He recommends an angiogram—inserting a needle into the groin—to better assess the intervention options: e.g., valve repair, stint or medication. The angiogram would look for something they think they can fix. However, if Ma will refuse any surgical intervention, there's no point in having her undergo the angiogram. (If you're not willing to eat at the restaurant, why ask for the menu?)

"We made an appointment for January to discuss medication—how it would help, and what are its side effects."

Dec 2, 2020: SANTA LUCIA, REBOOT

"I want to do something similar to Junie's driveway Halloween party on December 13th in honor of Santa Lucia day," Asta announced. "And you will wear the Santa Lucia white gown."

Ugh. I'll do this for her, but I will not sing.

She then proceeded planning the event with Elsa. Elsa sent candies and construction paper for the woven paper heart baskets that Swedish children learn to make in grade school (or did 80 years ago).

Last night, we sat in the kitchen with our craft supplies spread out in front of us. She had forgotten how to do it, so I looked it up on YouTube. In this way we were able to make a few baskets while conversing.

"How about if we thank June for the inspiration when we call her with the invitation?" I asked.

"No, no, no, no, no," Asta said. "This is *ours*. Don't give away credit."

"Okay, I won't say anything."

"Don't give away credit," she said several times.

Each time I answered, "Okay, I won't. I won't say anything."

"Giving away credit to other people for your ideas shows you have no self-respect," she concluded.

"Okay, okay. I won't say a *fucking* word," I said. I shouldn't have used the word 'fucking.'

"Who Are You? Are you my Daughter?" she stabbed.

I wondered, how should I answer that question? I stepped away and returned a few minutes later.

"I'm sorry I used that word, Mommy. As you request, I will not tell anyone that this is in any way, shape or form similar to June's driveway Halloween party."

"*If* we even go through with it," she said. Asta is self-conscious of the bump on her head and the consequent fierce black eye that she sees when she looks in the mirror. If it has not resolved by party time, she may not want to make a public appearance. But we will prepare just in case.

So I set her up with pre-cut construction paper pieces (like kits) that she can weave into baskets at her leisure, or we can work on them together again later. We'll fill them with candy and give them away as Swedish gifts. I'll wear the white gown, carry the candle and serve the coffee and cookies in front of our house.

I still think it's rude not to acknowledge that June's party provided the inspiration. It's totally a copy-cat event.

Dec 19, 2020: DAILY LIFE

For the second time in two weeks, I had Asta keep me company while I baked cookies, it being the holiday season. We used one of the bottles of eggnog that Lisa had sent last Christmas to make eggnog snicker doodle cookies. The batter was tasty, and Asta licked both beater spinners clean while I prepared the dough for the oven.

This evening she wasn't feeling so well, so I took her temperature which measured a low grade fever of 99 degrees. She ate little for dinner so I squeezed 30 fresh tangerines into a tall glass of pulpy juice for her to drink right then, and put three small glasses in her fridge in case she wants it during the night.

I tucked her in with a warm corn dog at her feet and will check on her again before I go to bed.

Dec 26, 2020: THIRD CHRISTMAS

While outside sunning herself the other day, Asta noticed that her toes looked red and swollen. She called me to look at them. Two toes on her left foot were purple, and three toes on her right foot were purple and swollen.

"I don't want to go to the doctor today," she said. She never wants to go 'today'.

"I think we should get them looked at," I said.

"Do I *have* to go?" she objected.

"Well, I don't think you're going to die tonight if you don't, but if it were me, I'd go sooner rather than later." She consented, and I took her.

Although the doctor found no crack in her skin or place where bacteria could have entered, and Ma had no injury to her toes, she was given an antibiotic ointment and told to return in three days, Christmas Eve.

On her follow up appointment, the doctor said he wasn't convinced it was cellulitis because she had it bilaterally. The blood flow to her feet was good in both extremities and on both exams. She was prescribed a conservative measure of oral antibiotics and instructed to come back in seven days. Ma is insisting on keeping the medication in her room, and I am insisting on making sure she takes it as prescribed and with something to eat.

Since it was Christmas Eve, after her nap I had her take the lead in making the traditional rice porridge. She tired easily from the stirring, but enjoyed the work of it. I was right there to prevent her from leaning her arm too close to the flame. "Don't fuss over me," she protested. And at Tony, who was picking up the scarf she was dragging and stepping on, she snapped, "What do you take me for, a Shild?" And ultimately, her verdict: "It didn't turn out as good as it should have. We used a different brand of rice than I'm used to."

For our family Christmas Eve dinner, I made my dad's famous Swedish Viking Stew (see March 27, 2020) and baked a loaf of fresh bread to serve alongside. After dinner, we sat in front of the lit fireplace and opened presents. Asta was as excited for the boxes as for the gifts that came in them. Boxes in varying sizes come in handy for her organizing and packing activities. Tony and I gave her a few music CDs, two pairs of palazzo pants, a tube of lipstick, a screen for her door, notebooks, a wall calendar, hoop earrings and a package of her favorite black licorice.

For the last hour or two, she's been relaxing in the enclosed space outside our front door with the dog. She likes that I am right here at her elbow, so to speak, ready to meet her needs.

"Get me a bottle of water," she called. "Can you bring me my sunglasses and hat?" "Help me back to my room. I think I'd like to take a little nap before dinner."

What we are doing is not remarkable. Lots of people take care of their aging parents in whatever way suits their circumstances. I consider myself lucky to be able to take care of my mother at this stage of her life. We've fallen into a rhythm: I'm able to anticipate her needs and we seem to be managing the issues to everyone's satisfaction. And I credit the Covid pandemic for quieting the talk of and tug back to Woodstock. That, and being able to work from home have made my life infinitely easier, and hers that much more secure.

PART II

APRIL 2021—NOVEMBER 2022

CHAPTER 7
DECLINE

Apr 11, 2021: PNEUMONIA

By February 21, Asta had gotten both doses of the Pfizer Covid vaccine. Tony and I had gotten both of ours by March 28. But Ma had grown more tired, winded from walking only so far as to the bathroom. She needed an escort and more assistance in the shower. She was seen by a few different doctors in the interim and no concerns had been noted.

And then she fell. She had insisted on washing her hair at the sink as usual, assuring me she could stand long enough. But after the rinse, her legs gave out and she began to fall. I lowered her to the floor and called out to Tony. He came running and had her rest against him while I ran and unpacked the wheelchair we'd recently had delivered to have ready at a moment's notice. The moment had come.

The fall resulted in a couple of skin tears on her arms that we cleaned up and bandaged. Otherwise, she was not injured. We assisted her into the wheelchair and she loved not having to exert herself by walking with her leaden feet.

The next day we noticed a little cough, and she agreed to allow me to take her to Urgent Care where she was diagnosed with pneumonia and put on antibiotics. Pneumonia in an over-90 year old is a four-alarm fire. I called Elsa and Chris and agreed that Elsa would come out first. We're preparing for any eventuality.

Asta now needs mobility assistance with the wheelchair and assistance with dressing and toileting. She's embraced having the commode in her room at night, and is enjoying the ease of getting around in the wheelchair. She is down to 95 pounds. Her doctor offered a blood transfusion, but for now, she is refusing. She'll have another blood test in two weeks, and at that time we'll revisit the subject.

Apr 11, 2021: EMERGENCY VISITS

Elsa flew out for a few days and provided heavy doses of companionship to Asta, even assisting her with the shower. I let her take over during the daytime, but continued with nighttime safety checks and management of the commode. As for Elsa-drama issues, there were some.

"Hol flabben, hol flabben," (Swedish for 'shut up'), Elsa hushed Asta when I entered the room where they sat talking.

"Hol flabben?" I asked. "I'll come back later." I backed out of the room and retreated to my office. Elsa came out quickly, acting guilty-sweet and utterly innocent of whatever rude things they were saying that I interrupted. Not wanting any conflict, I allowed the saccharine charade to play out.

Later, nobody wanted to cook so we were discussing what takeout food Tony and I would bring home for the four of us.

"Let's get Kentucky Fried Chicken," Elsa suggested.

"I love it but haven't been able to eat it for years. Too much grease," I said.

Elsa appealed to Tony.

"I can't tolerate KFC. Digestive system issues," Tony said. "How about El Pollo Loco? That's a good fast food chicken alternative."

But then, as we were about to leave, Elsa pressed $40 into my hand. "*Please*," she implored, "*for me*."

We brought home Kentucky Fried Chicken for Elsa and Asta, and then Tony and I went out to eat. When we returned home, Elsa greeted us with the longest, loudest, sweetest, fakest, sing-songiest "Hiiiiiiiiiiiii" I've ever heard in my life. Using hand gestures, I motioned for her to please tamp down the performance.

Drama aside, she worked hard to take care of Mommy full time for the three-day duration of her visit. We all put away the knives and made the effort to get along.

Apr 14, 2021: HYGIENE ASSISTANCE

I've been encouraging Asta to keep me company now that I'm working from home. On this Wednesday morning, while resting on the couch in my office, she conjured up a story. In it, I was 'forcing' her to take a shower. She felt humiliated to be in need of assistance in the shower. But since Ronnie and Angi are coming on Thursday, she agreed to a receive help with one on Wednesday night.

She can no longer stand long enough to take a shower independently. Getting into the shower, she grabs onto the glass door, which makes me nervous. She was indignant that I replaced the wooden shower bench with her commode (sans bucket) because it has handles. Since she can no longer stand at the kitchen sink to wash her hair, I wash her hair in the shower. Whether she tips her head backward, like at the hairdresser, or forward covering her face with a towel is up to her. "Whichever you prefer," I said.

Asta insists on wearing her underwear into the shower, to protect her modesty.

"I think you're being silly. It's not like I've never seen one. I have one of my own."

She accused me of dragging her into a horrible experience. "Dis is what dey do to patients in mental hospitals," she said.

"I understand it's hard to deal with the fact that you can no longer take a shower on your own, and can no longer wash your hair at the sink. But it isn't the end of the world. Are you refusing

the shower? Because I'm not going to drag you in against your will."
She has the right to refuse a shower.

"No, because Ronnie and Angi are coming tomorrow," she said.

"Mommy, it's just a shower," I said. "Please, put it in perspective." She allowed me to assist.

May 26, 2021: CAREGIVING EXPENSES

For all practical purposes, Asta stopped walking after the pneumonia. She cannot, in her wheelchair, independently cross thresholds in doorways. We no longer leave her alone, unless it's for a very short neighborhood errand. Tony and I made plans for an outing.

"Someone will be here with you the whole time we're away," I said, "so that you will have support and won't have to be afraid."

"Who's paying for it," she asked. "Am I paying half?"

"Actually," I said, "you're paying for the whole thing." I don't want to lie anymore about who was paying. It's time she smelled the roses.

"You're rushing me to my death," she accused. "My money was not to be touched for my care until I'm bed-ridden from a stroke or something. I'm going to move to Elsa's. Elsa needs the money more. Why pay for care I don't want? If Chris is on board with paying for my companion, then I'll hire a lawyer." I wonder if someone might be coaching her to think in terms such as these.

I escorted her to her room. She called Elsa. I called Chris.

"Elsa is eager to bring Ma back to Woodstock," Chris said.

"That's nothing new. I don't think it's in Ma's best interest on any level," I answered.

"Elsa said she won't ask for any monthly financial contribution."

"I'll believe that when I see it," I said. Elsa is drunk in love with the idea of taking care of our mother for free.

Chris tried to talk rationally with Elsa: "I asked who would take care of Mommy when she has to go somewhere, and she said, 'Oh, there's Marty, Axel, Tom, or I'll hire somebody.' I asked 'Who will pay for that?' and she said 'Mommy will.' 'So how is that different from what Suey and Tony are doing?" I asked her. She had no answer for that."

"Good luck getting Ma to allow *any* male to help with her care," I said. We're all dancing around Asta like puppets, trying to do the impossible: make her happy. I'm tired of thinking about it. Tired of hearing Asta criticize California and fantasize about how great living with Elsa would be. Tired of fighting the fire on which Elsa keeps pouring gasoline.

I signed a contract with an Agency.

A few hours later, Chris emailed me: "Ma told Elsa she doesn't really want to move to Woodstock. Elsa was sad but relieved. Ma knows she has it good with her spacious room, and she loves the hospitals and medical care in California. She's also afraid of how quickly Elsa might come to the end of her rope, again."

I went into Ma's room for the usual bedtime routine: brought in the commode, administered her eye drops, delivered her snack and beverage, and so forth.

"Elsa's door will always be open, but I will be staying here," Asta said, "as long as you're not kicking me out."

"We'll *never* kick you out," I said. "You just have to accept that Tony and I are going to come and go a little."

"I talked with Chris and understand I'll be paying for caregivers, but I don't want to pay for your dinners out or other activities," she said.

"Tony and I pay all our own expenses. You will only pay for caregivers when we aren't home. We want you to be safe," I said, feeling the headwinds from all sides.

June 6, 2021: PRESERVING DIGNITY

Asta's room smelled of urine when I went in to get her up for the day.

"I opened a can of anchovies last night. That's why my room smells today," she covered.

"Yes, it does kind of smell this morning," I admitted. I emptied her commode and picked up her wet dress from the floor.

"I slept in that dress. It's on the floor because I poured water onto my hands and it spilled onto the floor, so I dropped the dress into it so I wouldn't slip on the water," she explained. Plausible.

"Good thinking," I said.

I did her laundry and gave her a shower.

June 23, 2021: FALL RISK

When I entered Asta's room to escort her over for dinner, she was reaching for her wheelchair and already lowering her butt to sit on it, though the seat was facing the other direction. Had I come in five seconds later, she would've been sitting on the floor. She's at very high risk for falls.

"Take another step closer before you lean forward," I urge, time and time again. "I don't want you to fall and get hurt."

"Ja, ja, ja. But don't even whisper *physical therapy* to the doctor," she demands. "I don't want it and I won't do it."

July 6, 2021: TEAMWORK

Last night we took Asta to see the fireworks in Rancho Mirage. We met Floyd and Louise there and positioned Ma next to Louise so the two of them could talk. Tony hung out with Floyd. I moved around, took pictures and bought a souvenir.

"Let's stop for a hot dog," Asta said on our way home. Outings aren't complete unless they include a bite to eat. We went to Applebee's. It was packed, but they found us a wheelchair-friendly table quickly.

"When will you be going back to usher at the theater?" Asta asked over half-price appetizers.

"We won't be ushering this year," I said.

"Why not?" she asked. I hesitated.

"Because we can't leave you alone for the length of time it would take, and we'd have to go two or three times a week," Tony said. "I'm okay with it."

"I don't need you to stay home. After all, I sleep a lot," Asta said, "and you did it before."

"Yes," I said, "but you were more independent then." I'll be returning to the office in the mornings, and Tony will be refereeing some afternoons, but one of us will usually be home with her. Maybe she had a glimmer of awareness that we are in fact arranging our lives around her and her needs.

"I might live to 100…" she warned, inviting us to send her away.

"We're prepared for that," I answered.

"… and Elsa would take me in a heartbeat," she said.

"Moving is hard on people half our age. It wouldn't be good for you to make a big move again," Tony said. We're on the same page, Tony and I. I'm grateful for and proud of him.

Aug 6, 2021: TICKING TIME BOMB

Tony has been driving us to Asta's medical appointments to help me load and unload the wheelchair. His dropping us off and picking us up close to the entrance helps a lot. There have been a lot of appointments lately.

Currently, Ma has an infection caused by decay under her bridge and is facing a tooth extraction. She wanted reassurance that the extraction would not cause her carotid artery to burst, so we scheduled an appointment to find out.

"The ticking time bomb is your heart valve, not your carotid artery," her cardiologist said. "I recommend a new heart valve. It would be inserted through the groin and you'd be home the next day."

"I'm not feeling any symptoms," Asta said.

"That's because you're sitting in a wheelchair, not exerting the effort to move around. If you were to move around, you would feel chest pain, dizziness and shortness of breath. With a new heart valve you'd feel less tired, have more energy, and would be able to resume walking," he said.

"I have no intention of walking again," she said, "because of my feet."

"The procedure is not without risk, and I can't say how much longer you would live, given your leukemia and age," he said. "Take some time to consider this option and come back to see me next month. Meanwhile, your heart is not a barrier to getting your teeth taken care of. Go ahead and get that done."

Asta is optimistic that she'd survive a new heart valve procedure, but since it won't restore her ability to walk or reverse her blindness, and it comes with a risk of stroke, she's asking the reasonable question, "What for?"

"Maybe," she persisted, "I should yust live out the rest of my life, however short or long that might be, happily ever after without a heart valve replacement."

"Some people who come to crossroads such as these," I said, "choose hospice, which means they have all their care managed by one doctor whose purpose is to keep them as comfortable as possible."

"I'm not ready for that yet," she said. Confirmation that my efforts are aligned with her wishes.

Tony and I will support whatever decision she makes. Our focus right now is on getting her teeth taken care of so she can eat.

I sent a summary of the appointment to Elsa and Chris, and soon Chris set up a Zoom meeting for the three of us sisters to talk. In the meeting, we agreed to let Ma make the decision, and we agreed to have a Zoom meeting with Asta in attendance, so she can see that her daughters are talking and getting along.

CHAPTER 8

NO TURNING BACK

Aug 8, 2021: COLLAPSE OF THE HOUSE OF CARDS

Chris visited last weekend and witnessed how rudely Asta treated me with sarcastic comments and faces. Asta didn't trust me to satisfactorily put together the party for three friends we'd invited over. In her view, I'm not entertaining enough, don't know how to put on a proper Swedish spread, and don't know how to set the stage. I talk too fast, move too fast and work too much. I hire companions against her will at her expense. Like I'm the enemy.

In recent weeks, while Rosalva's been out of the country, I've had the agency send someone three times. Each time, they sent someone new. Three delightful and competent young women. Last weekend, I hired my friend Betty. The two of them got along very well. Every caregiver we've had has been top-notch. I'm juggling their availability and cost.

"Your companion this Saturday will be Betty again," I informed Asta.

"No!" Asta erupted. "I want the agency girl, Jeanette, who was here with me yesterday. I don't want Betty. I should have some say. Cancel Betty and bring back Jeanette."

"No." I wasn't going to undo what I'd gone to the trouble of arranging just because she felt like throwing a tantrum.

"I want out of here," she said, coopting another one of Elsa's phrases, and demanded to be taken to her room. Five minutes later the texts started flying.

"Just got off the phone with Ma," Elsa wrote. "If it's only a matter of making a phone call or two, couldn't you *please* try to arrange for the new girl, who she *really* likes, to spend the night instead of the other lady? It would make a difference in how she feels…" Elsa wants to make me do cartwheels.

"Two weeks ago she wanted Betty," I answered. "When you're in charge of her care, maybe you can satisfy her expectations. Don't construe this to mean I'm advocating for her to move, *because I'm not.* Betty will be here Saturday from 8:30-4:30, Rosalva will stay overnight the following weekend, and the next time I have to call the agency, I'll ask for Jeanette." Statement of fact.

"You need a vacation!" Elsa wrote.

"She's brutal towards Tony, and I could use my life back," I admitted, "but we're still willing to put it on hold." Tony and I talk about how we're making good causes and earning good karma, but at this point, frankly, I'm tired of painting a happy face on a difficult situation, and tired of the emotional gymnastics required to stay afloat.

The two of them pounced, like cats on a mouse at the corner of No and Return.

"We'll do the right thing and move her," Chris wrote. "Better late than never."

"I'm ready to retire anyway. My only worry is how soon I can fly out there," Elsa wrote.

"She has to be willing," I said, "and there's no rush. But I'll be going back to the office in December, and she'll fight me on that."

"I'll start looking into how to make my house better. I'll remodel my bathroom and build a ramp to the driveway," Elsa said.

"Lower bed, shower bench, toilet seat handles," I listed, "are little things. I want her to be happy. Same thing the two of you want." I so regret this moment, the one in which I gave up.

"Buckle your seatbelts!" Elsa texted.

Elsa is eager to play Florence Nightingale, Mother Theresa, Joan of Arc and Amelia Earhart all at once. Maybe Elsa can fatten her up with donuts and pound cakes, potatoes and gravy. Maybe they'll gossip and play all day. Me, I've run out of words and am tired of games. More than anything, I'm tired of competing with Elsa. The writing is on the wall. I've lost.

Aug 9, 2021: STOP THE TRAIN

Tony too had expressed frustration with Asta's tantrums and her constraints on our movement, so I was surprised by his reaction to the news that she would be leaving. He was furious. "It's insane to make her move across the continent at 93 years old and frail, back into Elsa's care," he said.

"Really?" I asked. "You think it would be best for her to stay? Is that what you're saying? Because I need to hear you say it."

"Yes," he hollered. "I want what's best for her. All I want is for her not to complain about your care or what we offer her here. All I want is to be able to go out on a date with you once a week, and for us not to have to catch hell for it from her or your sisters. That's it. That's all I want. It's crazy to move her back. You're all crazy to even consider it."

"Okay, then. Let's turn this train around," I said, and went in to see my mother and sat down.

"Mommy, I just told Tony you were leaving, and he just about hit the ceiling. He thinks you should stay here where you have such good doctors and excellent care. He just doesn't want you to complain about me," I said.

"I really don't want to leave all my good doctors out here and the fabulous Eisenhower system, either," Asta said. "I understand that I'll have the same problems there—being blind, unable to walk, and with a heart problem—but I like the idea of being able to visit Daddy's grave, and I like the idea of having the hospice nearby where Daddy died, in case I need it myself." She's willing to move for "husfriden's skull" (for the sake of peace in the home).

Tony came in behind me and said his piece. "I just want to go out with my wife and not have to feel guilty about it. We'll make arrangements with five-star people so you're not alone when we go out. And then when we come home you can ask us, 'How was your date? Did you have a good time? Tell me about it,' instead of complaining how long we were gone, or whether we're bringing in this caregiver or that one to take care of you. Elsa can't do what Suey does. It would be insanity for you to move there. We'll take care of you if you live to be 100. I just want to go out with my wife."

"He's got a point," I said to Ma. "You even said so yourself that you'd be better off staying here. He too wants you to stay, for your sake."

"It's too late," Mommy said.

"It's not too late," I said. "No construction has started, no tickets have been bought yet." Tony and I called Chris together.

"Why wasn't I included in the discussion?" he demanded.

"She's *our* mother," Chris said.

"But she's been living my house for three years," he yelled. Tony is my hero for fighting on Asta's behalf. Unfortunately, he threw expletives around to press his point, eliminating any chance of effective communication between them. I took the phone back into my possession.

"I'm changing my position," I told Chris, "We're advocating together that she stays."

"The battle over moving Mommy isn't over," she said.

Aug 10, 2021: THE FIGHT

"Mommy is all over the place," Elsa wrote in an email. "She needs to be reassured that the three of us are on the same page about her moving back to Woodstock. Are we? In one breath she says she will stay out of all the decision making, and in the next says she needs more time. I agree that we should wait till she has healed from getting her teeth pulled. In the meantime, I have already started looking into how to make my house handicapped accessible. She'll be happier here, if only for the weather."

The weather excuse is baloney. Here, we are entering gorgeous temperatures; there, they are entering winter.

"We are on the same page that we want what's best for her," I answered. "I'm sorry I led you both to believe I'd go along with moving her. Instead, I've decided to fight for her to stay. Tony is 100% for her staying, because it's what's best for *her*. So let's stop the train and go back to the station."

"The train has already left the station," Elsa wrote. "There are only three of us that get to make these decisions. You and Tony do not get to decide unilaterally what's best for Mommy. There will have to be more conversations down the road. And I too, am willing to fight for what's best for her." Elsa was determined to win.

Chris put in her two cents. "I agree that Tony should not be involved in our decision. She's not his mother, so he doesn't get a vote."

How is it that Chris—who was never willing to have Asta live with her—gets a vote, whereas Tony—who helped take care of her in his/our house, sacrificed his freedom and tolerated her criticism for three and a half years—does not? He's been a member of the family for 35 years. For them to dismiss him as irrelevant is profoundly disrespectful.

It isn't easy taking care of a dependent parent who complains (a lot). It's many times harder when the good work that's being done is undermined.

Tony and I agreed to stop talking to Elsa and Chris about the move. Anything we had to say on the subject we would say to Asta. She can relay to them whatever she wants. We don't want to participate in the fiasco of moving her back to live with Elsa. At the very least, I will try to ensure that Asta has a voice, and a choice, after all.

Asta called me crying. She had just hung up from a phone call with Elsa and wanted to talk. Tony accompanied me to hear what she had to say. Interestingly, the tears dried up the moment she saw Tony.

"Elsa is making all the arrangements and all she has to do is…" blah, blah, blah, she said. "And Heidi is skinny and has no teeth. I want to go see Heidi."

"It's deplorable that Elsa is playing the Heidi card," I said. "Elsa will bulldoze anybody who doesn't give her anything she wants."

"We think you should stay here, and we want you to stay here," Tony said. "We will take care of you. We won't be arguing with Elsa and Chris."

"They're rushing me," she said. "Elsa has already asked Lisa to fly with me to New York. I have to ask Lisa to slow Elsa down. I don't want to be rushed."

"There's no rush," I told her. "You don't have to go anywhere."

"If we thought that Elsa would take care of you, we'd be okay with it," Tony said. "But experience doesn't support that."

I called Chris.

"I want Mommy to be able to reach for the brass ring of happiness with Elsa," Chris said, "even if it's only a mirage. I understand that Mommy won't be happy wherever or with whomever she lives, but she should be able to go and die wherever she wants. For her to get closure, she needs to live out her final months or years with Elsa. Elsa won't accept any money—no monthly stipend, no funding for remodeling her bathroom or building a ramp, no contribution to the household food budget."

"I don't buy that for a minute, Chris," I said. "I don't care about Mommy's money, but it is fantasy to think that Elsa will do it for nothing."

"Mommy is aware of the risks she's taking," Chris said, "and she's scared. But she's been so bamboozled by Elsa's persuasiveness that she wants to go anyway. It's over, Suey. Don't force her to stay for the sake of care. She has the right to make the decision to move cross-country in pursuit of happiness."

"I think it's irresponsible to move her cross-country at this stage of her life and in her condition," I said. "How can you orient yourself towards happiness if first you're not safe and secure? Her needs for safety and security should be met first. Any happiness she can find would be a bonus."

So, we disagreed on what's most important, but Asta won't be held against her will—even if her will is just a carbon copy of the fiction Elsa's been feeding her for three and a half years.

I went in to speak with Asta. "You be sure to keep your voice and let people know you're still sharp," I said.

"How am I going to do that?" she asked, looking at me with resignation.

"I have no idea," I said, "Elsa is very domineering."

I have deliberately not sought a diagnosis of dementia for Mommy. Although she most certainly has it, she is entirely capable of expressing her wishes and preferences. A diagnosis of dementia would cause her to lose credibility in doctors' offices and in hospital. I predict Elsa will seek the diagnosis as soon as possible so that she can make decisions for Mommy.

"Why don't you postpone the move until spring," I encouraged, "so you won't have to deal with snow and ice on Elsa's driveway?" But my suggestion fell on deaf ears.

"I will ask my doctors whether they think it's safe for me to fly," she said.

"Great idea," I said. "Let's see what they say."

Aug 13, 2021: WORRY WART

"I'm sorry for throwing a tantrum about having Betty come over this weekend," Asta said while floating in the pool. "I understand that it opened the floodgates. That was not my intent. But now that the ball is rolling, I'm going with it. I like Betty and look forward to spending time with her this weekend."

We talked about the great team of people we've put in place to help us take care of her here: Rosalva, Betty, Jeanette. "Too bad you're leaving it behind. You'll have to start from scratch at Elsa's," I said.

It will give me no satisfaction to say 'I told you so' when something happens, either as a direct consequence of the trip, or when Elsa discovers she's bitten off more than she can chew. The tragedy is, this 'experiment' will be at Mommy's mortal expense.

"Don't worry," Mommy said.

"I can worry if I want to," I said.

"Try not to worry," she tried to reassure.

"I am going to worry. Elsa's not equipped for the job," I answered.

We talked about the different points of view:

- 'Safety and security' in which Ma can have confidence
- 'Happiness,' on which she can't count.

Yet she is choosing to take the risk. Maybe for the adventure, or for the project. Maybe it's her 'last hurrah.'

But first, her tooth extraction followed by a period of healing. One foot in front of the other.

Aug 15, 2021: BEST FOR WHO

There is no question that Tony and I would benefit by Asta's return to New York in the sense that we'd be regaining our freedom, yet we're the ones advocating for her to stay. Chris and Elsa are adamant that she move. Asta wants her doctors to tell her whether or not it's safe for her to fly with her leukemia and heart condition.

"You can stay if you want," Tony and I assured Asta. "We want you to make the decision on your own, without undue influence from anyone, including Chris and Elsa."

"I want to do what's best for everyone," Asta said.

"That's very nice of you to think of everyone else first," I said. "Just don't forget to think about what's best for you."

Later, Ma tried to reel me into a conversation about what Elsa or Chris had said. I extricated myself. "We don't have to keep having this conversation over and over again," I said. "You know where we stand. Whatever you decide, we'll support." I walked backwards towards the door and made my escape. She's got everything she needs for the night.

Her life is perilously close to the edge, and I don't want to push her over it. I'd rather walk with her down the hill. Tony and I can wait. Elsa, greedy for redemption or maybe impatient for her little bit of inheritance, apparently can't. Chris's judgement is clouded by the two fingers of 'happy' that Asta and Elsa have been pouring through the phone lines for the past three years.

Aug 22, 2021: AGITA

"Hello Sisters!" Elsa's email began. "I've been looking into ways to make my house handicapped accessible, and a company is coming over to give some advice. In the meantime, here is a cheap way to make your house more wheelchair-friendly. Installing this, or something like it, will help Mommy feel less isolated and more independent, and will take some of the pressure off Suey if Mommy can get around better on her own. Chris, you said that Ma doesn't have the strength in her arms to push her chair onto a ramp. Well then, let's look into a small motorized wheelchair. Since money is not a concern, let's spend some on her!" She attached an internet link.

In addition to not being strong enough to push a wheelchair up a slight incline, Mommy is essentially blind and would be unable to safely maneuver a motorized wheelchair, with or without ramps.

"Elsa, double check your house too," Chris answered, "because the door from the garage opens *in*. There's no way she could open the door at the top of the ramp and then wheel herself *up* the ramp."

I will not be responding to this idiocy. If Ma survives the trip and the first few weeks after landing, she will be as mobility-dependent there as she is here.

Aug 24, 2021: REASONS TO STAY

Asta asks me sometimes to play her voicemail messages for her because it's hard for her to move, hard to see. This one was a voice message from Elsa.

"I'm having a dental procedure done to prepare for an implant," Elsa said on the recording, "so I'll be uncomfortable and probably won't be able to call you for a day or two. Axel will be sleeping over here to help me while I recover from the procedure."

I asked Chris, "If Elsa will be so incapacitated by a dental implant that she won't be able to talk (or walk, cook, escort, or assist) and will need someone to stay at her house to take care of her, how on earth will she be able to take care of Mommy?" It keeps me up at night.

I envision Asta moving into Elsa's house and shortly thereafter being moved into an assisted living facility or a nursing home, where Elsa, with her connections, will waltz in, in full make-up, and pull rabbits out of hats to all the staff and residents' delight and entertainment. She will be the star of the show and will glow in the spotlight. Elsa will push anyone out of her way to get applause.

"As Power of Attorney, I won't allow Elsa to move her into congregate care," Chris said, but she's dreaming. I know how the system works. And so does Elsa's daughter, Lisa.

I escorted Asta to the patio and helped her put her feet into the pool. When she was ready, I helped her out of her dress and into my t-shirt so she could move a step deeper into the water. She enjoyed the scenery, the setting, the temperature, everything. We talked about how the weather is starting to cool down, and how we'll be squeezing fresh orange juice from our trees in two months' time. We agreed that last year's fresh pulpy orange juice may very well have kept her alive.

Inside, we sat having ice cream. "What would you like for your birthday next month?" she asked.

"Nothing," I said. "I can't think of anything."

"No, seriously," she said. "What would you like for your birthday? There must be something."

I thought for a moment and answered, "For you to stay."

Aug 25, 2021: KNOWING, ACCEPTING THE SYSTEM

Asta will let her doctors decide. If they say it's safe for her to fly, she'll go. The trip is only the first page of the final chapter of her life, but it's hardly the biggest problem with her returning to New York State.

"Maybe the time has come to make it happen," she conjectured. "We've been talking about it for three years."

"I won't hate you for moving back east," I said. I love my mother. She's got enough to worry about without having to worry about my feelings and me.

"I'm worried that something will happen to Elsa," she said, "like if she fell on the steps to the basement or something." A mother always wants to protect her child. It will be just the two of them in the house.

"Get in the habit of wearing your Lifeline button so you can call for help if either of you should need it," I said, giving Asta a sense of security and control. "And be on the lookout that Elsa might try to talk you into moving in with the nuns."

"If I put it in writing," she said, "Elsa won't be able to do that."

"It doesn't work that way," I explained. I tried to educate her on the levels of care—hospitals, rehabs, nursing homes, assisted living—and how none of those stops need be viewed as 'bad'. Each has their place and function along the continuum of care.

Dementia is another concern of hers, so as part of the education I downloaded and administered to her the 30 question mini-mental test. Granted, I'm untrained and may have been lenient because she's my mother, but she scored a surprising 29 out of 30.

"You passed with flying colors," I praised. "Don't let Elsa convince you or anyone else that you have dementia." She couldn't wait to call Elsa to brag.

Asta understands the risks of moving in with Elsa but wants to go anyway. Hoping her move will be successful, I offered her this advice:

"(1) Don't fight paying for the helpers, (2) Try to adapt to change (e.g., getting in and out of the tub) with less fight, and (3) Help yourself to whatever's in Elsa's refrigerator so that you can retain a little independence." She probably won't remember, however.

Aug 29, 2021: TALK ABOUT FAMILY

"Call me when you get a chance," Rosalva texted. "I want to fill you in on my visit with your mom. She gave me an earful last night about feeling locked up and about you and Tony. I told her, 'You have no right to judge their marriage,' and 'My mother would never say such hurtful things to me. She would never talk to me the way you talk to your daughter.' Your mom got very angry with me. She feels she has every right to say whatever she thinks, no matter how hurtful."

It's understandable that Asta would feel locked up when the thresholds keep her from wheeling herself out of her room.

"She doesn't trust me," Rosalva continued, listing her observations. "She doesn't believe what I'm saying. She doesn't want to hear anything different from her own opinion. She's very angry. She's so stubborn. She's not rational," and "She makes a lot of faces."

"Yes, I'm familiar with those faces," I said, not wanting to hear anyone criticize my mother. "I'm holding onto the memory of my mother as she used to be. She was a wonderful mother, vibrant, creative. This loss of independence is very difficult for her."

I called Chris. "Elsa's willingness to take care for Ma will likely evaporate pretty quickly, and I just want you to know that I won't object to the idea of assisted living in Woodstock, if or when it comes to that. Mommy might enjoy congregate living."

"Maybe they should invent a new way of taking care of people in their old age," Chris said. "Something affordable."

"They already have," I said. "It's called 'family'. The challenge is in getting the family to work together."

Sept 8, 2021: ASSISTED LIVING TOURS

I decided to educate my mother on Assisted Living. Maybe if she knows what to expect, it won't be so traumatic if Elsa moves her into one. I went ahead and scheduled tours at two such communities locally.

"What do you think of my idea?" I asked Tony.

"You might want to hold off on telling your sisters. Make the tours seem spontaneous for your mom, and have an email prepared in advance that you can send to your sisters the moment you get home."

I kept the tours secret until after her cardiology appointment and we were back in the car.

"I want you to see what assisted living looks like. It's not what you think, where people line the hallways and drool. Nor is it a place where people have to be independent. I've made appointments for us to have tours at two places. We're on our way to the first one now."

To my surprise, she didn't protest. First we toured one, then the other. At each, she saw residents gathered socially and companionably in common spaces. She expressed interest in and asked thoughtful questions of both of our tour guides. She decorated the rooms in her mind's eye and analyzed which place she liked better and why, and was surprised to learn that she could afford to live in either facility with her income and savings for as many as four years.

"But I will get it for free at Elsa's," she concluded. She has already started packing.

"I just want you to understand that if it gets too tough for Elsa, or if it wasn't working for either of you for some reason, assisted living would be a good option, one that you shouldn't and needn't be afraid of." As soon as we got home, I emailed my sisters.

"Hi Goils. Today I took Ma to see two assisted living communities here in Palm Springs. Although I would love for her to stay in this area with her excellent medical team intact and where I can continue to oversee her care, it is not my agenda to persuade her to stay, but rather to introduce her to the option of assisted living, should she (or you) need it or want it down the road."

"It looks like you did this with the best of intention, but…" blah, blah, blah, blah, blah, Elsa wrote, and "I will appreciate your advice when Mommy is living with me." Maybe I'll send her instructions on what she should cook to cure Ma's heart/blood/vision/hearing/ kidney/walking problems, and see how she appreciates that.

"Elsa was horrified that you took me there," Asta said, "and shocked when I told her I'd found it interesting and informative."

"I really don't care what Elsa thinks," I said.

Chris, sensing my struggle, tried to make me feel better with an invitation. "Maybe you and I should meet somewhere mid-continent sometime in 2022 for a weekend, just the two of us."

"Not ready to make plans just yet," I said. "Gotta recover from … this."

I am fighting bad attitudes, including my own, everywhere I turn. That I've lost some weight over the past few weeks doesn't have to be a bad thing. I'll get my appetite back later, and my enthusiasm.

CHAPTER 9
FINAL WEEKS

Sept 9, 2021: DOORMAT

"Asta has made it clear that she wants you all to herself," Tony said. He's been avoiding her since the November 13th date for her move was set. "She doesn't want a man around, so I'm giving her what she wants. I'm not being rude and nasty to you, but I'm not going to sit at the dinner table and pretend everything is fine. I don't care what your sisters think of me, and I don't need anyone telling me what a jerk I am. You take these next ten weeks and give your mother 100%. I'll take care of myself and stay out of everyone's way. This is the best I can do under these circumstances."

At 8 p.m., after Asta and I had watched an hour of TV together (through most of which she snored), I escorted her to her room. I was tired and had to get up early in the morning for work.

"So early?" she objected. "I assume the Big Baby wants you to be with him." She's angry with Tony for withdrawing.

She refused a stop on the way at the bathroom, so we went directly to her room. I performed my duties in her bedtime rituals and tended to her night-time needs. Then I laid down, exhausted, to read for a few minutes. Soon, I heard rustling and muttering in the hallway. She had gotten out of her wheelchair and used her walker to get to the bathroom.

"What a doormat you are," she announced, loudly enough to ensure that both Tony and I, who were in different rooms for the moment, would hear. Ignoring her rudeness, I wished her good night.

"Natti-natti (nighty-night), Mamma," I said. "See you in the morning."

"Ja," she spat, "god nat."

Maybe I'll have a doormat made that reads: "Doormats United," or make a bunch and see if they would sell. Perhaps there are others out there like me who are thirsty for dry comic relief.

Sept 10, 2021: CAR ACCIDENT

I sealed up the first three of Asta's boxes in front of her so she could witness me tape them securely, then drove to a Mailbox store and sent them FedEx to Elsa's. An hour later I got a call from Chris.

"Elsa was in a car accident last night and is currently in the hospital for observation," Chris said. "Her knee is banged up and she has a brain bleed. It's still possible that Ma will be able to live with her, though." I sensed a postponement coming, like a wave about to capsize my kayak.

"Ma's staying here beyond November 13th is no longer an option," I said. "But there is always assisted living." Chris balked. "If not assisted living," I continued, "she could move in with you. Just sayin'… in case her move to Woodstock goes sideways."

"Let's wait to hear how Elsa is first," Chris said. Pollyanna hopes Elsa will be able to lift Mommy's wheelchair in an out of her car and push her up and down ramps. She expects Elsa to bear the weight of Mommy's emotional demands when she herself is recovering from trauma.

"Visit the Assisted Living facilities in your area," I urged. "Educate yourself on how they look and feel. Honestly, I think Assisted Living would be the most loving choice for both of them."

Sept 14, 2021: FRAGMENTATION

Asta kept me company while I prepared and served a fairly elaborate dinner which she then barely touched, saying she wasn't hungry. During dessert and conversation, and while I cleared the table and tidied up, she began her critical and judgmental descent down the now all-too-familiar rabbit hole. I made an excuse and escaped to my bedroom briefly to assess and reassemble any fragments that might be coming unglued.

I escorted her to the bathroom and waited across the hall for 15-20 minutes while 'nothing happened' (no bowel movement) before resuming the escort to her room. Being backed in her wheelchair over the threshold, Asta saw Tony's and my open bedroom door.

"Oh, is Baby in his room?" she asked, and adding one more kick for good measure, "Or is Baby at a ball game?" I paused for a moment.

"I'll pretend I didn't hear that," I said somberly. She must know she's being rude and nasty. I don't want a big fight, or a small one. I won't miss this side of my mother.

Meanwhile, Chris sent a text. "I spoke to Elsa in the hospital," she wrote. "She wants you to know she loves you very much. I love you very much too."

"Yeah, well, Elsa's on some pretty good drugs right now. What's your excuse?" I joked.

Not catching my humor, or not knowing how better to respond, she gave a 'Hallmark artificial' answer and we awkwardly ended the conversation.

Sept 15, 2021: OLIVE BRANCH

I called Elsa to see how she's doing post-accident. When she heard it was me, she started bawling.

"Aw, don't do that. You'll ruin your make-up," I said.

"I'm black and blue and sore all over, but when I meditated yesterday, I felt an overwhelming calm and reassurance that I'll be okay," she said. "I should have died," she added dramatically.

"No, you shouldn't have, because Ma is on her way," I said.

"I'm looking forward to having her join me. How is she treating you?" she asked.

"She can be tough," I admitted, "but I didn't call to talk about Ma. I wanted to hear how you are doing."

"Not great, but okay," she said. "The good news is I can walk and am preparing for Mommy's arrival."

It was nice to hear her voice and to talk to with her for a bit. Getting ready to pass the torch. Honestly, I just want peace.

Sept 22, 2021: CREATING MOMENTS OF JOY

When Tony and I returned home from our day trip this weekend, Asta was lying on the couch and Rosalva was sitting in the kitchen. "I have a headache," Ma said, looking completely and utterly miserable.

"Want to keep us company in the kitchen while I put together a little snack?" I invited.

"No," she said. She's been refusing all my invitations of late. I took her word at face value and visited with Rosalva for a while. Once Rosalva had gone, I tried again.

"At least come outside for a while. You can rest on the poolside lounge." I gave her a fresh glass of juice to sip while I took a dip in the pool, and after drying off I brought out my ukulele and song books and played several songs for her. She always feels better when she hears music.

"At least you got a little fresh air," I said as we headed back into the house.

"And some music," she added.

"What could be better than that?" I asked. Here we are in this moment, with two things, at least, to be grateful for.

Two days later, we did it again, only this time I also draped my roll-up piano keyboard over her lap and brought out her old harmonica. And gave her a Popsicle (hydration). With a Popsicle in one hand and the keyboard under her other, she played along while I strummed the ukulele. For the finale, she performed a harmonica solo (a workout for her heart and lungs), which I video-recorded on my phone. A treasure.

Sept 24, 2021: FANGS AND WOUNDS

"I have a *big surprise* for Tony before I leave… and he's *not* going to like it," Asta announced through gritted teeth as I escorted her to her room.

"What do you mean?" I asked. She refused to elaborate. Awake at 1 a.m., I saw that her light was on, so I went in to talk about it.

"What were you threatening?" I asked.

Denial, denial.

"Whatever you do to Tony, you know, you do to me," I said.

Denial, denial.

"Your words and the tone of your voice were clearly a threat," I added. Finally she came up with something.

"I'm not going to give him a present when I leave," she said.

"Oh. No problem. He's not expecting one. Thank you for clarifying," I said, and went back to bed.

In the morning, she did not want breakfast in the kitchen, so I delivered her meal on the silver tray and went about my business—took a walk, ran errands with Tony, ran errands for her—with an upset stomach. I called Chris.

"I feel hurt by both you and Elsa. Knowing that Ma can be difficult, you both should have supported me in taking care of her. Instead, Elsa fanned the flames of discontent for three and a half years. And now the two of you have made the decision to move her to a new environment where she'll have to learn new routines. I'm still the best equipped to do the job."

"It was Ma's decision," Chris said.

"That's bullshit. Elsa talked her into it, and you endorsed it. It won't be better for Asta in Woodstock; it'll be worse."

"Give it a chance," she said.

I cried over the torment Ma has put me through with her chronic complaints and blamed it all on her daily gossip sessions with Elsa.

"I'm worried about you and the stress you're under," Chris said.

"Good, I'm glad somebody's worried about me." I said. I can't cry to Tony. It would just arouse his anger over the decision to move Asta. I'm dangling at the end of my rope.

"What can I do to help?" she asked.

"Replace texting with phone calls and conversations," I said. "I'm so sick of texting. It's good for sharing facts and information, but lousy for relationship maintenance."

"I can do that," she said.

"And make amends with Tony somehow, someday. He believes everybody blames him for Ma's failure to embrace living here, and he's angry with you for making the decision to send her back. But don't reach out now. Make it later," I said. "Right now we need time to heal."

"I'll try to come up with something," she said.

Oct 1, 2021: WINNERS AND LOSERS

I took Ma to the casino for my birthday. Not because I wanted to go, but because it was important to her that we celebrate my birthday, and because I knew she would enjoy it. We brought Rosalva along to help, and each of us gave Rosalva $20 to play.

I pushed Asta in her wheelchair from one one-armed bandit to another, looking for one that made a lot of noise and that didn't cost an arm and a leg.

"We're doing something wrong," she complained, blaming me for not finding a winning machine. She'd spent her $40, so I put in mine and asked her to play it for me.

"After all, you're luckier than me," I said. It didn't take any arm-twisting. She gladly pushed Play on my behalf.

When that $40 was gone, it was time for dessert, her treat. On the table sat a promotion that entitled us to $25 in free play.

"Let's stay a little longer tonight and see if we win anything on their nickel," I suggested. So after dessert, we did exactly that. Played a little bit longer.

This time, the three of us took turns pushing the button. Each time the machine made noise, that person got an extra push. Asta, being impulse-control compromised, snuck in a few extra pushes, having fun. We went home collectively $120 poorer, but my birthday was a night to remember.

Oct 12, 2021: TOO LATE TO TURN BACK NOW

"Elsa is promising lots of fun outings in the country, crafts at the dining room table, company coming and going, but she said it doesn't look like she'll be retiring after all," Asta said, worrying who will keep her company while Elsa is at work.

Of course Elsa believes she will be able to entertain Ma with activities and outings, and for a while, maybe she will… until Ma resists because she is tired, or doesn't want to get dressed or bathed. Elsa will have people coming and going, and at least some of them will be paid companions.

"I don't want to be dragged around against my will, and Elsa doesn't take no for an answer," Asta said. "She said she'd retire to be with me full time. I'm glad I'll be bringing my LifeLine system. I may need it when she's not home. I don't think she'll be able to give me as good medical care and support as I get here, but it's too late to change my mind now." She added, "And Elsa has decided to accept a monthly financial contribution."

"Well, it's reasonable for you to make a monthly contribution to the household expenses," I said.

Then, unable to resist the temptation to demonize whatever man happens to be by her daughter's side, Asta started criticizing Elsa's boyfriend, Tom.

"Don't do it, Ma. Don't start bad-mouthing him. It's partly up to you to make it work."

Oct 17, 2021: SEPARATION AND GRIEF

"Let me ask you something," Asta said when I went in to empty her commode. "What will happen to Rosalva?"

"What do you mean? Why do you ask?" I thought she might be asking if we were going to invite Rosalva to live in Asta's room after my mother moved out, but then again, I wasn't sure what she was asking. She was itching to say something. "Just say it," I said.

"I'm yust worried dat tings will go back to de cruel little world, Tony controlling, making you miserable."

"Ah, so it's not about Rosalva. Okay, I understand." What I understood was that I was speaking to Drama Mama, and it was my job to keep things cool. "Everything will be fine," I reassured her, and busied myself with tasks before Rosalva arrived and Tony and I left for our outing.

When we returned home in the evening, Asta and Rosalva were laying on the lounger by the pool.

"Your mother is giving me Swedish lessons," Rosalva grinned. They were clearly enjoying themselves. I sat down to join them.

"You don't have to stay out here yust to be polite," Asta said.

"But you don't mind if I do?" I asked.

"Oh, I wish you wouldn't take it that way," Asta said. I can't get anything right.

I look at my mother these days in search of the rest of her—the mom who would talk with me for hours at the kitchen table, endlessly interested in whatever was going on in my life; who could tell stories that kept you riveted in your seat, stories that would make you laugh, or cry; who'd write poems and songs full of humor, draw pictures both cartoon and realistic, play guitar or harmonica or mouth piano without inhibition; sing with a beautiful voice and remember every word from every verse of every song from her youth; who looked and carried herself like a movie star whether she was going to the grocery store or attending an elegant business function with Daddy.

I'm grieving and she isn't even gone.

Oct 23, 2021: IN THE RING

I'm back to work four days a week. Tony delivers lunch to Asta (which also serves as a safety check), but otherwise remains in avoidance mode. Asta complains that she's in solitary confinement, but refuses to join me to watch TV or to go for a drive or a walk.

"I have things to do in my room," she says, or "I'm tired." She's ready to move and I'm wishing the best for her. She continues to criticize Tony.

"Stop," I plead, wishing that word would be effective.

"No, I won't stop," she says, "It needs to be said. I should be able to state my opinion. I'm your mother."

"For my sake, Mommy, please stop," I beg.

"Okay, for your sake. But I yust want to say this…" And she continues.

The same thing happens with Tony.

"It's completely irresponsible of your sisters to move your mother," he says. "You are all disrespecting her by moving her."

"Tony, please stop," I say.

"No, I won't stop," he says.

"You're angry with them but you're taking it out on me. Honestly, I don't want to hear it." Yet he continues.

If either one of them were to cough out an "I'm sorry," it would most certainly be followed by the word "but" instead of "because." I'd rather everyone stayed in their own corner than enter the ring swinging swords.

Oct 26, 2021: SAFETY CHECK

"Tony will bring your sandwich in around noon," I said before leaving for work.

"Tell him not to bodder," Asta said.

"It's a safety check," I told her.

"I'm not hungry. I won't eat it." Not eating is an act of defiance.

"Maybe you'll be hungry by noon," I answered.

"It's his fault I'm leaving," she spat.

"Suit yourself. I'll bring your lunch in now," I said.

Tony may be in avoidance mode but stays close to home while I'm at work in case of emergency. My Tony Behind-the-Scenes.

Oct 27, 2021: WHAT'S IN THE BOX?

"Is there anything in this pile that you want?" Asta asked, pointing to the pile she was preparing to discard. In the pile was the cigar box onto which, many years ago, I painted a Swedish flag and gave to Daddy as a gift. He used to keep his cigarettes in it.

"I'd like this box," I said.

"Okay, it's yours," she said.

Inside, in giant-sized font, lay proof of Elsa's coaching in the art of confrontation, evidence of her determination to egg Asta into conflict. The article urged its readers to:

- "Speak up. Commit yourself to speaking up when confronted with a disagreement."
- "Be assertive. Instead of running from conflicts, run towards them."

Returning the article to Ma would have only given her reason to ruminate. Sending it to Elsa would be like giving a dog a bone to chew on and defend. I fed the article to the shredder instead.

Nov 6, 2021: ANYWAY, ALWAYS

Rosalva arrived just as Tony and I were getting ready for a night out.

"I'm dressed for my date," I said, presenting myself proudly to Asta and Rosalva in the kitchen. I thought I looked pretty.

"Suey, don't say you're going on a date. He's your husband," Asta said with her upper lip curved in disgust. She was equating 'date night' with 'sex,' and for many of her generation, sex is 'dirty.'

Not only is my sex life none of her business, but she missed an easy opportunity to give a simple compliment. Speechless, I gave her a 'you've-got-to-be-kidding-me' look and withdrew my pretty self from the room.

Asta will go to the mat to defend whatever frog comes out of her mouth, while I prefer they hop right out the back door. "I just want you to know," I said as I delivered my final words on this topic, "that I love you anyway. Always. No matter what."

Nov 6, 2021: CLICKER TROUBLE

Recently I had to ask Rosie for help because I had trouble restoring the television to cable after she'd been watching Netflix.

"Your mother can do it," Rosie said.

"Sorry, Rosie, but there's no way my mother can solve this type of technology problem. None." I was certain that any fix that Asta made would have to be accidental. I would have to call Spectrum for help.

A few evenings later when Ma and I were about to watch TV, again, I couldn't return the source from Netflix to cable. I fiddled unsuccessfully with the clickers for 20 minutes. Needing to step away from my frustration, I said, "I have to get something from the other room."

"Mind if I try?" Asta asked, mischievously almost.

Expecting nothing, but not wanting to deny her the chance to feel competent, I handed her the clickers. "Go ahead," I said, and exited the room.

Asta-Full-of-Surprises fixed it in less than five minutes. We celebrated her success with bowls of ice cream.

Nov 6, 2021: GARAGE SALE

Today was our annual neighborhood garage sale. The sun was shining, air warm. No rain, snow or slush; no coats, gloves or boots needed. I took Asta in her wheelchair for a two-hour-long shopping excursion among neighbors.

We met Jonas from Sweden. Asta enjoyed chatting in Swedish with him and sharing her recollections of his area of origin. Floyd and Louise were shopping the sale in their car. Asta was glad to be able to tell Louise in person about the duck lawn ornament she's leaving behind. Through the car window, Asta gave Louise a synopsis of the Ugly Duckling story, then instructed me to wash and deliver the ornament to Louise. I promised I would.

For Rosalva, Ma bought a simple, white V-neck t-shirt in a soft feminine fabric, and bought herself bought a sleeveless orange top with a wide elastic neckline and flounce. "I'll save it for Woodstock," she said.

"It'll be too cold to wear this top in Woodstock at this time of year," I said, feeling sad. "Might as well wear it here this week, or plan on putting it away until next summer."

Nov 12, 2021: GOOD BYES

"Why didn't you answer the phone?" Asta asked accusingly. I checked my phone for a missed call. There wasn't one.

"It didn't ring," I said. She wanted to talk about her upcoming move.

"I know what I'm giving up, and I know what I'm getting into," she said, trying to sound chipper about it.

"Well, Elsa had better take good care of you or she'll have me to answer to."

"That's what I wanted to hear," she said.

∞

"Elsa's not coming to meet me at the airport," Asta said, awareness setting in as to the differences between Elsa's and my caregiving styles. "She's sending Axel to pick me up. And I don't think the wheelchair lift in the garage is ready yet." Axel may have to carry Mormor into the house.

I just want her to be safe and well taken care of. I don't want her to fall, but if she does fall, I want her evaluated by a doctor. I don't want her to get sick, but if she does gets sick, I want her treated by a doctor, not some quack who prescribes potatoes. Of course she will die one of these days, but I don't want her rushed to her grave.

∞

I took Asta out for a going-away "sky-is-the-limit" dinner. We sat on the patio in the warm fall air under strung lights, among well-heeled diners (she will miss the Palm Springs life) and had a feast: two kinds of oysters on a half-shell, an antipasto, cups of chicken minestrone soup, risotto balls and a plate of shrimp scampi. No room left for dessert.

When we returned home, she found a card in her room that Tony had left her and asked me to read to her.

The outside of the card read: "I know that you have what it takes to survive this, and you'll come out even stronger" it said. Inside it read: "That's what makes you so Amazing!" It was a thoughtfully chosen card. He added a message of his own:

"Thank you for staying with us for 3 ½ years. I really enjoyed your company. I am sooo sorry that I was not able to meet your expectations and you became unhappy. Best wishes in your new life, safe travels — Tony"

Nov 13, 2021: DAY OF DEPARTURE

As I was assisting Ma on with her jacket and compression stockings, she said, "I decided to write something back to Tony." Reminiscent of the early days of her living here, it read simply, "Sonny, I got you babe, Cher."

"C'mon, Mommy," I said. "He writes something meaningful and you want to make a joke? You've lived under his roof all this time and that's what you came up with? You can do better than that."

Twenty minutes later she had written: "Dear Tony, Thank you for your nice card—I am sorry to (sic). You and Suey has (sic) been so very good to me. I hate to leave. But I hope you two will visit me in Woodstock. Sincerely, Asta. Good night, Sonny. I got you Babe. Cher"

"That's much better," I told her. "For what it's worth, I blame Elsa for sabotaging your stay here. Everyone knows you had excellent care. It's crazy for you to go back."

"I was lonely."

"Of course you were lonely," I said. "Anyone in your situation would be. But that didn't give Elsa the right to criticize Tony or me behind our backs and encourage you to do the same. Chris knows you'd be better taken care of here, but prefers the path of least resistance and tipped the scales in Elsa's favor. I feel betrayed. By both of them." Of course, I was crying.

"I'm sorry," she said.

"Yeah, I know. It isn't your fault, but now you know why it may be hard for me to forgive them any time soon."

We managed to assemble our faces before greeting Lisa at the gate. It took both of us to help Asta transfer into the SUV. Lisa and I hugged.

"I don't know how your mother thinks she's going to take care of Mormor by herself."

"I don't know either," Lisa shook her head.

"Well, she got what she wanted. I hope it works out," I said, and brought the subject back to the present. "Lisa, Asta can't stand. You have to stay by her side and assist anytime she's going to stand up, even in the bathroom." I got one last hug and we started the wave.

Back in the house, I went directly to my mother's room, threw out the trash, dusted, put the futon/bed back together with all its original pillows and cleaned out what was left in her closet. I emptied the storage drawers that had been hers in the garage, and emptied the garage refrigerator of her supplies. I cleaned her bathroom, the drawers, cabinets and cupboards, got rid of the Water Pik and Keurig machines, and since Chris had decided to cancel the service, packed up her Lifeline equipment for return.

Eventually, I took a break and found Tony.

"I'm going to make myself something to eat," I said. "Would you like me to make some for you too?"

"What are you going to make?" he asked, cautiously.

"I dunno. Maybe a sandwich?"

"What kind?"

"I dunno. Depends on what we have. Maybe bacon, lettuce and tomato?"

"Okay, I'm hungry."

"Me, too." I made sandwiches, plated them with chips, and served them with a bowl of canned soup on the side. We had a companionable lunch together in the kitchen and talked a little bit. "Welcome back to the table," I said.

Tony contacted Spectrum, cancelled the landline phone service that went to my mother's room and invited me to accompany him to the Spectrum store to return the modem. In the car, with the phone modem at my feet I said, "It's like an exorcism, getting rid of this thing."

Meanwhile, I texted Elsa a picture of Mommy's red "Go Bag" with instructions: "Falls are her biggest risk. She'll need to be seen by a doctor any time she has fallen. Promise me." I had to wait half an hour for her to reply, "Will do."

PART III

November 2021—January 2022

CHAPTER 10

LETTING GO

Nov 14, 2021: PASSING THE TORCH

Asta called gushing over how smoothly her trip went, giddy with excitement over all the newness and the project in front of her: moving in, unpacking, new faces and routines.

"Could you send me a picture of Ma's little Winnie Walker?" Elsa interrupted. "She's not crazy about the one I have for her here."

"I recommend a junior sized seated walker instead," I responded, and sent her a link.

"Yes, thanks," she wrote, expecting me to order it. It was her job now, not mine. I called her on the phone for a chat.

"Has Chris set you up yet with a debit card?" I asked.

"Not yet," she said.

"I used it to buy whatever Mommy needed and then immediately sent Chris a picture of the receipt, tracking every penny spent. You'll need to make sure Ma is not alone in the house for more than two hours without a safety check."

"It's going to be hard," Elsa said. "I may call you. And when I do, I'm calling for my sister, not for a solution."

"I know, Elsa. And I'll promise you this: I won't bash Tom," (I paused to let that sink in), "or you," (another pause) "or Marty, or anyone else, in hour-long daily phone calls with Ma. Because it's a hard job, and you're going to need support."

She can reflect on that. Or not. I'd said what I needed to say, and let her know that although I was angry with her, I was committed to not doing to her the disservice that she did to me. Then I called Chris to remind her to set up a debit card for Elsa.

"Mommy doesn't want that," Chris said.

"I suggest you not handcuff Elsa," I said. "It will be much easier for her to do her job if she has a debit card. She shouldn't have to pay out of pocket first." Then again, Asta's expenses are no longer my concern.

"I hope you'll begin to feel like you can breathe again soon. Your whole outlook will improve," Chris said.

I snorted. "I hope so too, Chris. Thanks."

"Did I say something wrong?" she asked.

"It's complicated," I told her. Because what I heard her say was that she thinks I'm negative and too tightly wound, and that I'm the one who needs to change. She, in contrast, must be very good at breathing, far, far away from hands-on responsibility, 24/7, with zero interference from people who think they know better.

Of course I will appreciate and enjoy the freedom. But I'm going to be angry for a while.

Nov 15, 2021: PRESSURE SORE

"What's going on with Mommy's heel?" Elsa asked in a text. I called her on the phone.

"I took Ma to see her primary care physician a few weeks ago and had him look at a dime-sized reddened area with a pin-prick sized blister on her heel. He diagnosed a pressure ulcer," I said. "Since then, she's been wearing a lamb's wool heel cup, and I've been checking it twice a week. Last time I looked, it was smaller, no blister, and barely pink."

"Now it's the size of a quarter, painful, and she's concerned," she said.

"Take her to a doctor," I said. "What was recommended then may not be adequate now. I'd take her to urgent care."

"Well, it's 3:30 p.m., and they're closing soon," she said. "She's got me running. I didn't think she'd need this much help."

"Yeah, well, now you know," I said, and sent her a link for the heel cushions. "I've been doing skin inspections during showers to look for skin breakdown, like at her tailbone, because she lays down so much. If you haven't already done so, you probably need to transfer Ma's medical records from here to there now."

Elsa didn't want to go to the trouble of getting Ma and her wheelchair into the car for a ride to Urgent Care, but she did go to some trouble for something else. An hour later I received a photo of Ma's hair in a French braid. Priorities.

I called Chris and enlisted her help to impress upon Elsa not to postpone a visit to the doctor. I was tempted to send a package of bacon with the message "I read on the internet that bacon cures pressure sores," but ordered a bouquet of flowers instead. It will be delivered tomorrow with the message: "A housewarming gift for the two of you, Love, Suey & Tony."

Dec 2, 2021: THREE WEEKS

Elsa sent a photo of Asta dressed and ready for a dinner with the Odd Fellows, a community service club to which Elsa belongs. The way Elsa had done Asta's makeup made her look like a cadaver, but I told Ma she looked beautiful.

Meanwhile, the National Guard has been deployed across NYS because nursing homes are so severely understaffed. I hope Elsa can keep her safe at home.

Dec 9, 2021: FOUR WEEKS

"Hello Sisters. I need your advice, especially yours, Suey," Elsa wrote. "Mommy is just as depressed, lonely, critical and judgmental here as she was in California. She is completely dependent on me for everything, and I realize how awful that must be for her. She turns on the smile when other people are around, but with me she is always frowning and sad. I only make it to work 2 hours a day (if that) but I still have doctors' visits and PT since the accident. I am here with her most of the time and doing everything I can to make her life easier, but she finds no joy in anything. We're both still in transition but the reality looks like she will not be happy no matter where she is. I had such high hopes. She keeps saying she'll be happy in April, like magic. Just thought you should know. I need your understanding and support."

"Hi Sisters," I wrote back. "First of all, forget happy. Your job is to keep her safe and clean, encourage her to eat, and tend to her physical needs. Whatever moments of joy you can create will be a bonus for both of you. I will support you by not fanning the flames of her discontent or by agreeing when she says how awful it is at your house. I won't mislead her into thinking it would be better somewhere else, like Chris's. You'll recall that Tony and I were opposed to this move. The two of you made the decision. The two of you need to figure it out. Hopefully you will not need to uproot her again. Do your best. Make it work. You can do it."

Let them talk. I called Ma.

"I know you don't want to hear me complain about Elsa or Woodstock, but it's hard for me not to," she said. "I'm lonely."

"Of course you're lonely. You're 93, blind, can't walk and are dependent," I said. "It's completely normal that you would feel lonely. Have you picked up your guitar yet?"

"No, I haven't," she said.

"Just please be careful not to fall," I said.

Having cooled down, I wrote a follow up email to my sisters:

"I called and spoke w/ Ma a little while ago. She sounds okay, and understands you need to have a life of your own. She understands she's not cheerful and that it will take time for the two of you to adjust and learn each other's habits, patterns, and what works. I suggested she ask you to hire a companion for a couple of hours at a time, twice a week. It would be something for her to look forward to and plan for. Of course she objected, but I planted the seed. It helped here, but it's up to you. I also encouraged her to pick up her guitar. Music from any source always cheers her up—like magic." I signed it "Guess who."

Dec 26, 2021: SIX WEEKS, SURREAL

"I'm realizing how difficult caring for Ma is becoming," Chris wrote in an email. Duh. She wanted my opinion on whether to hire a qualified caregiver for a few hours every day and have Ma pay for it, with or without her agreement. "As POA, I now have the opportunity to arrange for good care, in order that Ma can continue to stay at Elsa's and not have to go to a facility."

I called Chris on the phone. She started referencing 'what Lisa said about 'being a danger to herself or others.' I interrupted.

"Lisa is 3,000 miles away and will say whatever Elsa wants her to. I've hired hundreds of caregivers. So long as Mommy doesn't have any skilled needs, the qualified caregivers you are talking about hiring will be no more trained and educated than Elsa. Unless something has changed in the last six weeks, she needs meals, assistance of one person with ambulation and transfers, escorts to doctor appointments, and so forth, all of which Elsa is completely capable of providing. There's no need to have a caregiver in the house when Elsa is there. Elsa will have to arrange caregivers/companions around her schedule, which is probably all over the board. Maybe Elsa needs more pay to stay home and take care of Ma."

"Would *you* have retired for an additional amount?" she wrote back.

"Tony was home when I was at work, so I didn't need to retire."

"Elsa doesn't want to retire after all," she said, "so she'll arrange to get some help in for when she's working. Meanwhile, Ma didn't sound so good when I called her today. She says she's pretty weak and has to stop and rest after any small task like going to the bathroom. She has a bunch of appointments in early January, so I guess we'll find out more then."

Dec 26, 2021: LETTERS

Tony wanted to write an angry letter to my sisters, but I chose to write one myself. He wanted me to include the phrases 'you lied,' 'she'll live to 100,' and 'move her to South Carolina.' I spent several hours assembling my thoughts and words:

"Dear Elsa and Chris,

You both must know that I'm still feeling somewhat bitter about Mommy's move. I'm trying to move past it, and am hoping to bring closure for myself with this email. Please bear with me.

Those last ten weeks were difficult for Mommy and difficult for me. Tony asked me to apologize on his behalf for completely withdrawing for that period, but he felt his only other option would have been to express his outrage, which he did not do for her sake and mine. As far as I'm concerned, he owes no other apologies. For three and a half years he supported me 100% and helped Mommy to the extent she would allow, which wasn't much.

As you are now learning, Elsa, caring for a dependent parent is no easy task. You're on duty 24/7/365 and have to make many sacrifices. Tony and I were prepared and willing to do that here for the rest of her life. We did our best for her and made it easy for you. It's now been six weeks since she moved and here is where we are at:

By your own admission, Mommy is no happier in Woodstock than she was here. This was entirely predictable and was the basis for our opposition to uprooting her. We felt it was in her best interest to stay here given my experience in elder care and our combined willingness to share the responsibilities and our home. Naturally, we hit bumps in the road and complained from time to time as you, Elsa, now understandably will.

The two of you insisted on moving her anyway. Whether or not you retire, Elsa, is your business, but that you persuaded her to move on the promise that you would retire to take care of her (a lie or a ploy?) is unfortunate.

Chris, it's true that you gave me a shoulder to cry on now and then. In fact, you promised Tony you would support us by following my lead. Yet at a crucial moment, you came to the conclusion that you and Elsa knew what was better for Mommy and made the decision to move her back to Woodstock to live with Elsa—well aware that Elsa couldn't handle taking care of Mommy when she was ambulatory and living next door.

I love Mommy as much as the two of you do, and I want her to be happy as deeply as do the two of you. But more than that, I want her to be safe and secure. I have full faith and confidence, Elsa, in your ability to meet Mommy's daily needs, oversee her medical care and arrange caregivers as needed so that she can remain in your home for life (Tony believes she'll live to be 100). I believe you can do it if you choose to. However, if you, Chris, as POA decide you need to make other arrangements, will you choose assisted living or move her to South Carolina to live with you? I can't think of a better option that we haven't already tried. Please keep me informed. I'm going to practice listening and will learn to trust again.

I love you both. Please take good care of Mommy and yourselves over the holidays and always."

Elsa responded—retaliated—with criticism and hostility, while Chris parried with philosophical musings. They both need to protect their fortresses.

Dec 30, 2021: CHANGES

"Mommy's medication is being changed," Elsa wrote. "She's going to start taking a mild sleeping pill and will stop taking her potassium citrate because kidney stones take months to develop" (i.e., she doesn't have that long to live). "The doctor ordered Home Care, so a nurse and social worker will come over to evaluate her needs. That will save Mommy the effort of going to doctors' offices." In other words, Elsa has initiated hospice care. Didn't take her long.

"The doctor is changing my medicine," Asta told me that evening on the phone. "I'm down to 85 pounds. I want the three of you girls to get along, make (my end of life) decisions together, and make sure I have my final wishes, which include respecting my privacy. I want no pictures taken or put on Facebook."

"Yes, Mommy. We're talking," I said. I want her to feel like we can get along. It's her dying wish, and I will honor it.

"The doctor says I should take sleeping pills, and I trust him. It's not going to cure anything, but I might feel better," she said.

"It sounds reasonable. It's worth a try. And as far as leaving all decisions to the three of us, just keep in mind that as long as you're able to speak for yourself, the doctors should be asking you first."

A few hours later, Asta called again. "I yust had a big fight with Elsa about the medicine. I'm afraid of the side effects. I might not wake up and I wanted someone to know what was going on."

Asta used to like to stay up puttering at night. She'd make herself a cup of coffee and have a Danish or snack, and rummage in her closet and drawers. She'd pee in her bedside commode. Her nighttime activities made her feel capable and independent. Now when she can't sleep, she has to stay put so as not to wake or irritate Elsa. She's in Elsa's house now.

"If the doctor prescribed a mild sleep aid, that might be okay," I said. "Tony takes a sleeping pill sometimes, did you know that? And he wakes up in the morning, no different."

"He does?" she asked.

"And lots of other people take sleeping pills to help them sleep. Take ½ of one first and see how it feels. Tell me about it in the morning. I'll call you."

A few minutes later, a text from Elsa: "If we were together, we'd be laughing together. I was so hopeful."

"I hear ya," I answered. "On nights like this, I'd offer the baby monitors so she could just call my name if she got scared—but your rooms are so close, you might not need them."

"There's just a wall between us. She's refusing the medication."

"She may change her mind," I said. Getting Mommy into palliative care may be in Elsa's best interest, but Mommy enjoyed going to the doctor. I doubt she was expecting that Elsa would give up so soon.

In the morning, Asta told me she had taken the pill but didn't sleep a wink, and this morning she was unable to eat. She said, "Elsa may be trying to kill me with the sleeping pills." Indeed, Elsa may be greasing the hinges of heaven's gate or the steps leading up to it.

"I'm sure she's doing the best that she can," I offered as reassurance.

Jan 3, 2021: HOSPICE INTAKE

"I asked them several times not to use the word 'hospice'," Elsa said when she called to fill me in on the intake visit, "but they did it anyway. They ordered oxygen to be kept on hand. Mommy bragged about the Eisenhower hospital and medical system 'where they take care of the Rich and Famous, the hospital is so Clean and the staff is so Professional' to anyone who would listen."

Elsa has family and friends coming over often, and has enlisted a professional caregiver for when she has somewhere to go—like the funeral she's escaping to tomorrow for an hour or so.

I call Mommy every other day to touch base. "Heidi doesn't recognize me, I've lost so much weight," she said. She sounds tired, resigned, has lost interest in rummaging through her stuff.

Jan 4, 2022: WHO NEEDS HELP

"Mommy's having a meltdown over all the people that have been coming to the house from Hospice," Elsa wrote to me and Chris in an email. "Can you please intervene?"

I called Elsa on the phone and we talked for 15-20 minutes.

"I need help," she said. "I need Hospice support because I'm not a nurse."

"Do you need them for her sake or yours?" I asked rhetorically.

"She's so weak, I have to help her sit up," Elsa said. "I have to lift her to help her get up from the bed to a chair, or onto the toilet and back again."

"Is there any chance that might be due to the new medication she's on?"

"I don't think so," she said.

"Do you suppose Mommy is giving up because she thinks we're giving up on her?"

"It's too hard to get Mommy into the car," Elsa said, sidestepping my question. "She can barely get onto the toilet." She put Mommy on the phone.

"I yust don't feel good anymore," Asta said. "I have no appetite, I'm nauseous, I can't poop, can't sleep. I want it to be over with."

"It sucks to not feel well," I said. "Just let the people Elsa has coming over do what they do. Their job is to make you comfortable. Let them come and do their jobs."

"I'm yust tired, very tired. Nothing hurts, I yust don't feel good."

"Wish you were 19 again? Or 60?" I asked.

"70 would be good," she said. "I don't want to die, but I don't know how much longer I can live like this." Just talking for these ten minutes exhausted her.

"I'm glad Elsa stopped working," I said.

"For a week," Asta said bitterly.

"Is that all?" I asked.

"Ja."

"Well, call me if you need me or just want to talk, any time of night or day. You know I'm okay with that," I said, understanding that any of these calls could be our last.

Jan 7, 2022: GOOD-BYE

"Mommy just said she thinks she has lived long enough," Elsa wrote in a text. "She is barely eating or drinking. Hospice is tweaking her meds for anxiety, pooping and sleeping, and they gave her a commode, a hospital bed and a bed table. They said she could pass in the next few days or within a couple of weeks. Are you coming?"

"No, I've already had my time with her," I said.

Chris considered heading to Woodstock, but weather was an issue, as is Covid still. Elsa will have to take care of our mother herself.

I asked to speak directly with Mommy. She didn't want to talk, so I said I'd do the talking. I told her, for example, how very much Dawson liked the treats she sent him for Christmas, which she was glad to hear.

"I'm so sick," she said, the implication being that she knows she's going to die.

"I understand. Hang in there, Mommy. It's gonna be okay, no matter what."

"I can't breathe," she said.

"Why don't you use the oxygen? That's what you always said you wanted: to be able to breathe. The oxygen will help. Want me to tell Elsa to give it to you?"

"Maybe. Tomorrow."

"Okay, I'll tell her. I'll tell her you'd like to try the oxygen starting tomorrow. I love you."

"I love you, too," she said.

I called and discussed oxygen with Elsa and she agreed to offer it tomorrow.

Jan 9, 2022: IMPATIENCE

Asta is refusing Elsa's care and refusing medicine. Elsa is bemoaning that she needs help and has inquired about transferring Mommy to the Hospice facility. Chris and I discussed this by phone.

"Elsa is seeing the Mean Mommy who thinks Elsa is the enemy. If Ma were a little nicer, it wouldn't be this way," Chris said.

"Whether or not Mommy could or should be nicer is irrelevant," I said, "and this isn't about what's easier for Elsa. Mommy just needs to be taken care of by capable, willing people… who aren't in a hurry for her to die."

Jan 11, 2022: CONCLUSION

I called Elsa after work. She spoke sweetly to me but complained about how hard it is, and how she has to do it 'all alone.' Wah Wah.

"Yes, it is hard. But this is what you signed up for. This is what you wanted," I said. I didn't remind her how in our Zoom meeting she had romanticized the beauty of death and dying.

"I didn't know it was gonna be *this hard*," she lamented.

"Yeah, it's no party," I said.

"So, has your life changed since Mommy left?" she asked, inferring in stark contrast to her own, how she's carrying the burden all alone.

"Well, it's obvious," I said, and let that statement hang in the air, not wanting to blow wind into the sails of anyone's self-pity.

Paraphrasing a character on a recent episode of 'Life Below Zero': "When life kicks your butt, you can sit around licking your wounds and feeling sorry for yourself, or you can get up and do something productive."

A few hours later, at 5:20 PST, 8:20 PM EST, our mother died.

I wrote her obituary.

OBITUARY

Born in southern Sweden to Bror and Ingeborg, Asta was known as "Svarta Rosen," or the Black Rose, because of her remarkable beauty and tanned skin. She left home at the tender age of 14 and pursued a career as a licensed practical nurse, working in numerous hospitals across Sweden. She was known in that role for her spirit and competence.

In her early 20s, she met and married Ragnar Anderson, the dashing scholar and saxophone player who pursued her until she said yes. Always open to adventure, when offered the opportunity to live in America, Asta, Ragnar and their infant daughter, Elsa, sailed to Ellis Island to live in New Jersey for what they thought would be two years.

Within that two years another daughter, Chris, was born, and two years later, Suey. Meanwhile, Ragnar's career began to take root. Asta taught herself English and raised their three girls, teaching them to speak, read and write in Swedish, to draw, play, care for animals, be generous towards those less fortunate and take interest in those who are different.

Later, when Ragnar accepted a new position, they moved to a small town in Northeast Pennsylvania. Asta's job there was to remain beautiful and gracious and to entertain Ragnar's business associates. When asked where she got her tan she liked to say, "My husband gave it to me."

In the late 1980's, Asta enrolled in cosmetology school and learned how to cut hair. Ragnar never paid for a haircut again. She also worked for a time in daycare, nurturing infants as though they were her own, and spending countless hours on her own time creating colorful mobiles to enrich their environment. Asta was a natural-born artist and had a gift for decorating. Ragnar used to say she could turn a cardboard box into a castle.

At the age of 69, Asta and Ragnar relocated to Woodstock, NY. There, she took up writing and completed and self-published several books, including her autobiography in both English and Swedish. She would like you to know you can find them on Amazon.com. At 90, she moved to Palm Springs, California and joined the writer's guild.

Some of Asta's enduring qualities include her beautiful singing voice, her athleticism and her gifts for conversation. She could recite all the words and verses of hundreds of songs and hymns from her youth. She enjoyed the physical labor of yard work all year long, and was still building snowmen into her eighth decade. She loved dressing up for Halloween and for her roles as a gypsy and nun in Woodstock's local amateur theater.

Asta was predeceased by her husband, Ragnar, and leaves behind their three daughters, Elsa (Marty), Chris (Paul), and Suey (Tony), and four grandchildren, Axel (Mallory), Lars (Lila), Lisa (Jane) and Ronnie (Angi).

Services will be private and held at a later date. In lieu of flowers, Asta and the family ask that donations be made to an animal shelter or humane society of your choice.